REBEKAH ANN NAYLOR, M.D.

Missionary Surgeon
in Changing Times

CAMILLE LEE HORNBECK

Dedication

For Jeff, who always believed and unconditionally loves

What Others Are Saying About This Book:

Inspirational stories from missionary doctors long have been a mainstay for Christians excited to learn about what God has been doing in the world. Rebekah Naylor, one of the true missionary heroes of the 20th century, is sharing her life with a new generation of readers likely to turn these pages with great anticipation. Her story may be the next classic in the genre.

Robert B. Sloan, Jr., President
Houston Baptist University, Houston, Texas

I have been an admirer of Dr. Rebekah Naylor since long before I surrendered to missions myself. For the past seven years I have had the privilege of serving alongside her in Bangalore, India, and knowing her as both colleague and friend. Following in Dr. Naylor's path I have seen firsthand the remarkable impact of her life and ministry as a surgeon, administrator, missionary strategist, and servant of Christ. Camille Hornbeck's new biography of Rebekah Naylor allows everyone a glimpse into this amazing story.

David Garrison
Missionary leader and author

Rebekah Naylor's life is one of selfless service and sacrifice in God's kingdom. Listen carefully as it tells of her life and ministry to the beloved people of India. This series of stories will take you through the exciting journey that has been her life. Our world owes much to Dr. Rebekah Naylor. I pray that this book will inspire countless others in the generations ahead.

Frank S. Page, President
Southern Baptist Convention, 2006-2008

I have been challenged by the commitment of Rebekah Naylor since I learned of her service while I was a Southwestern Seminary student. Read this! Share this! God will use this great life and story to call others to go to the nations.

Rex Horne, President
Ouachita Baptist University, Arkadelphia, Arkansas

This volume sheds light on the remarkable life and ministry of a woman who was like the Great Physician who called her, marked by compassion for the lost and hurting. Camille Hornbeck does a masterful job of shaping decades of details into a compelling and inspiring volume.

Michael D. Dean, Senior Pastor
Travis Avenue Baptist Church, Fort Worth, Texas

This is a missionary journal that reads like a novel. Dr. Rebekah Naylor's life is more entertaining than fiction because it is entirely true and most remarkable. This book will inspire and challenge you to live every day for the King. I have had the honor of knowing the Naylor family for years. Her father was a friend and mentor during my years as president of Southwestern Seminary. Rebekah is a treasured personal friend and a true heroine of the faith.

Kenneth Hemphill, National Strategist
Empowering Kingdom Growth, SBC
Former President, Southwestern Baptist Theological Seminary

Most missionary biographies in a few pages become hagiographies, but Hornbeck captures the essence of a remarkable life without making Dr. Naylor a superhuman in the process. With a personal commitment to using her skills as a surgeon-missionary, Dr. Naylor learned to adapt to the far-reaching alterations that took place in Indian society during her time at the Bangalore Baptist Hospital. Hornbeck presents a well-written narrative of the life of an American woman who accomplished remarkable feats in difficult circumstances and did so from a commitment to serve God faithfully.

Rosalie Beck, Ph.D., Associate Professor of Church History
Baylor University, Waco, Texas

Dr. Rebekah Naylor's new book is a moving and fascinating glimpse into the life of one of God's most faithful servants. Any reader who has an interest in what God is doing in the world will be riveted by Dr. Naylor's moving account of her 35 years as a medical missionary in Bangalore, India. This book is a must-read for every Christian who desires to know God intimately and to serve Him faithfully.

Robert Jeffress, Pastor
First Baptist Church, Dallas, Texas

Dr. Naylor's story is a case study in the ever-changing challenges and roles of today's cross-cultural disciplers. She epitomizes the proverbial flexible spirit of the missionary—a servant of God who ministers to the physical and spiritual needs of the people of Bangalore, India.

Mike Barnett, Elmer V. Thompson Chair of Missionary Church Planting
Columbia International University, Columbia, South Carolina

The story of Dr. Naylor's life is one of extraordinary talent and commitment, but it also provides an incredible backdrop for understanding the depths of God's faithfulness. From the hospital halls of India to the church aisles in America, every location was an opportunity to see how God worked in her life and how she in turn was used in the lives of others. You will be blessed by every chapter.

Alexis Wilson, Freelance writer whose writing includes work for faith-based
    institutions, nonprofit foundations, and lifestyle publications
Based in Fort Worth, Texas

Just mentioning Rebekah Naylor's name causes medical students, veteran physicians, and others to stand at immediate attention. This newly written story of her life reads like an adventure novel and intimate diary at the same time. It is a fascinating and moving account of what God can do with a person deeply committed to Him.

Fred Lewis Loper, M.D.
Executive Director, Baptist Medical Dental Fellowship

Camille Lee Hornbeck provides an inspiring description of Dr. Naylor's exemplary life and work, outstanding character, work ethic, personality, and immense achievements in expanding and improving the medical and surgical care at the Bangalore Baptist Hospital. I strongly believe that the Holy Spirit has led her throughout her entire life and that we are all the better for her service.

Robert N. McClelland, M.D., Baldwin Professor of Surgery
The University of Texas Southwestern Medical School, Dallas, Texas

This beautifully written and painstakingly compiled story of how one small, refined, dedicated Christian woman dramatically impacts the subcontinent of India, often despite tremendous opposition, is a must-read. *Rebekah Ann Naylor, M.D.: Missionary Surgeon in Changing Times* is an amazing book with a fascinating title character.

Bernie Hargis, Associate Pastor, Service/Communications
Travis Avenue Baptist Church, Fort Worth, Texas

The extent of Rebekah Naylor's labors, the overwhelming obstacles she sometimes faced, and her determination to bring honor to Christ exude from this engaging chronicle. Even more obvious to the reader of this riveting narrative is the abundant supply of prevailing grace that her Savior gave her to fulfill His will for her life.

C. Berry Driver., Jr., M.S.L.S., Ph.D., Dean of Libraries
Southwestern Baptist Theological Seminary, Fort Worth, Texas

This compelling story of competence, compassion, faith, and transformation will deepen your walk with God. The incredible life story of missionary surgeon Rebekah Naylor will change you because nothing speaks louder than the testimony of a life totally committed to God.

David Stevens, M.D., Chief Executive Officer
Christian Medical & Dental Associations

I have been fortunate to follow Dr. Naylor's career from its beginning. She was the first woman to successfully complete general surgery training at the prestigious University of Texas Southwestern Medical Center at a time when women weren't expected to enter surgery. But that was only the start of the path less taken. The story of her inspiring journey will rivet you and show what a difference one person can make in the lives of many.

A. Marilyn Leitch, M.D., Professor
University of Texas Southwestern Medical School, Dallas, Texas

Rebekah Naylor has doggedly pursued God's calling in her life and has had a powerful influence on the lives of people all over the world. Her medical work in India has become the stuff of legend, and deservedly so, for she has labored exhaustively to ensure the medical success of the Bangalore hospital and to share the Gospel alongside her Indian and missionary colleagues. This book tells her story in ways that inspire others among us to emulate her example of service and love.

Dr. Robert N. Nash
Retired International Mission Board missionary

Rebekah has been an inspiring role model for many of us in the Christian Medical College and in the fellowship of Christian medical professionals in India. Her life has not only been challenging for the young and an example for her peers but also a sign of hope that points to Jesus Christ her Master. I am confident that this biography will be as stimulating as her life as a surgeon-leader in the Bangalore Baptist Hospital and will be read and remembered by many throughout the world.

Dr. Suranjan Bhattacharji, Director
Christian Medical College and Hospital, Vellore, India

Contents

Foreword

Twenty-nine years is a long time to have known a person. I first met Dr. Rebekah Ann Naylor in the latter half of 1979 when I joined the Bangalore Baptist Hospital as an intern. Since then I have had the opportunity to work with her as a senior houseman, junior consultant, senior consultant, and administrator. She has been a friend, mentor, teacher, and guide.

As a child she heard God's call to be a missionary and a doctor. She became a surgeon, moved in 1974 to Bangalore Baptist Hospital in India, and served for an amazing period of 35 years. Life must not have been easy for her—a single American woman in an alien country, living in a culture quite different from her own, working in a hospital that was situated on the outskirts of the city. Living alone on the hospital campus often meant being the only doctor on call and having to deal not only with surgical problems but also medical, obstetrical, and administrative problems. As if that were not enough, she had intermittent resident-visa and medical-license problems. Through all of this she never forgot her calling. She coped admirably. She became an example for others—an example difficult to follow.

Though she was a surgeon, she also performed duties in obstetrics and gynaecology. A constant shortage of doctors in that department existed. Dr. Naylor always pitched in to help. Over a period of time, she became renowned for her obstetric skills. Patients traveled from far and wide to have her deliver their babies.

Work was a passion. Her day began at 6.30 a.m. with ward rounds. She continued to work until late in the evening. After that she took night calls in surgery and ob-gyn. Even her interns found keeping pace with her to be difficult!

She always encouraged junior colleagues. Dr. Naylor was the one who helped and encouraged me to start the Department of Orthopedics in the hospital. Today it is a large department with a post-graduate teaching program. Her calling transcended the day-to-day healing without ever ignoring it. The hospital grew steadily in its capacity to help the community.

Her faith in God is absolute. Despite her hectic schedule, her spiritual ministry never wavered. She never forgot that she was here to serve God and show His love. She always made time to involve herself in the Pastoral Care Department, lead Bible studies for different groups of people, give sermons, pray with staff and patients, and help in the spiritual growth of the institution and its people. At the same time that her faith stayed unchanged, she adapted enthusiastically to the culture around her. She learned to read, write, and speak the local language—Kannada—and never was deterred by the accent. Where her calling required the mastering of a new skill or the engaging of a new community, she dove in. She was safe in the knowledge of God's guidance. She is the only American I know with the courage to drive in Indian traffic with confidence and élan!

To write the foreword for this book on Dr. Naylor pleases me greatly. Her story, a source of inspiration to all those who read it, will touch lives and make a difference, just as she touched ours and made a difference. Most people change according to the world in which they live. Very few people change the world in which they live. Dr. Naylor is one of the latter.

Alexander Thomas, MS (Orth), M. Phil. (HHSM)
Director, Bangalore Baptist Hospital
Bangalore, India

Be utterly amazed. For I am going to do something in your
days that you would not believe, even if you were told
(Hab. 1:5).

Preface

Write a book? Me? Write a book about you? Such an out-
landish thought evoked shock, incredulity, laughter. What provoked such a request? Lunch amidst the beautiful Mediterranean décor of Bistro Louise no longer tantalized me.
Avoiding a response, I drove home slowly. I drove southward
on Overton, wound my way through Westcliff, and found my
sister-in-law, Janice, and brother, Bill, talking with my husband Jeff. We're a close-knit foursome; they recognized something had transpired. I murmured, "Rebekah Naylor wants me
to write her biography."

Janice smiled, "Well, what did you tell her?"

We talked about the daunting project, my inadequacies, the
logistics, Rebekah's sterling academic record, intimidating
curriculum vitae, and résumé. Between a three-month
European jaunt and one to the East Coast Jeff and I enjoyed, I
visited Janice. Her first question was, "Well—I think I already
know the answer—what did you decide about the book?" I had
no answer to give—not a clear word from God, no direction,
nothing. Matt, my nephew, ever candid and exasperated at my
indecision and agonizing, blurted, "Did you even consider that
God would equip you in the process?" Jeff just smiled.

Little did I know of Rebekah's persuasive powers, tenacity,
or dogged determination. Cornering me between Sunday
school and worship service in February 2006, she extracted an
agreement that I would do the research for her story. She presented me with a plan! She organized the process! This was

not the shy woman I knew at Baylor nor the one who avoided people when she was visiting Travis Avenue Baptist Church. What had happened? Overcome, I embarked on the research. Jeff and I bought a laptop, a PDA, a voice recorder, and thick, spiral notebooks, and traveled to Richmond, Virginia; Columbia, South Carolina; even Bangalore, India! The interviews took me to people who know Rebekah the best—her brothers, Bob and Dick, her mother, Goldia, her missionary and medical colleagues and friends from Bangalore, the International Mission Board, and around the world—her college and medical-school friends, her professors and colleagues from University of Texas Southwestern Medical Center. Interviews were done through letters, emails, telephone calls, and personal visits. Some sent me letters Rebekah had written them.

Sandra Higgins and Judith Vernisky, the librarians at the IMB headquarters in Richmond, allowed me to roam throughout the library, use their copy machine and computers, and furnished coffee! Edie Jeter, the archivist, brought me all the archived materials on Rebekah; Tonya Caudle, the photo-section wizard, transformed Rebekah's archived pictures into digital format ready for the publisher! Bless you all. Drs. Jerry Rankin, Clyde Meador, and Van Williams gave me invaluable insight into Rebekah, Bangalore Baptist Hospital, and the International Mission Board.

Primary research included not only Rebekah's narratives from our many talks but also 4,091 letters she wrote her parents from 1960-2002. *Please keep these letters and they can serve as my diary,* she wrote in her very first letter, September 12, 1960. Mrs. Naylor saved them in chronological order, clumped by school semesters, school years, or time between furloughs. Each group was neatly encased in a plastic Kroger grocery bag with the date attached to the outside.

To facilitate my uncovering her life story, Rebekah, with the assistance of Dr. Berry Driver and Barbara Walker of

Southwestern Baptist Theological Seminary Library, employed seminary students to transcribe photocopies of her hand-written letters. Brothers Dick and Bob originally had suggested the value of the letters being available to mission students. The task, both monumental and costly, represents Naylor's commitment to having her story written. The electronic transcriptions have provided a unique nuance to this adventure. One evening I read the description of one of Naylor's frequent dinner parties. The menu listed *cheese guts* as the side dish to ham. A Texan who likes grits, I recognized the dish—*cheese grits!* Deciphering content typed by non-native English speakers created perplexity and some hilarious anecdotes. Reading Rebekah's diary continued for a concentrated eight months. Much of the content Rebekah had forgotten; as entertainment I sent her daily quotations from her letters. Rebekah has been patient with my constant barrage of questions. She has explained and clarified frequently—sometimes more than once an item. Actually Rebekah is the writer of this story. I'm just the organizer of the massive amount of material.

What to do! In Bangalore, Rebekah told those folks I was writing her story! Gradually word of the book leaked out at Travis. I was NOT happy about that. What if I never wrote a single word other than the title which her brother, Bob, suggested? If I did write, what if no publisher would touch it? Rebekah would be disappointed to the point of being inconsolable. I knew her reputation—no turning back if a decision is made. People knew my worst fear—I was writing a book, had no experience, didn't know how. I was teaching full time. My desk swayed under its load of other long-promised, unfinished projects—at least three of which had past deadlines. People knowing of my involvement, however, became a good thing—after they recovered from the shock, that is.

Even Cousin Sandy turned speechless that evening at Red Lobster! How clearly Jerry Rankin's voice rings in my head: "You've written a book before, of course."

"No," I whispered.

"First book? And it's about Rebekah?"

His incredulous, skeptical tone spoke what others must have been thinking. "Camille, you're an English teacher. Why do you think you can do this? Do you have any idea who Rebekah is and what she has accomplished?"

"I know; I can't," emerged the wee little voice. I probably should have borrowed and read daily my brother Bill's copy of *The Little Engine that Could.*

As a writing instructor I teach writing as process. I relentlessly demand careful research from credible sources, planning, outlining, drafting, revision, editing, peer review. (Thank you, Bay Area Writing Project and National Writing Project, Fort Worth Independent School District, Bob Reed, and Bonnie Dickinson.) These two years and this manuscript reinforce the knowledge of the recursive nature of writing and the absolute necessity of each phase of the process. Writing research indicates 85 percent of the writing must be in the pre-writing/planning stage. I can testify to that! No plan—big chaotic mess on paper. Literal cutting and pasting of the pieces of paper are not obsolete for this writer!

This project I did not complete without help. Janice, Matt, and my niece, Angela, continued to be solicitous; their unwavering support was encouraging and comforting. Friends Amy St. Clair, Carolyn White, Frances Mallow—a two-time author herself—and Mary Ann Hamilton talked me through the project. They offered salient suggestions and advice. At one dinner Angela and Jay served us curry and told us the meal was in honor of the approaching foray into India.

Even Elle Jacobs, my great-niece, was part of the effort. One day she played with her toy telephone. Her mother, Angela, asked her to whom she talked,

Said 2-year-old Elle, "Aunt Camille."

"Oh, really. What's Aunt Camille doing?

"She's writing the book."

When I repeated the story to Rebekah, she sighed, "I wish!"

As the process stretched over almost two years, many of you helped. The readers—Rebekah, Mrs. Naylor, Cousin Sandy—gave invaluable suggestions, found all manner of potentially embarrassing glitches, and corrected data. Sandy read first drafts; what an act of unconditional love! My brother, Bill, a physician, became my SME (subject-matter expert) for medical schools, internships, residency, UT Southwestern and Parkland, and medical terms. Once, in a bit of consternation at what I'd read in a letter, I asked Bill why firemen from Harvard would be doing research at Bangalore Hospital. He laughed uproariously and defined *firemen* in the medical context—specialists, very respected in their field, who travel around giving lectures. Drs. Chuck Nixon, Scott Middleton, and Louis Carter assisted. They have taught me much. Whatever errors remain are my oversight, not from my sources or my readers.

With the gig up, word out proved fortuitous. More friends flocked to both Rebekah and me. They enthusiastically embraced and endorsed this story. They prayed, encouraged, and overlooked my poor attendance, non-participation, absentmindedness, tearfulness, and, yes, whining. They listened and sent funny cards and sweet notes. Jeff folded laundry, bought the groceries, brought in dinner, zealously guarded the social calendar, and even chided and rejoiced over each completed chapter. My students asked about progress. English Department Chair Dr. Ruth McAdams and Dr. Judith Gallagher, division dean, graciously understood my need for time away from the classroom. At their Friday meetings Jeff's breakfast group inquired about the book. They and their wives upheld us in prayer. I'll never forget Roland Larson taking my hand and saying, "I'm so proud of you for writing this book about this missionary."

The folks at Hannibal Books have guided, edited, arranged, designed, planned, and answered myriad questions kindly and patiently. How essential they have been to this entire process! Thank you, Louis and Kay Moore, Katie Welch, Greg Crull, and Jennifer Nelson.

Just as Rebekah thinks of herself as bi-cultural, so is her story. The book will be released in both America and India. The text employs British-Indian spelling and terms, especially in the context of Bangalore Baptist Hospital and Rebekah's life in India. The letters, rich narratives of Rebekah's everyday life, her work, her travels, and her travail, as well as the 40-plus years they document, are exact replicas of the original manuscript. They appear in italics that are followed by the original letter's date. The Bible verses, each selected by Rebekah—her personal favorites and those most meaningful to her—are quoted from the New International Version of the Bible. Rebekah and I have furnished a glossary; Matt Lee created a splendid map of the hospital compound. The pictures are from Rebekah's personal collection, Jeff's series from our 2006 trip, and the IMB archives. Jeff put the photographs into digital format. He's the photography department.

God did equip me. When I was at my most perplexed and most discouraged, I prayed, especially as I went to sleep and again the next morning during my quiet time. Without fail, the problem became resolved—not always that morning and often not until the fourth or fifth draft of the chapter. Organization became logical, wording became clear and effective. No doubt, simultaneous with my prayers, those faithful praying friends were also praying, for they have been on their knees for two years. They are Beverly Lea, Carolyn Coggin, Celia Rice, Billie Talmadge, Millie Kohn, Linda Gregory, Jack and Susan Keen, Larry and Charlene Willcoxon, Beverly's Sunday-school class, and countless others. Without their support and prayers, this story would remain locked in letters and memories.

The story stands before you—an imperfect retelling of Rebekah's life, achievements, trials, and successes, but a sincere effort, only because of those who have given so freely of themselves in assistance and because of God's grace. In her presentations Rebekah often quotes Habakkuk 1:5. This book is a perfect example of God's work. Rebekah's life work is amazing. Rebekah as a person is amazing. God has done the amazing. He has equipped. My prayer has been and continues to be that this piece of writing glorifies God and that Rebekah's story inspires others to follow the call as she did.

Truth time. These two years have stretched, frustrated, humbled, amazed, and overwhelmed me (4,091 letters, 30-plus years in India, numerous buildings, a school named for her, countless awards and parties!). I'm glad she gave me this opportunity.

Dear reader, please meet my friend, Rebekah Ann Naylor, M.D., Missionary Surgeon in Changing Times. Mrs. Naylor, here's your little girl's story. Oh, how I hope, Rebekah, dear friend, you recognize yourself in THE BOOK!

Camille Lee Hornbeck
April 2008

Introduction

The mass of humanity was overwhelming, the poverty heart-wrenching, and the sights and smells attacked the senses in a culture shock for which I was unprepared. I thought idol worship was something relegated to an Old Testament era and was long-since abandoned by any modern, 20th-century society. Surrounded by deformed lepers pleading for a handout and taxi drivers competing for exorbitant fares, I felt the anxiety of a panic attack that was not soon to vanish.

I had just arrived in Madras on the southern coast of India as a part of my college summer-mission experience. After an assignment in the Philippines, I had an intense desire to see other mission fields. The call to missions had happened early in my life. Now, with a strong confirmation of that future direction, I was on a tour of Asia to see if perchance God would impress me about my future field of service.

My heart was drawn to every place I visited, but something happened when I landed in India. With visions of opening medical work, Dr. Jasper McPhail, a cardiovascular surgeon, and his wife, Dottie, had just arrived as Southern Baptists' first missionary to that vast nation. His unique credentials had finally opened the door after many years of rejected appeals. To think of joining a pioneer effort to evangelize this subcontinent was exciting.

I was impressed by the spiritual darkness; in fact, the oppressive nature of this Hindu culture was something that could be felt. The environment was not an inviting one for anticipation of bringing one's family and planting one's life in the midst of the stifling heat, poverty, and disease. But something drew me to these people. Their very depravity was evidenced in a spiritual hunger that readily embraced a pantheon of beliefs. I realized I was seeing in a microcosm what represented hundreds of millions of people who were living a life-time and going to hell—not because they had rejected Jesus Christ but because they had never heard of God's love and had no opportunity to believe on the One Who died for them.

The chaotic traffic in the cities and massive slums of mud houses plastered with cow dung would have repelled anyone from contemplating the option of living there. As a classical British writer once said of India, "You cannot look at it, but you cannot look away!" Something magnetic that had to be interpreted as a divine compulsion to give my life to them drew me to these people.

As I finished college, enrolled in seminary studies, and gained the needed experience for missionary appointment, I never could dispel the impressions of that brief visit in 1963. However, when time arrived for my wife and me to be com-missioned for service abroad, that our visa to India would be denied was evident. Only medical personnel were being allowed entry on our Southern Baptist platform. With the door closed, God led us to Indonesia for the church-planting assign-ment for which we were gifted and equipped.

Throughout the years that followed, I wondered why God had allowed me to experience such a deep personal burden and passion for the people of India. I struggled with the doubts about God's providence and why a sense of His will could be misinterpreted. I did not realize that He was preparing me for an enlarged ministry that in the future would include a nation-wide ministry in India and all of South Asia.

However, my personal pilgrimage is not the point of this book. God was moving in the hearts of others. Doctors, nurses, hospital administrators, and lab technicians responded to God's call to join the fledgling medical ministry in India. A hospital was built in Bangalore. In 1974 Rebekah Naylor fol-lowed God's leadership to contribute her surgical skills to this challenging field. Through the mission programs of Girls' Auxiliary when Rebekah was a young girl, God had planted the seed of a missions call. Her parents had nurtured an attitude of submission to God's will to the point that disobedience was not an option.

Her stellar academic record in college, medical school, and through surgical residency confirmed her potential success in whatever direction she chose. Her teaching role at University of Texas Southwestern Medical Center in recent years reflected a professional competency and reputation in her field that others would envy. However, without reservation, she left it all to give herself to the people of India.

Missionary colleagues arrived and went, but Rebekah stayed. She persevered through visa denials and removal of her medical credentials. Friends of influence intervened and appeals were made, but invariably, the inexplicable and miraculous hand of God would restore her work permit. The Bangalore Baptist Hospital continued with mission support long after others had been nationalized. Although other Southern Baptists found creative channels to work in the country, for many years she continued to hold the lone missionary visa.

During that tenure my personal journey converged with that of Rebekah Naylor. Years later I began an itinerant role as church-growth consultant for the emerging work in Bangalore and throughout India. This grew into an administrative assignment as area director for South and Southeast Asia. This gave me an opportunity to know and work with Rebekah throughout a span of 25 years.

I was awed to find my original call being fulfilled through extended excursions into the country as I trained pastors and evangelists, coordinated human-needs ministries, and led strategic planning among our missionary contingent and national co-workers. I had known Rebekah by reputation through common friends and my acquaintance with her father as president of Southwestern Baptist Theological Seminary.

However, on those early trips to Bangalore I was not prepared for what I found. Although I did not enter the surgical ward, my wife and I often were invited to join Rebekah for breakfast in her apartment next door to the guesthouse only to find that she had spent the entire night responding to emergencies. We saw her as a gracious hostess as she planned receptions and entertained staff and friends from the community at dinner parties.

I was surprised to see her leading chapel on Sunday mornings as she used a flannel graph to communicate skillfully a Bible story and share the gospel with hospital patients. As an accomplished musician, she never abandoned her piano skills. She provided accompaniment for hospital musical functions and in local churches. She later organized a hospital choir which developed to the point of recording a professional album and presenting televised concerts.

Outside her surgical specialty, she took pride in establishing the Nutritional Rehabilitation Center, a village replica behind the hospital in which mothers could bring malnourished children and be mentored in restoring them to health. She loved to train Indian nurses and interns and eventually saw the Rebekah Ann Naylor School of Nursing established as an adjunct to the hospital.

Weekends often would see her going out to the villages with hospital evangelistic teams as a growing network of churches expanded throughout the city and in the area around the hospital. Rebekah persevered through the administrative challenges of employee strikes, threats of Hindu radicals in retaliation to the conversions that were obviously taking place, and the incessant and complex government red tape that was required to keep the hospital going.

The time arrived when her Indian medical license was finally and irrevocably denied. Rebekah faced an unprecedented personal crisis. As I counseled with her, she could transfer to another mission field and continue her medical practice, as numerous locations existed at which doctors were critically needed. Or she could remain in India to fulfill her missionary calling which would entail relinquishing her medical practice. Which was pre-eminent—her call to missionary medical practice or her call to India?

I was as surprised as others when she chose to stay in India. After all, she had planted her life there. She had bonded with the people. Being exposed to the pervasive lostness carried with it a responsibility and accountability to God. Having adapted to the culture and speaking the language of the people, her life and India had become inextricably intertwined.

She stayed and rode a new wave of changing mission strategy which brought in new personnel and swept far beyond Bangalore in an evangelistic impact throughout the nation that now includes more than one billion people. She received training to become the strategy coordinator for a major unreached people group. She used her relationships and networking skills to mobilize teams of national workers and Stateside partners to plant churches in places being penetrated by the gospel for the first time. And, of course, God honored her obedience by enabling her to continue to offer support, training, and encouragement in the medical field among colleagues at the Bangalore Baptist Hospital as well.

Rebekah Naylor is not a saint. I had to mediate many conflicts between her and co-workers. But she is a person of strong conviction and deep commitment. Administrative policies in themselves were not enough; she had to be convinced of the rationale behind them. Still, they existed to be challenged. She was a person of such integrity that she had little tolerance toward those who failed to fulfill promises or carry out responsibilities.

Her tenure on the mission field spanned an era of transition as she adapted her work to the vision and strategy of three mission-board presidents. She went to a field ingrained in a traditional, patronizing mission strategy of subsidies and foreign leadership. She will retire having been a part of a movement toward nationalized medical work and innovative church growth.

Most missionaries gain acclaim and recognition only many years after their deaths. Bill Wallace, Lottie Moon, and Amy Carmichael are revered names and heroes of faith that capture our imagination. I would not identify Rebekah Naylor as a living legend, for to those of us that know her, she is quite human. But she has had the honor of serving her Lord in a unique calling and in a part of the world that stands out among peers. She has distinguished herself by tenure of service and extraordinary obedience to God's call by persevering in circumstances that sent others home.

As you read this biographical account of her life and ministry, you will be impressed by a gifted and multi-talented individual who chose to give her life to something other than personal dreams and success. You will get to know a compassionate person who risked relationships and contentment to champion a cause in which she believed. You will be touched by testimony after testimony of how God worked, often in miraculous ways, in the lives of multitudes of people touched by her ministry and witness.

But most of all you will be impressed by a God who is faithful. The victories won were not anything that Rebekah Naylor did but were the evidence of the power of her Lord who chose to work through her. You will be blessed by testimonies of how He led and provided guidance in hopeless situations and will rejoice in this account of a life lived for His glory.

Jerry Rankin, President
International Mission Board, Southern Baptist Convention

The Littlest One

Infant Rebekah with her parents; brother
Bob is at left; brother Dick is at right.

The Naylor home in
Arkadelphia, Arkansas

Rebekah, age 3

Rebekah, right, on front yard of
the Naylor home in Columbia,
SC. At left is friend Janey.

Rebekah, age 8

29

Rebekah in her high-school
cap and gown as she graduated from Paschal High
School in Fort Worth

Rebekah as a Baylor
University student

Rebekah and her brothers Dick, left, and Bob, with their
parents, Goldia and Robert Naylor, in 1998 family photo

O Lord, you have searched me and you know me . . . you have laid your hand upon me (Ps. 139:1, 5b).

The Littlest One

"I feel like Jesse. Samuel, in response to God's direction to anoint a new king of Israel, was sent to Jesse. He asked Jesse for his son. One by one the ancient prophet rejected the sons— first Eliab, then Abinadab and Shammah—seven sons in all. When Samuel asked if these were all the sons, Jesse, in honesty, replied, 'There is still the youngest.' And so God asked for my youngest, my little girl, not the big strong boys—not Dick, not Bob—but Rebekah, the littlest one."

Robert Naylor spoke of having to reconcile preaching about the call of God and following that call with the giving of his only daughter—the baby of the family—to God, to missions, to that clarion call of God. Each time she returned to India, he wept as if he were at a funeral when he said goodbye to his baby girl and looked to his wife, Goldia, for her words of assurance that "God can take care of Rebekah there as well as here."

Just as God called Jesse's youngest one, God did call Naylor's littlest one to be a missionary—a surgeon, a single woman to faraway India, a country in which she lived and worked and witnessed for more than 30 years amid constant change in an ever-changing world. Herein lies her story.

Rebekah Ann Naylor, the third child and only daughter of Robert and Goldia Naylor, along with brothers, Bob and Dick, 12 and 10 years, respectively, older than she, moved frequently until the family transferred to Fort Worth, Texas. During Rebekah's childhood, Robert Naylor, understanding and accepting God's call, was pastor of four churches.

Rebekah was born in Arkadelphia, Arkansas, January 3, 1944, while her father served at First Baptist Church, Arkadelphia. He had been called to there in 1937. When she was a baby, she and the family moved to First Baptist Church, Enid, Oklahoma (1944); three years later to First Baptist Church, Columbia, South Carolina (1947), and in five more years to Travis Avenue Baptist Church, Fort Worth (1952). Dr. Robert Naylor became president of Southwestern Baptist Theological Seminary in 1958. He served in this position for 20 years.

Robert Naylor, an Oklahoma native with ties to Texas, at an early age learned about God and education. His Tennessee-born grandfather (1835) moved to Texas. George Rufus Naylor, who was always called G.R. Naylor, was born near Dallas, Texas, into a family that was not particularly religious. A farmer with a few cattle, he once attended a revival service at which he was converted and called to preach. Realizing that he could preach more effectively if he had a better education, as a Baylor University student he completed one year of intensive Bible study. After that study, he went, some six years before Oklahoma gaining her statehood, to the Oklahoma Territories as an association missionary of the Southern Baptist Convention's Home Mission Board. He served throughout the southeastern part of the territory in a position somewhat like that of an itinerant preacher. Thus Robert Naylor's parents emphasized education to their children; all seven of G.R. Naylor's children attained bachelor's degrees and succeeded in their respective careers. Two of these were Bill Naylor, who became a retired United States Air Force officer, and Robert Naylor, pastor and president of a seminary. Robert himself graduated with an English degree from Oklahoma's East Central State Teachers College (which he entered at age 16). He also was a member of the debate team. During his junior year in college, Robert heard God's call and determined he must follow the directive to become a preacher. After his 1928 college graduation, he entered Southwestern Baptist Theological Seminary (SWBTS). He graduated in 1932 after he worked his way through the four years.

Goldia Dalton Naylor, Rebekah's mother, was one of four children reared in the family home in Galax, Virginia. With greater financial resources than that of the Naylor family, Goldia had been encouraged toward higher education. Goldia graduated with an associate degree from Virginia Intermont, a Baptist women's college in Bristol, Virginia. Because of her musical talent and interests, she wanted to study under Andrew Hemphill at the Conservatory in Chicago. Hemphill, however, was wooed to the new Southwestern Baptist Theological Seminary (SWBTS) as voice professor. Although her father was not a religious man, he thought her pursuit of more musical training a worthy endeavor and allowed her to study at Southwestern under Hemphill. Thus Goldia, too, found herself at the seminary in Fort Worth in 1928. Because both were only 19, one year younger than the accepted age for matriculation, special permission had to be secured for them to enter SWBTS.

While Robert worked his way through school, Goldia's experiences were far different. Being from her somewhat privileged and sheltered background, she had little preparation for the life of a seminary student in a dormitory. With a laugh and a sparkle in her clear, blue eyes, she describes the shock when she was told that no one was around to do things for her. Washing her own clothing was nothing she'd done; soon enough she learned to do such things for herself.

Goldia tells of her first meeting of Robert, a young ministerial student. As the accompanist for voice students, she played for the young men when they had to sing for the professor of church music, a required course for all divinity students. On this particular day, after the student sang, she commented to the professor, "The young man looks all right, but his voice surely isn't much." Little did she know that she and the "young man" would meet that same year (1928), court, fall in love, and marry two years later in 1930.

Robert and Goldia Naylor moved from being seminary students into the role of pastor and wife, with Goldia holding positions of church organist in Arkadelphia and choir director in three different churches. Bob, as Goldia affectionately calls Robert, was pastor at Oak Avenue, Ada, Oklahoma, while he was a student; First Baptist Church, Nashville, Arkansas, 1932-1935; and First Baptist Church, Malvern, Arkansas, 1935-1937.

In time their family grew. Two sons, Robert E. Naylor, Jr. and Richard D. Naylor, were born, 1932 and 1934, in Nashville, Arkansas. According to Goldia, in the fall of 1943, the four Naylors sat at the kitchen table. The parents began to talk with the boys about an important event. Goldia was going to have a baby. The boys, aged 10 and 12, seemed to think a baby was all right but immediately began to discuss names for this baby.

Asked Dick, "What shall we name the baby?"

"*Caesar*," Bob responded, "because Caesar was smart."

"No, I think *Mary*. I don't know anyone named *Mary*."

"Yes, you do—the girl across the street," chided elder brother Bob.

The parents carefully instructed the boys that this information about the new baby was to be their secret. The boys thought a secret to be great fun. In their earnest youthfulness, they pledged secrecy; nonetheless, they were quite excited about the advent of a baby. The very next afternoon, Dick's teacher visited Goldia and related an announcement that had been made in her elementary schoolroom: "'We have a secret. We're going to have a baby in our house.'" Needless to say, in a town as small as Arkadelphia, the news of an expected baby in the Naylor family spread with lightning speed throughout the houses there.

When this baby arrived, her name was neither *Caesar* nor *Mary* but *Rebekah*. Goldia wanted a name that began with *R* to complement the boys' names, *Robert* and *Richard*. A debate between the names *Rachel* and *Rebekah* ensued. Finally *Rebekah* was chosen because of Goldia's love for the Old Testament story of Rebekah and Isaac. This baby was named *Rebekah Ann Naylor* and would be called *Rebekah,* with no nickname, although her brothers' names had been shortened to *Bob* and *Dick* just as their father's name was *Bob*.

Unlike the boys, who were light-haired and blondish, Rebekah had black hair and dark eyes. Petite and bright-eyed, she wore her hair in pigtails until she was in elementary school. Goldia says Rebekah not only looks like her dad, Robert Sr., but also walks like he did and replicates his mannerisms. Her forthright speech, her direct look in the eyes of her audience members, her posture with head tilted just so in the lectern or pulpit do bespeak of Robert Naylor.

The family members shared the work load. When the Naylors lived in Enid, Oklahoma, the Naylors had a four-story, white house. Because of World War II, they owned no washer and had no household help. Washing became a family chore. The parents, carrying the baby and her walker and followed by two little blond boys, went to the basement to the three big tubs. Daddy operated the scrub board, Mother rinsed, and Bob and Dick did the wringing and hanging of the clean, wet items. Baby sister moved about in her walker; no doubt her bright, black eyes took in all the activity.

With their father pastor of the church, the children attended all the services with their parents. Rebekah sat between her brothers. One particular evening service, Rebekah, rather than playing quietly with her doll as she usually did, wiggled—first on the pew, then in the floor, back on the pew, down in the floor. Bob and Dick were quite perplexed; from the choir Goldia could see the activity. At that moment in his sermon, Robert's voice boomed "Rebekah"; his text was from Genesis

24, the story of Rebekah and Isaac. Thinking her father called her name in reprimand, little Rebekah popped back onto the pew, where she stayed throughout the remainder of the service. Her mother observed that after that, Rebekah "behaved." Perhaps the most endearing story of Rebekah and her dad in a church service during her earliest years concerns the morning he preached with the pulpit committee from First Baptist Church, Columbia present. The committee members had attended to hear him preach; he recognized this sermon was a test—one in view of a call to that church. As he began the invitation, the tiny, pigtailed, 3-year-old Rebekah flipped out of the pew and down the aisle toward her daddy. He scooped her up and continued the invitation without missing a beat.

Big brothers Bob and Dick found time for her and watched tenderly over her. Often the parents had commitments after church. They took the children home so their offspring could be in bed at proper times. When the parents returned home after their commitments were met, the boys would have rolled Rebekah's bed between their twin beds; the three would be fast asleep and holding hands across the beds. Goldia says the brothers taught Rebekah to play dominoes, to count, and to spell using her building blocks printed with the alphabet letters. As a little girl Rebekah won over many of Bob's university friends. Growing up, the children had access to books, for those were favorite gifts. Both Bob and Rebekah are avid readers. They listened to classical music—their mother's classical 78 rpm record collection. Their times together didn't last as long as that of siblings in many families. When Rebekah was only 6, Bob was at Harvard and Dick at The Citadel. Their time together was limited to the brief and infrequent holidays from school.

Although her brothers left home and Rebekah until that time had been dependent on them, according to Goldia, Rebekah was not lonely. She had a dear little friend, Janey Jacobey, whom she met when they were 3. Janey lived in the house next door on Wacammaw Street in the Five Points area of Columbia. Rebekah and Janey have remained friends through the years. Her mother says that Rebekah didn't like big groups but always had one or two friends. That preference continues even now. Painfully shy and withdrawn, Rebekah announced in her forthright manner that she didn't want ever to be a flower girl in weddings again; thus, she was not. By the time Rebekah was 8 and the family had moved to Fort Worth, Rebekah cried and begged not to be made to attend the parties for Sunday school. She remembers praying that her parents wouldn't make her go to church camps in the summer. She much preferred her brothers' friends and grew up in an adult world. She made her books and her music her companions. When she was only 11, she traveled with her parents and three other couples on an around-the-world tour. This trip set a pattern for the future.

Just as education stood paramount in both Robert's and Goldia's backgrounds, so did it in their home. As Bob Jr. asserts, "Going to college was a given. We never stopped to think about whether we would or wouldn't. We knew we were." He led the three siblings. Bob describes his education experience and expectations to complete school as "clear from my earliest memory. Education followed a natural progression of elementary school, junior high, high school, and college. The family lived in a town with two colleges. Colleges were part of the landscape. Even Arkadelphia had a college." As Bob neared the end of the 11th grade, because his class was the first to have 12 grades, he and his classmates were given the opportunity to go straight to a South Carolina state college if they passed the optional exam. Most of the students he knew were taking this option; he did also. As a result, at 15 he entered undergraduate studies at the University of South Carolina, lived at home, and paid tuition and fees of $40 per semester. He graduated at age 18 with a bachelor of science degree with double major in chemistry and mathematics. Bob emphasizes that the parents never pressured the boys as they selected universities but supported them. South Carolina offered four excellent schools: the University of South Carolina in Columbia; Clemson, an all-male school at the time; Winthrop; and The Citadel, also all-male in the 1950s. During his last year at University of South Carolina, he began to wonder what to do after graduation. In the spring of 1951 Bob was awarded a Rockefeller Foundation Fellowship. Not wanting to attend a Southern school and having the option of one year at any school of his choice, he followed his dad's suggestion that Harvard had a good reputation; thereby it was the only place to apply. "Chemistry seemed the easiest discipline to pursue, so I completed both a master of science in chemistry and a Ph.D. in chemical physics and chemistry, defending my thesis before professors from both departments." He completed both degrees halfway between his 23rd and 24th birthday. His career as a research chemist for DuPont led him to Buffalo, New York; Wilmington, Delaware; and ultimately to Philadelphia, Pennsylvania.

Likewise Dick completed higher education after he graduated from high school in 1950. Although he entered The Citadel in Charleston, South Carolina, he remained there only two years. For his junior and senior years, he transferred to Baylor University with an Air Force ROTC scholarship. After receiving his bachelor's degree and officer's commission in the U.S. Air Force, he was stationed at James Connolly Air Force Base in Waco, Texas. He not only worked in the Judge Advocate's office at the base but also attended Baylor Law School, from which he graduated at age 23. For more than 26 years he practiced law in Pecos, Texas, and currently practices law in Austin, Texas, as an assistant attorney general.

Time mandated that Rebekah embark on her educational journey. She did so in Columbia, South Carolina. At age 5 in 1949 she began first grade in a private school with three friends—Jane, Michael, and Henry—as her classmates.

Perhaps the most notable experience that year was her first kiss! Henry pulled her behind a tree and kissed her as he did so. For second grade Rebekah entered public school, A.C. Moore Elementary School. She remained there until early in the fifth grade (1950-1952). Her second-grade teacher, Mrs. Todd, insisted that Rebekah have pictures with each of the stories that she wrote. Rebekah didn't like drawing pictures and couldn't make straight lines as Mrs. Todd insisted. But the most traumatic event that year occurred on her 7th birthday. Tomato soup topped the menu for lunch. Rebekah did not like tomato soup and stands convinced to this day that the tomato soup she was compelled to eat made her sick and caused her to miss her own birthday party! She was promoted to third grade after that January 3, 1951, birthday.

Her public-school years continued in Fort Worth, where her parents moved in 1952 in response to her father's call to be pastor of Travis Avenue Baptist Church. Lily B. Clayton and Westcliff Elementary Schools prepared her for McLean Middle School. She graduated with highest honors and as valedictorian from Paschal High School, class of 1960. Like her parents and brothers before her, she began college at a young age — a mere 16.

Although Rebekah was young, she knew in her heart and mind exactly what her course of study would be. She entered Baylor University at Waco and prepared herself to be a doctor. She steadfastly clung to the belief that only excellence in all work proved an acceptable standard and performance. Her mother says, "We told the children that whatever you choose, you should do your best. We didn't insist on perfection." Regardless, Rebekah had a drive to achieve excellence, for she worked untold hours on her studies. Her letters recount the exact hours in the various laboratories, the study of class lecture notes and textbook materials, and the visits to the professors. She mentions her goal of a 4.0 for the semester and the coveted *A* marking on each and every exam, essay, and laboratory write-up. She rued grades less than that. This relentless drive perhaps stems from within—perhaps to be part of the family that fostered and modeled academic success, perhaps to be part of this family that perfection seemed to be ever so prevalent. As her friend of more than 40 years and fellow student from Vanderbilt, Dr. Godela Iverson, observes, "Giving up or failing is not in her vocabulary." Letters speak of the satisfaction and pure joy she experienced each time she was recognized for academic excellence, whether it be a tea at the dean's, a dinner and award evening, or membership in Baylor's Laurel Society.

The various programs and events at which she received the awards became highlights of those letters. They conveyed the joyful anticipation, the careful descriptions of the event, her outfit for the occasion, and the accolades presented and spoken. Letters written during spring of 1963 tell of the tapping for Laurel Society, a prestigious honor reserved for the few—the elite.

> *Tomorrow is Women's Day and that banquet. I will know then about Senior Women's Laurel Society. I feel deserving, but I am trying not to get my hopes up because I don't have the other qualities it takes.* (March 27, 1963) *Each year Laurel Society, the senior women's honor organization, sponsors this day honoring the women on the campus. The girls all wear heels and Sunday clothes. The highlight of the day is the awards banquet in the evening. The organizations, clubs, and dorms all present awards for various things. Laurel Society then recognizes 12 outstanding senior women. As the very last and most exciting and important part, they have the Tapping Ceremony of new members. Members come up behind the new member and place a wreath on her head. Of course, this is a surprise to everyone concerned. Toward the end of the list, this*

*one member tapped me on the shoulder. I nearly fell
out of my chair. Only 12 of all potential seniors are
chosen. It isn't just grades but also character, leadership, and service. I just can't get over the fact that it
would include me out of all those people. It is such an
honor. The group is very active in many campus activities. This morning at 7 they had an informal pledge
ceremony followed by breakfast. It was very, very nice.
I have been so excited all day. It just doesn't seem real.*
(March 29, 1963)

*As a pledge of Laurel Society, I have been wearing
a little green ribbon representing growth and opportunity. The pledge ceremony Friday morning was very
nice: repeat the pledge, sign, light our candles, have
our ribbons pinned on. I received a note from Dean
Marshall inviting us to her apartment at 6 p.m.
Tuesday evening, April 9. Monday evening when I got
in I found a beautiful long-stemmed white carnation
and a congratulatory note from ØBM. Very touching.
Tonight I got a note from the Baylor Chamber of
Commerce. I am really being honored. There was a
meeting this morning at 7. We will have a pledge meeting for officer election next Wed. at 7 AM.* (April 3,
1963) *We new Laurel Society members had been invited to Dean Marshall's apartment for dessert and an
opportunity to get better acquainted. Her apt. is lovely.
She is a nice woman, too, and I am glad that I am
going to have opportunity to get better acquainted. She
served coffee and orange-coconut pie—lovely china
and the silver service. A very nice experience.*
(April 9, 1963)

*Laurel Society met to go out to the home of Mrs.
Lois Murray, an English prof, for our initiation. She
lives several miles out in the country west of Waco in a
beautiful rather modernistic home that is beautifully*

decorated and furnished. We had our initiation first
with each of us initiates standing in a semicircle. After
repeating the vow of membership, we knelt and
received Laurel wreaths on our heads. Miss Marshall,
the dean, was there, as well as Mrs. Herring, wife of an
Eng. Prof. and a Mrs. O'Brien who is an author and a
noted citizen of Waco. She invited us all to tea this
coming Wednesday at her house. After the ceremony
Mrs. Murray served light supper: congealed salad,
nuts, cookies, and punch. It was a lovely buffet—silver
and the works. We left shortly before 7 after a lovely
occasion. (April 20, 1963)

At 3 we Laurel Society girls met to go to the home
of Mrs. Esse Forester O'Brien for tea. Her home is
located on Lake Waco in the north part of town. You
turn off the main road into this private road (dirt)
which winds up and up this hill. Suddenly you turn a
curve and the house is before you. It is new and so as
yet the fountains and grounds are not complete. The
house seems rather large but not overwhelming. I was
a little disappointed. We walked up to the front door,
entered, and one of the most unbelievable sights you
have ever seen greeted us. Through the entrance hall
you could see this enormous room entirely glass at one
end, on a sloping bluff, directly overlooking the lake.
The room was 40x50—huge. Covering the floor was
one of those gorgeous rugs imported from India. There
was an Oriental flavor somewhat to the house. She had
a huge marble fireplace in this room and an multitude
of sofas and chairs. The view was quite impressive. The
entire house followed the same pattern—bedrooms
overlooking the lake. She spent 2 1/2 years completely
designing the house herself. Scattered around were
beautiful pieces—figurines, cut glass, china. The maid
served us tea with sandwiches, crackers, cookies, and

plums—real style to it. We stayed until after 5 and it was all quite an experience. (April 25, 1963)

Spring 1964, Rebekah's final semester at Baylor, marked another high honor—that of Premedical Student of the Year. Once again the letter home, chock full of minute details, tells of the occasion, the attendees, the honor, and the accompanying emotions.

Thursday night when Brad called he asked me what color dress I was wearing—I carefully told him that the boys were not buying flowers. Yesterday evening there turned up a beautiful corsage of 4 baby orchids and it was beautiful. He had done the selecting himself. We had a very pleasant drive down. The dinner at the Stagecoach Inn was typical, absolutely out of this world. After dinner the first thing was presentation of the Pre-med of the Year Award. Before much comment on qualifications was made, Dr. Tweedie called me to the front as the recipient. The award consisted of the plaque with my name added to the list. It was such a high honor. Despite the wise cracks I had made, I really honestly did not expect it and was very surprised. Especially for a girl this is something. Dr. Tweedie was most complimentary. The speaker of the evening was Dr. Charles Shellenberger, a local pediatrician and Baylor trustee. (April 11, 1964)

On May 22, 1964 Rebekah graduated *magna cum laude* from Baylor University. She entered Vanderbilt University School of Medicine, Nashville, Tennessee, that fall. Farther away from her dear parents than ever before, she continued to pursue with dogged determination the degree of medical doctor. At the end of her second year she writes: *I now have the 'M' after my name.* Medical school presented challenges—

some similar to those she encountered at Baylor, some new; the hours in classes and on duty stretched on seemingly endlessly. The difficult subject matter, the tedious labs, the unfamiliar environment, the lack of friends, and the finding of a new church also challenged. Overarching each and every endeavor hovered the desire to excel—to achieve the highest grade or score: *I feel a certain tenseness over the upcoming exams, not just for the grades but the material I need to know.* In the copious letters Rebekah comments often that Vanderbilt, although chosen sight-unseen, proved itself a perfect fit for her. Toward the end of her four-year study at Vandy she commented that *Only God could have planned it this way* (March 16, 1968). She knew she had a first-class education and recognized the valuable contributions the faculty had made in assisting her along the way. The goal of the school and thereby the staff and faculty was to equip and ascertain each student's success in the program. The organization and philosophy undergirded that promise. Indeed those professors and advisors made themselves available not only to Rebekah but also to other students. Often she mentions both Dr. Billings and Dr. Brittingham. She needed the contact and feedback from the professors and instructors for reassurance, clarification, and sometimes explanations. The endless hours on duty, both in the various clinics and with patients, provoked sharp criticism and appeared in the usual recitation of activities, duties, and tasks that comprise the bulk of many letters. One particular letter, however, gives insight into the rationale behind the duty required when she was on call and to Rebekah's goal of learning the most and accomplishing total mastery of all material: *I am really tired. But I learned a great deal and this [hospital duty while on call] is the only real way to learn it and remember these practical things.* Yet after a period of time with few in-hospital hours and many hours in lectures halls and studying for exams, she reveals her passion: *All this studying is for the birds—I am ready to play doctor again.* (April 12, 1968).

44

The time to graduate from medical school arrived. *The cap, gown, and hood ordered April 10,* a comment marked with several exclamation points in her letter of that date, signified Rebekah as a graduate of Vanderbilt University School of Medicine. Her parents and brothers attended the festivities, which included a reception at the home of the dean of the medical school, Dr. Batson. Rain fell heavily that day, so the family members availed themselves of valet parking. The group of Naylors, after leaving the reception, presented the ticket stub for the car, but the car didn't arrive and didn't arrive and didn't arrive. Finally the attendant explained the delay. The Naylor car, stuck in the mud, could not be driven to them. The dean himself called a cab for their trip back to town; the next day, a much drier one, they returned to retrieve their car. Interestingly enough, the debacle with the rain and the stuck car remains paramount in her memory; the graduation exercise itself does not!

At Baylor Rebekah did face challenges beyond the academic ones. As the only child living at home in a disciplined, orderly environment that included classical music, entertaining, gracious living, and travel, suddenly she was in Ruth Collins Hall—the non-air-conditioned, six-storied dormitory for freshmen women from all walks of life. The dorm mother, renown for her inspections and insistence on cleanliness and tidy rooms, took her position seriously. Unfortunately Rebekah did not always have roommates who had the same standard for meeting the weekly inspections. Writes Linda Dunlap, her friend from college years, "Rebekah followed the rules. If the room was supposed to be dusted, beds made, and floor mopped, she was the one student in the whole dorm that set the standard. Basically, she was disciplined, organized, and not one to challenge authority for no good reason."

During the summer after the freshman year, Linda, Rebekah, and a third student—Kathleen Fisk—talked and agreed to be roommates for their sophomore year. This decision proved to be prudent. The three became good friends and have remained in contact, although their last reunion was at Baylor Homecoming in 1976. Both Rebekah and Kathleen were bridesmaids in Linda's wedding.

Linda shares that "we were all three very compatible in temperament, quiet at that time, and eager to do well in our school work. It is remarkable that three would get along so well since two usually end up being better friends, leaving one out, in such an arrangement . . . Despite being primarily devoted to her studies, particularly that sophomore year, she never showed favoritism and was a remarkable friend to both Kathleen and myself. I did not have the manners or 'polish' that Rebekah and Kathleen had, but there was never a hint of any hesitation to be the best of friends equally with either [of us]."

Linda shares another bonding experience. "I am not sure which year Rebekah brought a car to Baylor, probably her sophomore year, but both she and Kathleen had vehicles there. It was not unusual for us to take a study break during a long strenuous time of studying by going to a local restaurant [Sam Coates] for a treat, usually something simple like rolls or dessert and then returning to hit the books for a few more hours. I had a good time with these two roommates and consider them to have been just the best roommates possible."

That Linda narrates candidly from her recollections from her student days indicates the quality of the friendship. No doubt Rebekah was grateful.

Following her pattern from childhood years and college, Rebekah made friends in medical school but had few close ones. Two of these remain dear to her today—Jacqulyn Anderson and Godela Iverson. Anderson worked at the Baptist Sunday School Board and attended First Baptist Church, Nashville. She gave Rebekah a quiet place, home-cooked meals, and restful sleep opportunities away from the dormitory. Godela, a fellow student, offered and received almost sisterhood and became a frequent lunch and dinner companion as well as one who went along on shopping and town excursions.

Iverson writes her memories: "The two of us shared work on a cadaver in anatomy lab. Only two students on a cadaver and two women at that was highly unusual. This gave us an opportunity to become well acquainted and provided a quiet, intense learning environment. [We] shared many meals in the hospital cafeteria, studied together. Rebekah was an outstanding student, usually finished exams long before anyone else . . . I feel we have a mutual understanding of our life's work and personal lives that has given us both support and encouragement. Her parents have been like second parents to me."

The Ford Mustang Rebekah brought back to Nashville her third year of medical school allowed her to move about the city for her favorite pastime—eating out—and to attend church more easily. When Rebekah graduated from Vanderbilt University School of Medicine, Godela and she parted. Godela went to her residency and Rebekah to hers. Nonetheless, the friendship continued.

Both Linda Dunlap and Godela Iverson speak of the close relationship Rebekah and her mother shared then and now, their interdependence, and Rebekah's young age on entering Baylor. When Rebekah lived at home, each morning before class Mrs. Naylor styled Rebekah's hair; however, when Rebekah entered Baylor, she relied either on the beauty salon in the Student Union Building (the SUB, as Baylor students in the '60s called the building) or on a roommate not only to style but also to set her hair. During her years at Baylor, Rebekah wore her long hair in a French twist—no small feat to accomplish or to learn in a short while. In these later years of Rebekah's life and amidst the accolades and successes as well as the difficulties she has encountered, little challenges of normal life often are overlooked.

Lamenting leaving the beauty of the Vanderbilt campus and Nashville, Rebekah writes: *I am more aware every day how much I will hate to leave Nashville* (April 19, 1968). But move she did—into an apartment in Dallas—a new city—in preparation for five rigorous years of hospital duty, being on-call, and learning surgery. Unique experiences awaited her. Whereas in Vanderbilt she and Godela were partners in labs and in studying and had each other for companionship, in her residency class she was the only female student selected for the 1968 class. Furthermore she was the only female surgical resident in the entire school; that would be the case for the 10 years after her completion of the program. The pattern that she developed years ago of having one or two close friends followed her through the Dallas experiences. One friendship, however, grew from outside her medical world.

As Linda observes: "Rebekah was ALWAYS in church for services, no matter what else was going on in her life. [We were] sitting in the center of Columbus Avenue Baptist Church [Waco] one Sunday and my concern [was] that Rebekah was going to fall asleep and not be able to sit up straight as she always did in the pew. I believe the lack of sleep was the result of long, endless hours of studying for some horrific chemistry test the next day."

Millicent Kohn, children's minister at First Baptist Church, Dallas, concurs. True to her regimen Rebekah did not miss church unless duty prevented her from attending. She met Millicent the day she joined First Baptist Church in 1968. Kohn began to watch for Rebekah to enter (generally late) the sanctuary for worship service; thus Millie saved a seat for Rebekah. Millie often took Rebekah to her home for lunch, dinner, a nap, or conversation and invited her for an overnight just to provide Rebekah with a respite from the frantic pace of hospital duties. Out of these gestures of kindness the two became fast friends. Through Millie, Rebekah had the opportunity to observe one-on-one witnessing; teaching about the

Bible, Jesus' love, and the plan of salvation; and discipling new believers.

Despite Rebekah's wiggling as a wee child in that one church service, she was a quiet, reserved youngster who was more comfortable with adults than with children. Billie Talmadge writes that Rebekah grew up "a child in an adult world." Regardless of being 18 years apart in age, during her childhood in Columbia and then in Fort Worth, Rebekah held Billie as her best friend. Indeed Billie was a friend. Not only was she Dr. Robert Naylor's secretary in Columbia, she was a family friend. Billie stayed with Rebekah. Often Billie has traveled from South Carolina to stay with Goldia Naylor so that Rebekah can make her twice-yearly trips to India. Billie moved to Fort Worth after the Naylors left Columbia. She worked as Dr. Naylor's secretary first at Travis Avenue Baptist Church and later at the seminary.

With Billie Talmadge and Millie Kohn as personal confidantes and mentors Rebekah bravely persevered through the personal challenges and demands those five years presented. They encouraged, listened, and ministered through letters, the occasional telephone call, and birthday and Christmas packages. Today Rebekah counts them as dearest of friends. Historically she has confided in these two rather than in her parents information that might have unduly alarmed or created anxiety for her parents.

The determined march through Baylor, the triumph at Vanderbilt, and the prestigious surgical residency at UT-Southwestern and Parkland Hospital in Dallas, however, sprang not from Rebekah's own choosing or design. Missionaries, who were frequent visitors in the Naylor home for weeks at a time, at the various churches, and on the seminary campus, told their stories and intrigued Rebekah. She knew them personally. When she was young—maybe 6 or 7—

Rebekah read the biography of Dr. Ida S. Scudder, an American woman surgeon in Vellore, India, who was a missionary from the Reformed Church. Fascinated by Dr. Scudder, Rebekah memorized the details of her life's work—how she graduated from Cornell Medical School in the first class in which women were admitted and returned to India to establish Christian Medical College and Hospital, a tiny hospital that today is well over 2,000 beds. Dr. Scudder also established a women's medical school so that more care could be given to women.

In her direct manner Rebekah succinctly tells of God's call. When she was 13, she recognized God's tap on her shoulder and His voice telling her she should be a missionary and a physician. Striving to follow God's direction, Rebekah prayed; she responded affirmatively and yet hesitated in telling her parents. She—the baby, the littlest one—was well aware of the bond between her and her parents. Finally at age 15 she talked with her parents. Older brother Bob, when asked what he thought about his baby sister going to some foreign country and the long years ahead in the pursuit of a medical degree and specialty, stated unequivocally: "The call came. The call takes precedence. The call is real. And being a doctor? Why not? She could do that. The thought of questioning her decision or doubting the call never entered my mind. One must understand the significance of the call in our family."

Just as her grandfather and her father had done, Rebekah chose to follow God's call, even if it meant being far away from home. Thus on May 29, 1974, Dr. Robert Naylor's "littlest one"—now Rebekah Ann Naylor, M.D., surgeon and Southern Baptist Foreign Mission Board missionary—found herself in Bangalore, India.

The Cutting Doctor

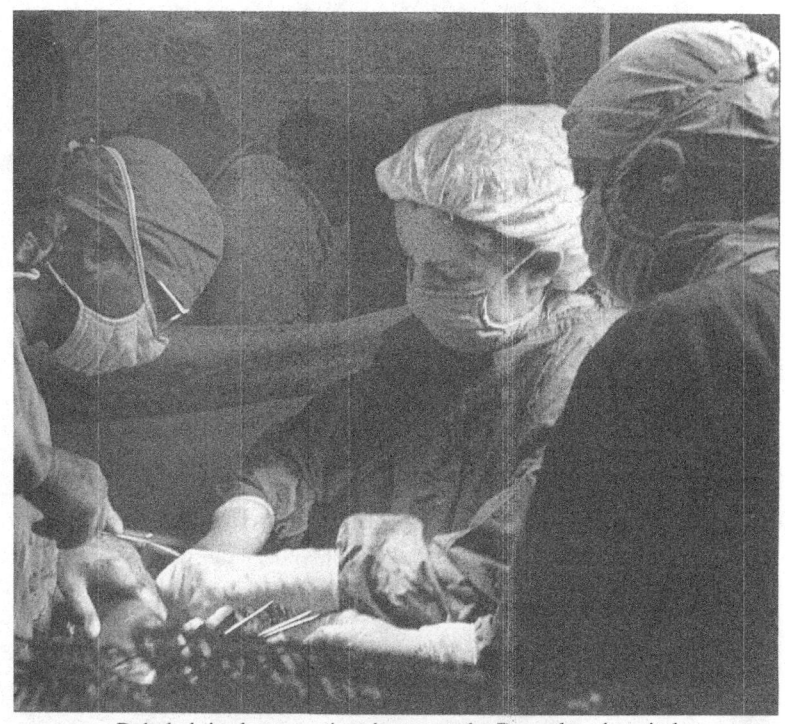

Rebekah in the operation theatre at the Bangalore hospital

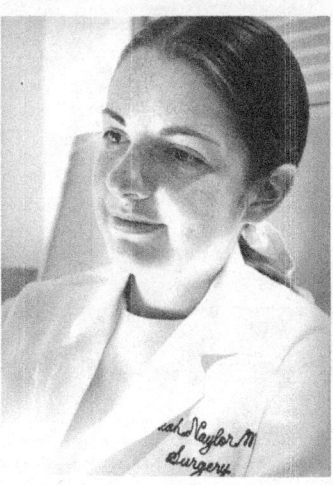

Rebekah in lab coat at Bangalore Baptist Hospital

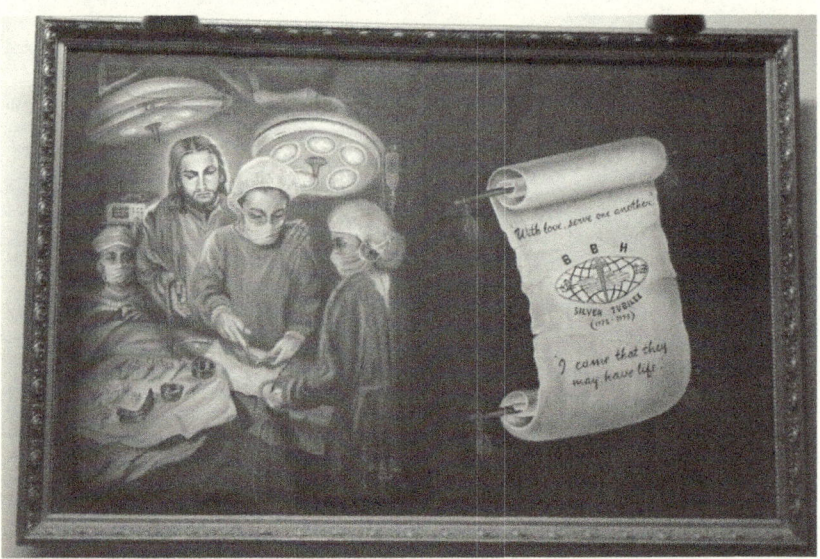

Painting by surgeon and artist Dr. Anita Thomas depicting Jesus watching over Rebekah's shoulders as she performs surgery. Painted for BBH 25th anniversary

Rebekah, second row, second from left, during residency
at University of Texas Southwestern Medical School

Trust the Lord with all your heart and lean not on your own understanding; in all your ways acknowledge him, and he will make your paths straight
(Prov. 3:5-6).

The Cutting Doctor

"The Cutting Doctor is here! The Cutting Doctor is here!" rang through the little Tamil village. Pastor Anthony Jacob, former chaplain at Bangalore Baptist Hospital for 13 years and recently retired director of India Baptist Society, and a small American woman in traditional saree carrying a white canvas bag holding her red leather-covered Bible and medical supplies alighted from the little gray van. Singing the announcement children scurried about houses; a crowd gathered. In Tamil, one of the many languages in the state of Karnataka, India, no word exists for *surgeon*; the word for Naylor's specialty translates literally into English as *cutting doctor*. For more than 30 years, to these illiterate and poor people, Rebekah Naylor, M.D., surgeon, has been "The Cutting Doctor."

Making her initial trip to India to function as Rebekah Naylor, surgeon, "The Cutting Doctor," Naylor had myriad emotions. Because of a 13-week orientation for the mission field by the Foreign Mission Board (now the International Mission Board) of the Southern Baptist Convention, a semester at Southwestern Baptist Theological Seminary, and travel to India, for 11 months Rebekah had not practiced or in any way had the opportunity to be involved in medicine. She expressed great concern about being out of touch with routines and patient care. She writes in her travel journal:

The arrival at the designated place of work has been anticipated in a vague way for years and specifically for many months. I can hardly believe it is at hand. There is plenty of apprehension and uncertainty mixed in, too, but I will be glad to get there. (May 25, 1974) Then in July of that year she continues: *I guess I still feel like I am losing ground professionally and it is very hard to keep from bothering me. I have to believe something else is more important.* (July 21, 1974)

Greetings from Bangalore! I arrived safely last night—finally. After I wrote you Monday in Madras, I remained quietly in the hotel until Tuesday afternoon . . . I left for the airport at 4 in order that I run no risks at all. There was an Anglo lady also there who has lived in Bangalore almost all her life. She had very little luggage and counted my bags on her ticket so I had to pay no extra. Also it provided some security to have her around in that airport. We took off on time at 6:20 in a 2 motor prop plane—55 minute flight. The equipment was old and a little dilapidated and [the flight] was rough in spots, but we got here. Everyone was at the airport—Linda [Garner] first. Dr. and Mrs. Hughey [Foreign Mission Board area secretary for Europe and the Middle East]. James Kirkendall—FMB field representative; John and Barbara Wikman—Suzanne and Laura. Richard and Frankie Hellinger—Dick, Amy, Laura, John, Beth and Frank who is their nephew; their oldest child Fran who is away in school; Frank and Dick are home on vacation from boarding school; Bill Mason, our hospital administrator—his family was to have come Monday but have been delayed one week; John and Winkie Watts from Serampore College [Calcutta]. And Dr. Fowler [Medical Consultant for the Foreign Mission Board]. I don't believe I have left anyone out. They had so many garlands of flowers which they draped on me. The men took care of all of the bags—took my tote bag away and all. That was most appreciated of all—to once more be looked after. I noticed instantly when I got off the plane the freshness of the air—probably close to 80 but very pleasant. It was dark, by the way, at that time. We all loaded up in cars to come to town. Linda's driving is doing fine—I wonder if I will ever learn. The car, by the way, is running as of the present. We went to the Hellingers for home-made ice cream—it was a jovial party. By the way, I had had no food or drink for many hours; the ice cream was very welcome. Finally after 9 the party broke up and we went home. The Wikmans had all my luggage so they came by. (May 29, 1974)

I am so impressed with the facilities and will be eager to show them to you. Understandably John and Richard are very proud of it. Slowly I am beginning to get some inkling of all that has been involved not just the building, but every piece of furniture, every solution, every uniform, and on and on. There is still an endless amount to be done but it is amazing that which is here. I may have already mentioned that just prior to my arrival the new well they were drilling struck water—4 times as much yield as they needed or had hoped! Another answer to prayer. The property contains several acres (bought in 2 segments). The hospital is on the front of the piece. Currently a nurses' hostel and a guest house (duplex) are being built. The next proposed building is a male hostel. It is a marvelous place of roses and other flowers. Bougainvillaea is blooming along the fences. The gate is closed and guarded 24 hours a day. You know I can't draw, but I shall make an attempt. Also I have taken some pictures.

We will send them to Bombay tomorrow and when they come back I will send some to you if they turn out. All of the hospital is 2 floors—there are 3 wings. Clinic—5 examining rooms—a treatment room—a minor surgery room. Our pharmacist is Theophilus—fair variety of drugs—hardest to get are injectable drugs. X-Ray— good equipment—we do the major studies—bowel, kidney—ourselves. Read our own films. We need a radiologist to come for a month to teach us and help us get this going. I do not have any contact I can think of in this specialty. All of the halls are wide—spacious. The lab is probably one of the best in the city. Our pathology specimens we send to the Catholic med. school—2 to 3 day service which is great. Sam Taylor is a fine Christian young man who is primarily in charge of the business office. Grace [Solomon] is one of the Christian ladies who does much of the evangelism. I think one of the greatest things that happened was having Bill Mason to come as administrator. (May 29, 1974)

Wing 1 will be surgery and OB-GYN. Wing 2— medicine and pediatrics. Wing 2 is a little larger than Wing 1. Right now all patients are in Wing 1, but June 17 we will open Wing 2. Please pray that this will really happen. I feel we will quickly build up our census. Already we are full with present space—census over 30 ever since Friday!! The rooms are private, semiprivate, or 5 bed wards. All food must be provided by the hospital kitchen—none from outside. Visiting hours are enforced which greatly helps the cleaning problem, noise. They hope to open ICU about a month after Wing 2 if we can staff it. ICU has room for 3 or 4 beds and I believe I mentioned the monitoring unit we have. The recovery room is the front 2/3 of the ICU—big

area. There is room for 3 or 4 beds in labor and then
we have a well equipped delivery room. The OR's are
fine—2 air conditioners in each—good tables. Freeda
runs the OR—excellent—a good scrub nurse too.
Annamma is in charge of OPD (outpatient depart-
ment); she also is excellent in the theatre (as the
British call the OR). The nurses wear white sarees, the
aides white with a green border, and the ayahs (clean-
ers) blue. I may have mentioned all that before.
Monday morning I made rounds with John [Wikman]
and then spent most of the day trying to get oriented. I
went to the pharmacy and looked at drugs—need to do
some studying on that. I also followed John around in
clinic. We had 140 yesterday! It was almost 2 when we
finished. Dr. Justus is one Indian doctor and Dr. Moses
the other. We then had lunch at the hospital at the same
time as staff meeting. The food was relatively bland
that meal and I did OK—it was a vegetarian lunch that
meal—sometimes she does have meat for those who
can eat it. I can't describe everything since I didn't
identify it. We discussed some policy problems, opening
Wing 2. There are numerous things to be set up, decid-
ed; something new pops up almost everyday. The
phones here are unreliable . . . Sometimes the nurses
cannot get John or Richard. Now we are busy enough
that it seems mandatory that someone stay in the hospi-
tal. There will be 5 of us (including the 2 Indian doc-
tors). After Wing 2 opens we will begin a rotation sys-
tem probably. Until then I have been assigned no call
nights. (June 4, 1974)

The letters from Bangalore Baptist Hospital arrived at
Rebekah's parents' house and gave intermittent reports of
patients, work load, and mission activities. Without a doubt,
surgery suited Rebekah well; she loved those days she could

be in theatre doing both "big cases" and "small cases," as she classified the various surgeries.

As a medical student, Rebekah deliberated whether to enter medicine specialties or surgical specialties—a paramount decision for a medical student. Training in medicine specialties would allow her to know and treat diseases, an important area of the medical field. On the other hand, "surgery is so definitive in scope," according to Bill R. Lee, M.D. "A surgeon fixes things immediately. A Parkland general surgeon can take care of malaria or kidney infections, but an internal medicine doctor can't do surgery." One summer, Rebekah's choice became easier to make.

Applying for and receiving a Smith-Kline and French Fellowship for medical students after the junior year of medical school, Rebekah worked at Baptist Hospital, Bangkla, Chacheungsao, Thailand. During these three months of 1967, she spent countless hours in OT and on rounds with Dr. Harlan Willis, a surgeon. As Willis shared the needs of the hospital—needs common to the majority of mission and rural hospitals—he emphasized the worth of a general surgeon who also could do medicine. A person in medicine, however, would have only rudimentary training in surgery; that doctor's limitations might hamper patient care, especially in a rural, mission hospital. Enroute to Thailand she wrote back home about the Baptist work she observed in Hong Kong: *Tuesday morning I got a tour of some of our work. At 11 I went to the hospital and Dr. Lewis Smith gave me a tour. I talked with all 3 of the doctors. They, too, emphasize the ability to do everything. I may get the internship [residency and specialty] decided at any rate!* (June 13, 1967)

Returning to Vanderbilt to complete her senior year, Naylor reflected on the experiences at Bangkla and Hong Kong, listened to advisors Drs. Billings, Brittingham, and Franks, and searched her heart. Today she avers that the summer at

Bangkla was a "life-changing one" in that general surgery became her chosen area of study. Without surgery she would have had no procedural skills for the patient care required in Baptist Hospital. Secondly "the summer affirmed my call to missions, that I could adjust to being in another culture far from home and my parents. I had no disillusionment with personnel difficulties or relationships." Finally on November 4, 1967 she wrote to Dr. and Mrs. Naylor:

> *Internships don't help any. This has really been a very trying fall in that respect—and it isn't over yet. All the "realistic" advice from all these men, whom I greatly respect and appreciate, has left out the big factor of God's will. This is most important to me and yet something I cannot bring them to understand. I have reminded myself several times that on my own I would have a Master's right now and be trying to start a teaching career in piano. Yet I couldn't be any happier now that I am where I am. Isn't this much the same choice again? The very fact that I was so sure about internal medicine seems to make my reversed choice even more important. I can't help but think that I ended up where I did this summer and with those people for a big reason other than happenstance. If that really is true, then I have to believe that I made a correct choice and act on it until something occurs otherwise. Enough of that—I realize that I never had made this firm statement to you so I thought it could stand clarification.* (November 4, 1967)

The various advisors and instructors frankly told Rebekah that her chances for acceptance into surgery residency were limited because of her being female. Surgery was not a medical field into which women were easily accepted. Concerned yet knowing the decision was right and God's will was paramount, she continued the quest for the perfect program for her—one that would train her for the challenges of being in a mission hospital situation—one that saw every kind of need. She realized the demands of such a program: five years, with the first year serving as the internship and the last four years those of residency.

Even though Dr. Scott at Vanderbilt had assured Rebekah that she was on "top list" for a surgery internship at Vanderbilt followed by a residency, she explored other programs. December 19, 1967 found her with Dr. G. Thomas Shires at University of Texas Southwestern Medical School, Dallas. She was interviewing for an appointment to the school's general surgical residency program. On January 14, 1968 she mailed her rankings:

1. Parkland Hospital University of Texas Southwestern Medical Center, Dallas
2. Medical College of Virginia, Richmond, Virginia
3. Vanderbilt University School of Medicine, Nashville
4. Johns Hopkins Hospital, Baltimore, Maryland
5. University of Rochester, Rochester, New York
6. University of Virginia, Charlottesville, Virginia

The agonizing choice between surgical specialty and medicine specialty made, the interminable wait for appointment began. Finally on March 4, 1968 a note from Dean Chapman announced a meeting for Monday, March 11, 10 a.m., for internship announcements, with the rest of the day off from school. No doubt the next seven days stretched longer than the first semester of that senior year. On March 11 the wait and suspense ended. Rebekah's appointment to a surgical residency at Parkland Hospital, Dallas (University of Texas Southwestern) confirmed her instinctive reaction to the program at Southwestern being well-suited to her needs on the mission field and affirmed the choice of hospital for this vital part of her medical training. A week later she reflects on her choice of Vanderbilt and now Parkland: *Only God could have planned it this way.*

Dr. Chuck Nixon, general surgeon, one year behind Naylor at Parkland Hospital, explains the program at Parkland as "perhaps unique in the nation in the '70s. Second-year residents were not sidelined so much as apprentices but put immediately into the surgical operation theatre. They operated early in their program under close supervision rather than playing an understudy role for two to three years while watching the senior resident (a fourth-year trainee) do the cases. Then in the resident's third year while rotating on various subspecialties such as OB-GYN [obstetrics-gynecology] or orthopedics, the surgery resident had by that time accumulated so much first-hand technical expertise that the weight he or she carried onto the subspecialty services was considerable and made the rotations much more enjoyable and productive. For example, Naylor didn't need a urologist to teach her to remove a damaged kidney because she had already done that procedure before under extremely challenging and life-threatening circumstances. Most surgical programs were still placing the operating responsibilities mainly on their fourth-year residents whereas the Parkland second-year resident operated in the primary position while the seasoned fourth-year resident served as a junior staff instructor and operated only the biggest cases which at that time were vascular in nature."

That Naylor's choice of surgery proved to be one she could not only learn but also perform ably is noted by her peers and juniors. Nixon remembers Naylor as "an excellent surgical technician with genuine rapport with her patients as well as with Dr. Tom Shires, the program department chief. She had the brain power and the nimbleness of her fingers working in tandem to perform the surgeries. She was smart, kept her mouth shut, did her job efficiently, and stayed out of politics.

Naylor seemed shy and to stay by herself." Dr. Lee also commends Rebekah's choice: "Although rare for women to go into surgery during the '60s and '70s, Naylor chose well. Surgeons are gutsy people. They are not scared of gunshots or stab wounds, so a caesarean section won't affect them adversely. General surgery suits the missionary doctor well."

Similarly Dr. Scott Middleton, surgeon, of Corsicana, Texas, gave his observations of the diminutive Dr. Rebekah Naylor, intern. A senior resident at the time, Dr. Middleton knew Rebekah only limitedly. Dr. Shires sent him to help her do her first surgery at Parkland; it was an inguinal hernia repair. Like his colleague, Dr. Nixon, Middleton observes that Rebekah became "the first female surgical resident at Parkland, and physicians in those days were not gender friendly, surgeons among the worst." In subsequent years Rebekah has not only been with Dr. Middleton in the OT, but also he has recently sat in with her during Grand Rounds at Parkland Hospital. During one of her furloughs he even took her place in Bangalore Baptist Hospital as a volunteer.

Nixon commented that Naylor "seemed reticent to share her faith initially." Nixon, an evangelical Christian himself, didn't understand this tendency, since she was headed for the missionary field. He finds her "a changed woman now . . . warm in personality, verbal in her faith, and outgoing not cautious and quiet." Perhaps her association and broadening experiences with First Baptist Church, Dallas during those five years of the residency program produced these results; perhaps her confidence and the growing realization of the importance of her faith prompted the boldness. All for the better, she changed and grew.

The hospital changed and grew as did the young surgeon. At the dedication of Bangalore Baptist Hospital in January 1973 the hospital was an 80-bed facility. The hospital could serve 7,000 outpatients and 6,000 inpatients per year. At the time Rebekah arrived in May 1974, however, the census remained low—only in the 20s, occasionally reaching 30. By August 1974 numbers of patients reflected an increase. An August 11 letter notes: *The census is up to 45! . . . Policies need to be set.* In April 1975 the surgical recovery room opened; it was equipped and run efficiently under Dr. Naylor's direction. The tiny clinic in a converted chicken coop behind Dr. Ralph and Lynda Bethea's home emerged as an ever-expanding medical facility that serves the needs of the nearby community.

The Cutting Doctor reports surgical cases:

I can't believe I'm here. My first surgical case in Bangalore—tubal ligation, 4 days post-partum on Uma, a Hindu lady with many children. She must stay in the hospital until 10 days after delivery because of the Hindu idea that a woman [is] unclean and should be isolated during that time. She does speak some English. Has a cute baby girl.

We continued with the perplexing diagnostic problem of the 13-year-old boy who weighed 20 kilograms and had severe abdominal and back pain, vomiting, and weight loss for 1 year. We were getting nowhere in diagnosis until Friday when we did an Upper GI-obstruction in second part of duodenum. He had had upper GI bleeding twice earlier in the week and was losing ground. We set him up for surgery Saturday a.m. He had an inflammatory mass in right upper quadrant area of duodenum. As we Kocherized the duodenum and dissected around, we found posterior perforation X 2 of duodenum involving the ampulla and distal common duct with severe inflammation in the head of the pancreas. The more we looked the more evident it became that a Whipple was the only alternative—no

*way to repair the duodenum or put any kind of jejunal
limb up there. We did it—6 hours total operating time.
I was the surgeon. It was an exhausting day but every
aspect of the case went smoothly. Now after over 48
hours he is still doing well and, in fact, is far more
comfortable postop than preop.*

Descriptions of cases continue over the years—caesarean
deliveries, leg amputations, cancer of the tongue resulting in
the removal of half the tongue, removal of worms from the
intestines, mastectomies, appendectomies. From limited expo-
sure to the operating room no more than two mornings per
week in those first few months of assignment to Bangalore
Baptist Hospital in 1974, The Cutting Doctor progressed to
extended hours in the operation theatre several days per week.

Early in Naylor's tenure at Bangalore Baptist Hospital she
felt frustration that patients during the clinic examination did
not give commitments for needed surgery. If a patient did give
consent and scheduled an appointment, frequently the patient
did not keep the appointment. Yet these surgeries were essential, not elective. After being in the States for furlough, Naylor
commented January 20, 1984 that *I have had to readjust to
frustrations of refusal of surgery and failure to keep appointments.* That patients do not agree to the needed surgery or do
not keep their appointments today frustrates the physician.
Lives could be saved, better care provided, and health
improved for many people if only the treatment could be
given.

Despite the frustrations and perhaps because of the realiza-
tion of the need for early treatment, in early 1999 Naylor
organized and instituted the first breast camps in the villages.
Taking a team—Mary Sundari of nursing services, Beulah
Sundra, a practical nurse, and Carol Moore, a registered nurse
(R.N.) from the United States—Naylor went into rural areas

and city slums not far from the hospital to teach women about breast cancer. Using a flip chart she designed, she gave instruction on cancer of the breast as well as on the process of performing breast self-examination; she then did exams on hundreds of women. Sundra remembers that at the first camp more than 350 patients attended—so many that the police finally closed the gates so that the crush of the crowd didn't impede the examinations. The team repeated the visits every three months. These initial camps segued into regular occurrences under the aegis of Community Health, which was already a viable, integral department at Bangalore Baptist Hospital years earlier. Sundra herself has continued to work actively with the breast camps and Community Health, although in 2003 she moved to the newly formed HIV department as a counselor.

The Community Health department's beginning was a mobile clinic driven from village to village. The first van arrived Monday, December 8, 1975. Of that event Naylor writes in her December 10, 1975 letter: *This week we began a feeding program in our initial village . . . well received. Actually it is exciting to think of possibilities. Already much education has taken place.* Because of the great number of attendees, the half-day camps extended to full days.

Regardless of the years of training, the elite medical specialty of surgery, or her position as chief of medical staff, Naylor placed patient care first and never thought herself above any duty nor found performing any duty beneath her. Sundra observed that a patient in ICU (Intensive Care Unit) needed an emergency surgery. Naylor, the physician on call, ran from her quarters to the hospital. The only operating-team member present, Naylor prepped the patient and the OT (operation theatre) herself. By the time the surgical team members arrived from their homes in Bangalore, all preparations were complete. Surgery could commence. Freeda David, the OT charge nurse, told of similar instances in which Naylor regularly worked as a team member within the theatre. Naylor helped the nurses scrub, then helped the anesthesiologist scrub; only then did she herself scrub for the upcoming procedures. Between surgeries, she cleaned the OT as well as brought in the new patient; she never relied or expected someone else to perform those tasks. Dr. Naveen Thomas, currently the deputy director, tells of an obstetrical delivery patient with a prolapsed cord. Naylor took the trolley to OT, gave the anesthesia, and performed the caesarean section. Dr. Thomas, an internist and not a surgeon at that time, helped before the anesthesia. Sister Flora, director of nursing, spoke of her initial experiences as a registered nurse in OT. Generally Naylor reached the hospital first and assessed the patient in the emergent situation ahead of the OT team's arrival. She would have taken the patient into the theatre and have the packs and anesthesia ready when the team arrived at into the hospital. "She doesn't wait for others or think herself different; she is ready to do what it takes to do the job," avers Sister Flora.

Both Sister Freeda and Sister Flora pointed out Naylor's teaching before, during, and after the surgery. She listed patiently more than once the supplies and equipment needed for each particular type of surgical procedure. Before each surgery, she explained what she would do during the surgery and what the nurses should do. Then after each surgery, she quizzed the nurses on what they had learned from that particular procedure and that case. She taught them anatomy and how to assist in the theatre and aided them in becoming the efficient, capable surgical nurses they are today. With a smile Sister Flora announced emphatically that Naylor has "compound eyes like a butterfly. She looks everywhere at once—on respiration, on me, on the patient."

Nurses and other physicians concur on Naylor's habitual practices in surgery. First she prays with each patient before the surgery. As she started the surgery, in Kannada she said,

We are going to pray to God. Please close your eyes. She allowed others to pray; often the team members took turns. According to Sister Flora, Naylor "understands many languages and always knew when to say 'Amen,' regardless of the language." Secondly her team members and fellow physicians echoed Drs. Nixon and Middleton's characterization of her as a surgeon. She was fast in surgery, correct in writing orders, efficient, and tireless.

Naylor's various titles and names reflect respect, admiration, even awe, and definitely her position as physician. At the beginning of her term at Baptist Hospital the nurses called her *Sister* as they do each other and as others refer to the nurses. Sundra calls her *Naylor Amah,* the same title Mother Teresa was given. Hannah Sinclair, the secretary in the administrative office, calls her *Doctor.* Naylor did convey the image of a physician, for she wore her lab coat, a three-quarter length, long-sleeved, white poplin, button-front coat with her name embroidered in black above the top left pocket: *Rebekah Ann Naylor, M.D.* Wearing this coat whenever she was officially serving as a physician and therefore representing the hospital, she was unmistakably *Dr. Naylor.*

Initially cases trickled into both surgery and the hospital. After the 10th anniversary of the hospital in 1983 other surgeons belonged to the staff. Cases a surgeon with a particular specialty within surgery might do, Naylor did. For instance, she removed the gallbladder of an 18-month baby with peritonitis, whereas in the United States a pediatric surgeon might do the same surgery. Naylor writes her parents to reassure them she was functioning as a surgeon:

Thursday I was in surgery all day—big cases. Two of them were pediatric patients, one with two big cysts in his liver and another with apparent tumor. Both did OK. The liver case was especially stressful. Dr.

Viswanath's wife had a breast lump and I did a biopsy—no report yet—hopefully benign. Then last night I had a lady with an abscess of her pancreas. Today all are stable. But a wearing day. (June 19, 1992)

The letter dated August 21, 1994, states: *I have done quite a bit of surgery since my last letter. Thursday I operated on Dr. Prathap's cousin who had cancer of the colon. The surgery went well and I was able to remove it. So far she has done OK. We are waiting on the pathology report to know the extent of it. She is a very nice lady. I had another small case also. Then Saturday we had a lady (PC or private paying patient the hospital terms Private Consultation)— who actually came to Dr. Joy for what had been diagnosed in Singapore as an ovarian tumor. These people are with Campus Crusade, live mostly abroad, have children in the States. She decided to have her surgery in Bangalore and wanted us to do it. I was to help Joy from the general surgical side. It turned out not to be ovarian despite so many fancy tests done abroad. She had a large tumor apparently coming from her rectum and lower colon. It was quite extensive and not resectable. We ended up doing biopsies only. The lady had not had any symptoms—it was found on a checkup. And the husband is stunned. Joy and I spent almost half hour with him after the surgery. This morning she wanted to know exactly so I told her. They are wonderful believers and very nice people. We have prayed with them numerous times this week. It has been emotionally stressful. I had two little PC cases besides that big case on Saturday. Friday night there was a man with a perforated ulcer who also was obstructed. And there was a C-section Friday night. I have done 7 cases the last 3 days. I also saw 8-9 PC's in clinic*

*Friday morning. And a man came to me also with a
thyroid lump which I will operate on the 1st. I also
have cases to do this coming Thursday.*

In December 1995 she pens these words: *Surgery is
going through another bad cycle—not quite so sick as
Christmas but almost. I am involved in 3 ICU patients
just now—at least one of whom we do not have a diagnosis except malaria and we cannot explain all on that.
Then last night a lady came with severe abdominal
pain. She was white as a sheet. She was unmarried.
She had no trauma. She denied any sexual activity ever.
She had blood in her abdomen. Well, I pushed in 4
units of blood and at 2 AM took her to surgery. She had
a ruptured tubal pregnancy. She is fairly stable now.
Lying nearly cost her life. Today I had to operate on a
lady with severe abdominal pain—she had TB all over
her abdomen—she is fairly sick. Then Tuesday I helped
Fred [Job] do a very difficult major case—the man had
a block in his bile duct. Fred never dreamed I would let
him do it. His technique is very good. I walked him
through the procedure. He was thrilled. He and the
patient did well! Now after this long description, have
no doubt that I am doing general surgery.*

Once again, Naylor stresses and assures her parents that
she wasn't losing her skills or growing stale within her chosen
field but instead was utilizing them and the nine years of training almost daily and many times per day.

Regardless of the frequency of *very sick patients*, the term
Naylor used to describe those deemed beyond critical, and
large numbers of patients with one of the ordinary medical
problems, Naylor never adjusted to deaths and some conditions. Summer and fall 1982 brought several such experiences,

one after the other. Two amputees happened in May. She removed a leg filled with maggots from one who lived; the second died. She writes: *I was not affected but was bothered enough after all these years that I had trouble sleeping . . . strange after all these years.* The Truebloods—Tom and Mary Jo, teachers at Kodai in the English-language private school— had been in India only one year. They traveled to Bangalore for dental appointments. While there Mary Jo began bleeding; it was a recurrence of a previously diagnosed medical condition. Surgery had been recommended. Since Dr. Prabha, the obstetrician who performed the earlier D and C, was off-duty, Naylor took the case and admitted Mary Jo to Baptist Hospital Saturday afternoon. The letter of August 19, 1982 gives the account:

I gave blood on Sunday and she improved. I told them she could not put off the hysterectomy. Tuesday morning we did it—the surgery itself was no real problem. But she apparently had a major transfusion reaction to blood we gave during surgery. About an hour after surgery things began to fall apart. Just everything went wrong. By late afternoon her blood pressure was unsteady, lungs full of fluid. She seemed to stabilize in a rather precarious state but at 6 p.m. got worse. Again she stabilized. I finally went home at 11 only because Dick was the duty doctor plus I had a big case on Wednesday morning. Dick called at 1:30. She was worse. I went back. Sarah [Williams] came also and sat with Tom and their 17-year-old daughter. She was unconscious all night. It was one of the worst experiences I have had. I sat with the family most of the time as there was not anything more we could do for her. Finally she died about 9:30 a.m. Wednesday. At 8 when I had to start surgery, I told Tom that I had to go and Dick would be there. Already he knew there was no

hope and was crying. But he embraced me sobbing and
said "Thank you." I had stayed together until then . . .
Emotionally this has been terribly difficult for me plus
I am tired—long hours in surgery this week.

Tom hugged Rebekah! What a witness to the non-
Christians among hospital workers and visitors and patients to
have a committed Christian thanking the doctor despite the
loss of his wife and soulmate!

In late November a 15-year-old boy who had fallen off a
tractor that had in turn run over his abdominal area was
brought into Casualty. Naylor comments: *The pancreas gland*
was cut in half. I so rarely ever care for trauma. He's doing
OK after all that [injury and surgery].

A practical, truthful person and physician, Naylor carefully
chose her words in advising patients of optimal care and treatment. Many times patients who had medically compelling reasons for needing surgery either delayed or never had it.
Patients might not follow careful and precise instructions.
These instances provoked blunt reactions: *I went for surgery at*
2 p.m. Sunday and it took all afternoon. This young woman
was started on TB treatment in our hospital early in 1981.
After 3 months she stopped and never came back. Now she had
been 10 days in some outlying hospital with acute abdominal
pain. She was so terribly ill. She had a bowel perforation and
died at 8 p.m. Came too late—no compliance with treatment—
all could have been prevented. That is the every day sadness
that is here.

Not all accounts were dismal nor sad but easily could have
been. The following certainly reveals the Indian environment
that is far different from that of the United States:

Friday afternoon I was about to go home at 5 when
a man was brought in from Kogilu, our main rural

clinic village, having been bitten by a cobra at 3 p.m.
They had been trying to get transport all that time.
About 1 minute after he arrived, he stopped breathing.
Cobra venom causes paralysis of all voluntary muscles
so that is what happened. He was bitten on the hand.
Nirmala was on duty. Russ [Rowland] was still here.
With real teamwork we got a tube in his trachea and
started breathing for him. We had 6 vials of antivenom
which was not enough. I called Bill [Mason] to find
some. He rounded up 6 more vials from 3 other hospi-
tals in town. I would not have given you 2 cents for his
chances. The men had brought the cobra with them in
a bag. This man was trying to catch it and sew its
mouth closed when it bit him. He had done this before
and had never gotten hurt. All this confusion took place
during the middle of visiting hours and the whole hos-
pital was in an uproar! Well, Russ and I left about
6:30—the man was unconscious and making no respi-
ratory effort on his own. By 10 he was awake, breath-
ing, and I was able to pull his tube out! Since then his
hand has had much swelling and pain. He tried to stop
breathing again while I was eating lunch yesterday, but
today he looks good. We told him even Friday night
who had saved him. This is quite a story. If he contin-
ues to do well, this will be fantastic for PR in the vil-
lage. (June 27, 1976)

Fewer than 30 patients per day may have been the norm in
1974 and ample reason for concern for the fledgling hospital.
The numbers, however, increased. On August 27, 1976 she
wrote home: *Today the census is at 86—patients on cots!*
We've put extra beds in the wards. By 1982 overcrowded conditions prevailed. The hospital indeed was known in the community! The more seasoned Rebekah Naylor, M.D., general
surgeon, commented: *I did still another C-section during*

lunch. We have 14 newborns on the ward as of now! Today we had 85 patients and 13 newborns on the census—just running over everywhere! The 29 days of February 1984 recorded 125 OB/GYN cases, with 14 in the first two days of March that year—all performed by Naylor and Dr. Prabha. In 1998 the rate of yearly occupancy amounted to more than 80 percent or no empty beds. Although one of her goals for her fourth term as missionary surgeon in India was to *build a stronger surgical practice*, the letters and official reports show clearly that The Cutting Doctor had ample opportunity not only to hone her skills but also to use them frequently at Bangalore Baptist Hospital.

Administrator

At left, Rebekah in her office at the
Bangalore Baptist Hospital

Below, Rebekah with nurses
at Baptist Hospital

With Naveen Thomas, left, and Dr. Khan

Above and at right, Rebekah with U.S. Health and Human Welfare Services Secretary Dr. Donna Shalala on Shalala's Bangalore visit as part of India tour in 1997

With Richard Celeste, U.S. ambassador to India, during Dr. Shalala's visit

*The Lord himself goes before you and will be with you; he will
never leave you nor forsake you. Do not be afraid;
do not be discouraged*
(Deut. 31:8).

Administrator

*I feel in some state of numbed exhaustion. The day of mission
meeting is now ended. I am now chairman of India Baptist
Mission (IBM) . . . A real bombshell came . . . unanimously
they agreed that I should be the new chief of medical staff.*

The Foreign Mission Board (FMB) of the Southern Baptist
Convention in the 1970s as well as now organizes its work
systematically. The first division was by geographical areas
into seven worldwide areas, which then were subdivided into
smaller regions—missions—such as a multiple country group
or one country. An area director lived in Richmond, the headquarters for the FMB, and coordinated the operation of the
missionaries within the area. Dr. J. D. Hughey, former missionary to Spain, was area director of the Europe and Middle
East area, of which India was a member.

In the mid-1970s the mission in India carried the title *India
Baptist Mission* (IBM). It represented the cooperative efforts
of both Southern Baptist missionaries and the Indian Baptists
throughout the country.[1] The field representative, the FMB in-
area director, was James Kirkendall. The missionaries in
Bangalore were considered a station. The station (Bangalore),
working under the aegis of the FMB and within the provisions
set forth by the property deeds and agreement with the Indian
government for the foundation and building of the BBH, oversaw local money matters, living quarters, property management, goal-setting, evangelism strategy, and operation of day-

to-day activities for the community of missionary personnel and mission employees.

When Naylor joined the group in 1974 missionaries in Bangalore were few: J. Allison and Sue Banks, Jack and Sharon Everhart, Cindra Huffman, Margaret Ann Hunt, Carolyn McClellan, Robin Ritger, John and Barbara Wikman, Richard and Frankie Hellinger, Bill and Mona Mason, Russ and Betty Rowland, and Linda Garner. Assigned directly to the hospital as medical personnel were Wikman, Hellinger, Rowland, and Naylor—physicians and each a medical board fellow; Bill Mason, administrator; and Garner, who had a master of science in nursing. In the local mission office, Florence Charles, office manager, coordinated many of the mission activities. Individual missionaries, elected by their peers, held offices such as mission chairman, vice chairman, secretary, treasurer, and hostess. By sharing and dividing responsibilities, no one missionary need assume the sole responsibility for the smooth and orderly operation of the mission as well as serve in the primary missionary role to which he or she had been appointed.

From the outset government policy about foreigners, especially Christians, in India was uncertain. In January 1975 Dr. Hughey wrote: "We cannot expect to send missionary evangelists to India, but we can hope for visas for unusually well-qualified medical and educational specialists whom the government regards as needed."

Additionally, the goal was to "avoid in India a buildup of permanent dependence on Southern Baptist money and missionaries. This is paternalism. Such dependence is not good for individuals, churches, or other institutions. The present tendency towards Indianization is an attempt to correct this. The future presence of missionaries in India and even the importation of funds are uncertain. What we do must be done in such a way that it, or the resultant good, will live on after Southern Baptist missionaries have gone and the funds cease . . . Our task in India is not to carve out a Southern Baptist area of influence, but rather to contribute to the growth of God's kingdom . . . We must avoid any suggestion of Southern Baptist superiority or imperialism. Indian government policy limits the admission of missionaries; many Christian leaders also favor Indianization . . . [The] prestigious Christian Hospital and Medical College of Vellore, India, invited a Southern Baptist missionary to join the faculty. Southern Baptist Convention relationship to Vellore is being renewed now through a missionary professor of anatomy. A Southern Baptist missionary is on the theological faculty of Serampore College, near Calcutta, the school founded by William Carey . . . [A] visiting Baptist agriculturist has served on faculty of University of Agricultural Sciences in Bangalore. Southern Baptists cannot establish a medical college, a seminary, or an agricultural university in India. But in existing institutions are splendid opportunities to serve the Christian cause as Baptists."

Hughey explained two primary goals for the work in Bangalore:

"1. cooperation with existing respected Christian institutions and established Baptist churches and general organizations . . .
2. concentration on state of Karnataka (formerly called Mysore) " ("A Strategy for India." *The Commission*. January 1975. 19-23.)

Thus the institutional approach to evangelism, similar to the methodology practiced by the FMB in other parts of the world, served as guiding principle for the work. Although one purpose for the hospital was and is to bring medical care to those who seek it, another of equal if not greater, importance was and is the commitment to share the story of Jesus and salvation with each patient, staff member, and visitor. (*The Commission*. January 1975)

No one—not even a newcomer—was exempt from serving within the mission organization. At the first meeting Naylor attended in June 1974, she was elected secretary. She quips: *But I can't type. Florence will type!* Florence Charles faithfully transcribed Naylor's notes. Other missionaries arrived the following year: John and Kathy McNair, Van and Sarah Williams, Maurice and Nancy Cook. By 1976 they, too, were elected to key positions: Van Williams, pediatrician, mission chair; John McNair, vice chair; Mona Mason, secretary. All missionaries except Linda Garner, two journeywomen, and Naylor were married.

In April 1979 Naylor found herself elected as chair of the India Baptist Mission. Naylor, in her new position, learned quickly that Bill Wakefield, now area director for Southeast Asia, the area to which India was shifted, would be invaluable. A seasoned career missionary accustomed to the daily operations of a station, a mission, or an area, he could advise in financial matters which remained a major concern since the facility opened; in focus and direction; and in personnel issues. Wakefield's visit provided Naylor with confidence, encouragement, and direction:

> *I am so grateful and pleased for the way Wakefield has related to us, his positiveness, his perceptiveness, his understanding, his listening ear . . . We were able to cover almost all major immediate problems. Strategy planning and decision—he communicated clearly his philosophy and approach but agreed with us that we had to get our objectives and then policies clearly stated. We would aim to finish it by mid-1981 according to furlough schedules. He clearly got the picture that because of our unique size and situation, we needed more outside direction. He proved more than willing to assume it . . . Instead of a field representative (he does not like that concept). He decided we only might need a*

"consultant" to come in 2-3 times per year, serving
many of the same functions. He proposed Jerry Rankin.
(October 12, 1979)

Indeed Rankin did assume the position of consultant. This began what would be a long-term friendship as well as an employee/supervisor relationship for Naylor and Rankin. *Jerry will be a consultant to us as set up by Wakefield, comparable to field representative but not called such. I felt that we had a good meeting and a good discussion about many subjects. Jerry and Bobbye have been well received by the entire group.* (January 18, 1980)

The mission limped along; it was composed primarily of physicians or teachers, none of whom was trained or equipped to lead administratively or to see the overall picture relative to strategy for evangelism or operation of the business portion of the station. One great accomplishment of the group was the completion of the policy manual—a big step toward preparation for the yearly mission meeting. When Naylor resumed office of chair in July 1983 the missionaries on station were few: Jason and Carolyn Lee, Dick and Joan Fox, Van and Sarah Williams, Glenda and David Travis, Dwight and Emma Baker, and Naylor.

Mission meetings involved participation and attendance of all the missionaries within the mission of India as well as the consultants and area director. Often these meetings were held in lovely resorts or mountain retreat centers such as the beach of Goa or the hills near Kodai. Bible studies provided by an outsider to the mission allowed the missionaries to be led rather than having to prepare and present. The time away from station furnished change of scenery, change of pace, and relative freedom from the normal schedule and responsibilities. Naylor anticipated with some dread these annual meetings. Perhaps her shy, introverted, and retiring personality didn't lend itself to groups. Perhaps she felt somewhat defensive about her role, strong opinions, and forceful leadership. Perhaps she sensed different philosophies and priorities placed on projects and functions within the mission. She notes that the mission meeting June 21, 1984 was very difficult. The Board of Church Development, which supervises evangelism, had been restructured to be more positive and better controlled. The mission drafted these strong statements to the trustees:

- length of stay at Bangalore Baptist Hospital
- lack of interaction with and reporting to mission
- new approach to language and orientation
- after 1985 no increase in hospital subsidy
- giving to world missions from United States churches is grim
- Charles Stanley President of SBC—concern that he has only independent missionaries in his churches

The meeting provoked action and produced changes. Florence Charles, administrative assistant and office manager, was to work and not talk with missionaries during business days. Naylor, as chair, must keep her office hours in the mission office (a separate building from the hospital facility)—an additional stressor. How could she cover hospital emergencies, be in her BBH office, and be in the mission office? Although Naylor again was re-elected mission chair, she commented that *the people in India do not support me; others who do are back in USA.*

Jerry Rankin serving in his consultant role visited in September 1984 and discussed developments within the mission and the hospital—radical changes. Personnel dwindled: Van and Sarah Williams and their family returned Stateside in 1984 because of educational needs of their children; Dick and Joan Fox in 1985, Dwight and Emma Baker in 1987, David and Glenda Travis in 1988. Naylor states: *Steady loss of*

missionary personnel occurred until finally I was the only resi-
dential missionary from 1991-1996. Wakefield, realizing the
loss of personnel and the financial difficulty of the hospital
and mission, told the missionaries all programs except the hospital and church development—the two essential portions of
the work in Bangalore—were to cease.

Although in June 1985 Rankin moved to India in order to
take over National Indian Ministry (NIM), he remained actively involved in the work at Bangalore. The dramatic, tumultuous action at mission meeting bespoke another huge change.
*The first topic was structure of the mission for the year ahead
in view of only five people. Jerry had drawn up a proposal as
to how that would work if we decided to do it. We will do our
jobs, answer to Jerry—no committees or boards . . . Jerry will
be talking with each of us this week and then we will have
another general session on how we will function. Someone will
be asked to be coordinator and the liaison with him and the
FMB.* (January 15, 1985) The three missionary units on station—David and Glenda Travis, Dwight and Emma Baker, and
Naylor—reported directly to Rankin. By April 1987, however,
Rankin, now appointed area director, moved to Richmond
under IMB policy. Les Hill from the Philippines replaced
Rankin as associate area director.

Although the plan under which work in India began was
labeled the *institutional approach*, by 1984 a shift seemed to
be occurring. Hospital trustees discussed the possibility. *Phil
and I began thinking that maybe we should have a national on
a permanent basis. Phil does not want to do that if it meant my
not returning. I said it definitely did affect what I would do. I
was disturbed and yet I could see that as the answer (possi-
bly), an answer we had not been open to. I do believe in seeking God's will we have to be open to anything . . . Nationalization seems to represent philosophy of the new FMB Board.*
(March 4, 1984)

The tiny mission station made financial plans. Les Hill visited Bangalore on March 19, 1988, to meet with the Lees and Rebekah. Funds were limited and personnel few; therefore, the extra vehicles needed to be sold. Maintaining an office building in Bangalore seemed an unnecessary expense; the building should be vacated the end of the year. National leadership within the Indian Baptist Society needed to become more responsible for the evangelism and community work.

Bangalore Baptist Hospital, a separate operation from the Mission, had a trustee board and a personnel organization. Missionary medical personnel held key positions on the staff, but nationals also filled various positions such as nurses, technicians, dietary workers, *ayahs*, drivers—all the people necessary to operate and maintain a medical facility. Articles in *The Commission* magazine from February 1973 chronicle the opening and dedication of the hospital and state the hospital's mission:

The hospital "was officially opened and dedicated January 15, 1973." The general medical and surgical hospital "is to benefit all," according to the dedication announcement, but "the primary purpose is to serve the poor; 75 percent of the beds will be reserved for indigent patients." ("Missions Update." *The Commission*. February 1973)

SBC President Owen Cooper presented the hospital to the people of India. Chief Minister of Mysore State in India, D. Devaraj Urs, cut the ribbon across the door of the new BBH. This marked the culmination of a Baptist effort that began in 1964. Baker James Cauthen, FMB executive secretary, gave the dedicatory address:

"The doctors who have come to serve in this hospital are doctors of distinction who have stepped out of medical professions in our land and have come just because of their hearts' being motivated by the love of Jesus for mankind. The basic motivation is the example of the Lord Jesus Christ, for he came and went about doing good. And we who love him would like to be as he was. We would like to follow his example. Medical staff will include both American and Indian doctors. The two Southern Baptist physicians now on the staff are John H. Wikman, Jr. [surgeon] and Richard J. Hellinger [internal medicine] . . . Baptist Hospital will not only attempt to minister to the poor, but will also serve as a teaching facility, sponsoring internship and residency programs and later an outreach program in community health and a nursing school." ("Bangalore Dedication." *The Commission.* April 1973. 22-23)

As Dr. Hughey and Dr. Cauthen explained, one avenue of access to India was through this teaching medical institution.

April 1975 marked a significant change in Rebekah's career—one that affected her both as a doctor and missionary. On station as missionary less than one year Rebekah indeed was fulfilling the role indicated by the M and D behind her name. The annual Bangalore Baptist Hospital Trustee Board meeting occurred that April. Myriad emotions flowed:

> *Our hospital board meeting was just excellent— long and tiring in the heat. Discussions were superb. The trustees were excited by what had been done. They commented, as did Linda, that one year ago almost everyone literally was crying—including Dr. Hughey— over the absence of patients. Absolutely bleak discouragement . . . As chief of medical staff not only am I responsible for our current doctors, but also any new ones hired, lab, pharmacy, x-ray, medical records. The trustees demanded that I pursue contacts with the local medical community. And the beginning of our teaching program is my opportunity. All conferences are my job. I must admit that I am inwardly pleased and foresee*

*many possibilities. I may yet be doing that for which I
thought I came.* (April 27, 1975)

The most dramatic, earth-shattering, devastating change for
Naylor, the one who had continued to work despite shifts in
policy from the institutional approach to nationalization, loss
of mission personnel, shortages of funds, scarcity of medical
personnel dropped: sell the hospital! Sell the hospital? The
very avenue for Baptist work in India? The lifeblood and life
work of Naylor? Ah, but the impact on her personally as she
reflected on the past 14 years and contemplated the future.
Fast on the heels of this announcement dropped the staggering
report that all regular budget funding for Baptist Hospital from
the Foreign Mission Board throughout the following 5-10
years would be on a diminishing scale until none was given.

Naylor searched for a buyer for the hospital. She traveled
into Northern India, to Madras, to Calcutta. The various facilities could not understand why the sponsoring organization, the
Foreign Mission Board, wanted to sell the hospital. How could
the founding entity sell this property? The conclusion those
approached reached was that the hospital must have serious
problems with finances, personnel, quality of care, legal standing. Not one hospital or sponsoring mission organization was
interested. Naylor doggedly persisted; she was determined to
find a viable plan for selling the hospital rather than closing its
doors, all the while praying and pleading with her U.S. prayer
support to pray with her. She and the nationals in Baptist
Hospital felt betrayed, marginalized, undermined. Those in the
U.S. who knew her personally and knew of her work were
sympathetic to Naylor's predicament and feelings.

Another directive arrived—this one more definitive, more
final, yet strangely more positive. Naylor's words on October
11, 1987 give record: *[I had] a call from Jerry Rankin Tuesday
morning . . . He did say that I must pursue the possibility of
Vellore taking over management and the finding of a national*

administrator. (June 11, 1987) Shortly, she received the pronouncement: approach Christian Medical College and Hospital of Vellore about the purchase of the hospital. On October 1, 1987, Naylor visited with Dr. Pulimood, director of Christian Medical College of Vellore (CMC), when he attended an alumni meeting of the college in Bangalore. The two doctor/administrators discussed the idea of BBH as a peripheral hospital of CMC Vellore besides various ways in which the two facilities could be related and helpful. Finally Pulimood *suggested that we prepare a working paper on a model that could be worked out of a relationship between the two institutions. I felt it was a good beginning of discussions and he is very open to ideas.*

The meetings occurred regularly between Naylor and Pulimood, Baptist Hospital personnel and trustees, and CMC staff and trustees. During this discussion and negotiation period at least two volunteers from the United States gave valuable directions and shared their expertise in administrative concerns. Norman Roberts, senior vice president of Baptist Health in Little Rock, Arkansas, explained the concept of a satellite hospital—one of his administrative duties within the Arkansas Baptist Hospital organization. He went several times to Baptist Hospital; each trip was of tremendous assistance to Naylor as she struggled with concepts totally foreign to her in her isolation within India and separation from changes in American hospital-management practices. Cecil Hamiter, hospital administrator of Baptist Hospital, Gadsden, Alabama, and the epitome of a Southern gentleman, helped during his visits and extended stays. Perhaps Naylor's letters tell the story best:

The biggest event has been my trip to Vellore yesterday [November 7] and Norman's 3-day visit there. Norman and I had a meeting with the top leaders at the hospital [CMC] including Dr. Pulimood, the director. Norman presented the concept of satellite hospitals from his experience. To our astonishment they were already prepared to discuss our situation specifically. Norman wrote a paper while there on some considera- tions of relating the 2 institutions—a management con- tract was one aspect. By the time I arrived on Saturday they were talking very specifically, even as to who. The idea is that the FMB would own the hospital and par- ticipate in overall policy. Then CMC would manage it on contract (5 years at a time). CMC would appoint the top 2 or so officers and would manage it. Norman and I both had such an overwhelming feeling of God at work . . . Incredible. (November 8, 1987)

We are excited and somewhat overwhelmed by the events at Vellore. Sunday afternoon Norman and I went and had tea with Stan and Ragini [Macaden]. We wanted a special personal chance to talk to Stan. Monday we told the Administrative Committee. Last night Norman and I presented it to the mission. All response is mostly positive. The administrative commit- tee expressed quite reasonable concerns but not in a negative way. Stan was very excited about the possibili- ties. We shall do the necessary work and leave it in God's hands. The FMB and CMC hierarchy still must decide. (November 11, 1987)

On February 4, 1988 Naylor again writes of steps toward progress:

Cecil and I spent a long time going over the Vellore proposal. I finally called Dr. Pulimood in Vellore and Cecil and I will go there to see him on February 17. Last night I talked to Mr. Raghavan our lawyer about that and he is quite willing to handle it and has started working on the papers we have.

I certainly would be the first to admit that though I feel so positive that we are doing the right thing, it is not easy to think of the hospital going other directions. I can only pray those directions will be positive and to God's glory. Maybe the place can be even better. I do feel affirmation that our direction is right in that step by step we make progress when I thought such a thing was impossible. Les Hill speaks as though he has had indication from Jerry and even Bill Wakefield that we need to move in this direction. I am not sure yet whether the FMB is really ready to let go and hand over. I am comforted by the fact that because of my hard effort it is in better shape to hand over than ever before. Yesterday Earl, Les, Cecil, Stan, and I went to Vellore. We had a very good day. Earl and Les had never been there so Dr. Pulimood himself gave us a brief tour which I also greatly enjoyed. Then we met for 2 1/2 hours—7 of them and we . . . The people we are dealing with in Vellore are all so nice. Dr. Pulimood, the director, obviously now has a better understanding and trust of us. He no longer feels that control of the board is necessary to manage the hospital. But his colleagues still do and that still has to be worked out. Each time we talk, there is more understanding on some issues, and less on others . . . Rumors have now become rampant in the hospital here so I think Earl and I will talk to the medical staff before he goes. The plan is now to present it to the FMB and the CMC executive council. If the two can agree to agree we will negotiate all details and try to have a final agreement ready in 6 months time . . .
(March 20, 1988)

Earl was finally able to reach Jerry by phone on Monday morning. Jerry is very positive. He will

*present it to FMB in the April meeting. Earl and I met
with the administrative Committee Monday afternoon
to discuss details of talks with CMC last week. Then we
went to the lawyer with further questions about
property. I now must go to the mission lawyer to
straighten out the issue of a deed in question. He has
been working on it over a year, obviously not working
hard. Earl told me to tell him to do in 30 days or I
would go elsewhere.* (March 23, 1988)

*I went to Vellore Thursday morning . . . It was
incredibly hot . . . 105. The meeting began at 10:30
and . . . went on all day. Afterwards we met the 3 students we are sponsoring and visited with them until
6:30. Dinner at 7. Asleep at 8:30—despite the heat I
stayed in bed 10 hours and much of that asleep. I had a
fan but the bed radiated heat. What part of me was
down was sweating. They did discuss with their
Executive Committee on Wednesday the negotiations.
They did not go into specific detail. Thursday at 4:30,
last agenda item of the day with everyone hot and
tried, our thing came up! Dr. Pulimood, the director,
gave a summary of the hospital—excellent and concise.
He explained our predicament. He called on me to
speak without warning! I emphasized the young age of
our hospital and the inability of our churches to
assume responsibility. A very lively discussion followed. In general those doctors running hospitals were
upset and opposed— jealousy—and to my surprise the
church leaders seemed very favorable. In fact 2 or 3
bishop types made some very complimentary remarks
about our hospital, the need for continued witness. The
debate was heated. The only decision was whether to
negotiate—no commitments made. When at last the
vote was taken, it was almost unanimously in favor of*

going on with negotiations. I think this fairly well sum-marizes my trip and the events in Vellore. (March 27, 1988)

By April 1988 the discussions between Naylor, CMC, and the FMB were occupying even more of Naylor's time. Even Dr. Keith Parks, president of FMB, became involved in working out the legal agreements. Just as they had in the early stages of the discussion, personnel of CMC Council gave excellent advice and sent administrators and lawyers to help Naylor and other administrators and trustees with Indian law and the hospital organization, structure, constitution, and bylaws. Finally by July 1988 both Baptist Hospital Trustees and CMC Council had agreed to the major points concerning a management contract: subsidy, length of agreement, reviews, board structure, pastoral care department, name. Naylor writes: *We will proceed to prepare a draft of a legal document to be ready by late September. This will be presented to CMC's executive in September, to our trustees, the FMB, and the CMC Council in October. If OK, the final document will be prepared and signed. We will plan to implement January 1, 1989.* (July 10, 1988)

Thinking positively Naylor was sure that plans were moving in the right direction for the management agreement with CMC and that FMB supported the plan. Not so! In September Naylor learned that FMB had issues with the contract—specifically with the stress on the hospital's autonomy. She writes:

> *And this is the very thing we have defended to the last—retaining our identity of who we are and not being swallowed by CMC. I felt this was important for the continuing Baptist ministry . . . The counter proposal blew my mind. The leadership of FMB decided the best thing was to GIVE CMC all the property and*

hospital—just make them the owners also—then as
owners they would have to be responsible. The FMB
would still want all the same requirements in the agree-
ment—missionaries here, pastoral care . . . Basically
he [Jerry Rankin] said the FMB does not intend to
continue a curative health ministry in India. Life surely
is interesting. (September 26, 1988)

New conditions of the management contract with Baptist
Hospital and CMC were the major topic of discussion during
the hospital board meeting. Baptist Hospital would become a
legal society under Indian law. All property would be given
over to the hospital society; this would free the FMB from lia-
bility. *I feel we still can retain much of our autonomy and
identity. All of the points previously agreed about missionaries,
pastoral care, the name would be included in the agreement.*
(October 15, 1988)

At the CMC Council meeting the presentation of terms
took much of the meeting time. Naylor writes that

*the Council members, especially a few bishops
seemed most upset . . . They could not believe our hospital was not sick. They could not understand about
our Baptist churches. They were quite critical of a mission board that would wash its hands of a hospital
refusing capital funds or future support (after 5 years
of tapering subsidy). I despaired of the agreement ever
passing. But when the vote was taken, it was 77-3 in
favor of relating the two institutions as we have proposed. Another miraculous event. And another step
taken . . . We have agreed to try to finalize all documents immediately with CMC and BBH lawyers together and send it to Richmond. The next FMB meeting is
in December, 2nd week, and the CMC executive is
December 19 for this purpose.*

By November 10 Raghavan and CMC attorneys had revised the agreement contract; both BBH and CMC approved the terms. The documents left by courier Saturday, November 12 for the FMB in Richmond. Then December 16 the call arrived from Jerry Rankin after the FMB meeting December 13-14. Hear the joy in Naylor's letter dated December 16, 1988: *I finally had a call from Jerry this evening. He said all went through swimmingly positive, no question, pleased, supportive. Miraculously it is done.*

The biggest announcement of all flew back home in the January 6, 1989 letter. *But the greatest thing was that the CMC papers are signed by me! I went, got them all notarized, and the courier collected them. They will be in Richmond Monday. [Carl] Johnson [FMB vice president for finance] will sign them all and send them back. I will send them to CMC and we will be done! At the same time we have amended our rules of the society and this must be sanctioned by the local government. That has been submitted. PROGRESS!*

In the years after this tumultuous chapter of Baptist Hospital's history the decision to nationalize Baptist Hospital under the management plan with CMC is deemed wise, solid, providential, and a method for securing the future. Dr. Santosh Benjamin, former director and also acting director and CEO of BBH during 2006, noted that CMC Vellore brought in administration, put the hospital on firm foundation, and gave administrative and professional help to Baptist Hospital. An additional potential threat of no funds for operation was also avoided. The Indian government disallowed U.S. money entering India. Since FMB was the major support financially, this new government policy could have been disastrous for the hospital's operations. No one knew the ban would last only five months; no one knew when the ban once again might be put back in place. Benjamin also pointed out that when India gained her independence in 1947, some 700 hospitals funded and operated by mission organizations were in operation with more than 40 percent of all hospital beds in India mission facilities. "Administration was slack, vision was lost, and some 60 years later only 300 exist and all are struggling and marginal facilities. BBH, on the other hand, remains vibrant."

Rankin avers that the move to contract with Vellore and move Baptist Hospital from being a hospital under the aegis of the IMB was positive. Nationalization secured the future of the hospital. He recognizes that the change and the negotiations were a difficult and challenging time, with misunderstandings, questions, and even thoughts of abandonment of Naylor. Yet he praises the hospital: "The strength of BBH is amazing. A new wing has been built after IMB was no longer supporting the hospital and nationals were managing it."

In a recent reflection about the takeover of management by CMC, Naylor wrote the current director and CEO of BBH, Dr. Alexander Thomas, the following commentary on the positive effects of the arrangement:

> *The bottom line is that the relationship probably saved BBH. As other mission parent organizations left, we know what happened to so many mission hospitals. This tripartite agreement allowed BBH to continue and survive, not as some altered or different place with another purpose and name but with the same intent and direction as it has had from the beginning. The IMB has been able to continue to participate and share and minister without supporting or being solely responsible which it could not continue to do.*
>
> *1. Financial viability and achieving self support in operation—that was a primary concern from day one. CMC said we had to have private patients and staff housing. They pushed us in the raising of funds and the*

94

outlay of money to achieve viability

2. The education programs—I doubt that otherwise that would ever have happened. This vision for education emerged—it was there but dormant until then—being done in a small scale only (like interns).

3. Rapid growth of services and facilities. BBH had always moved forward and been a leader in the community (gastroscopy and ultrasound as examples) but this process became more rapid.

4. Administrative consultation—wise counsel based on their long experience—and yet never forced or imposed. This has been invaluable over and over again. This has indeed strengthened policy and financial management.

5. Professional consultation and development and equipping of our own staff—participation in the evaluation of services

6. CMC's reputation enhanced our own status in the community.

I think the retained autonomy of BBH is important, even its name and who we are and total respect for our opinions and ideas and vision. (October 13, 2007)

Baptist Hospital, like other medical facilities and the Indian Baptist Mission, has an organization that oversees day-to-day operation, employs personnel, and plans for future expansions. In the hospital's early years, the 1970s and 1980s, two major officers divided much of the work—the chief of medical staff and medical superintendent. The chief of medical staff, a physician, functioned much like a chief of staff at an American hospital. (*Administrator*, the American organization term for the superintendent role, is not used in the Indian-British system). According to Indian tradition, the superintendent position, held by a physician, carries legal responsibilities.

The executive committee composed of the chief medical officer and superintendent as well as heads of departments met
weekly. A board of trustees approved and set policy, salaries,
and pensions; appointed personnel to key positions; and oversaw long-range plans for the programs and operation of the
hospital among other duties. The trustees numbered only three:
a staff member from Christian Medical College and Hospital
Vellore, a person from Bangalore, and a representative of the
Foreign Mission Board. The hospital administrative team generally attended the meetings. Naylor, shocked to think she was
elected to the position of chief of medical staff in 1975, indeed
became medical superintendent just 10 years after her arrival
at Baptist Hospital. Big growth happened not only because of
medical and scientific advances and needs as well as financial
gains and patient numbers but also, and primarily so, because
of Naylor's leadership. As the head of the hospital, direct
responsibility for the programs of the hospital fell under her
supervision. Those areas for which provisions were made even
before the hospital's building and opening slowly became
realities.

At the inception of Baptist Hospital an agreement between
Baptist Hospital and Christian Medical College of Vellore
existed. Part of the agreement allowed two staff members of
Baptist Hospital to sit as members of the General Council at
Vellore and represent the Foreign Mission Board. Secondly
membership on Vellore Council allowed BBH to sponsor students in all levels of health-care training. Those sponsored
then work at BBH for two years in compliance with the contract between the ones sponsored and Baptist Hospital.
Children of staff personnel and children of Indian Baptists
received first consideration. The current deputy director of
Baptist Hospital, Dr. Naveen Thomas, a physician sponsored
by Baptist who has subsequently sought advanced specialties,
continues to work by choice at BBH. The appointment of the
first sponsored student occurred August 1976. Naylor in her

administrative role became directly involved with interviews and the appointment process.

Naylor and Baptist Hospital received affirmation of personal, professional, and medical worth. *I have been put on the Executive Committee of the Council. I was so shocked. Actually I was rather pleased. I will enjoy the relationships with the people and CMC. I feel rather honored that those guys thought I knew enough to contribute something. They want to have the December meeting in Bangalore so that they can see our hospital.* (October 21, 1988)

In preparation for the management agreement with CMC Vellore, Baptist Hospital formed a legal entity required under government policy and regulation—Bangalore Baptist Hospital Society. The trustees, a managing board, would carry the title *governing board*. Six of the seven voting members are from CMC Vellore: the director, general superintendent, principal, and treasurer of CMC organization plus two others according to Baptist Hospital needs such as nursing service or other ancillary medical services. The seventh member, currently Richard Folkerth, represents the International Mission Board. Sitting on the board in the non-voting membership capacity are three Baptist Hospital personnel: the hospital director, one member of the Administrative Committee who is elected for a two-year term by that team, and Naylor, representing the International Mission Board.

The original plans and the property deed called for the hospital to be a teaching facility. Wheels turn slowly in India, however, and each bit of change evolves over time. On April 11, 1978 Naylor writes of her visit with a cooperating medical school program: *I went to St. John's to see Dean Francis about internship programs. We will start with medicine and pediatrics—only 2 or at most 3 students at a time.*

The approval from the health minister in the national administrative office in Delhi allowed the intern program to move forward. Allocation of funds to pay two interns at a time allowed the first students to apply. The government regulations for the training and certification of a physician within India sets a compulsory internship of one year, which can be followed by further training in a specialty for six months or more. These doctors in further training hold the position of senior house officer and receive a stipend. Of particular significance to the program is that one of the first interns from 1979, Dr. Alexander Thomas, now serves as director and CEO of the hospital.

Excitement rings in Naylor's announcement marking the advent of the intern program at Baptist: *Big news—the intern program is picking up at last. We are getting people from other medical colleges in the state (government). One is to start this next week—a girl–she will start on surgery!* (June 22, 1979)

A second training program for doctors desired by Indian licensing boards and national regulatory agencies is the residency—years devoted to learning and perfecting one's medical specialty. In 1993-94 Baptist Hospital received approval from the National Board of Examinations for residency training programs in medicine, paediatrics, obstetrics/gynaecology, and surgery. In the first class of residents, Baptist took three young physicians—one in each of the fields. Since that initial class, however, the numbers have risen. In fall 2006 approximately six per department were in the residency program. Additionally, residency now also is available in orthopaedics, family medicine, and anesthesia.

Other departments were added to the hospital for medical care, education, and evangelism. In an article written by Naylor herself, the August 1978 edition of *The Commission* chronicles the beginning of the nutrition program ("On the Front Lines: Battling Malnutrition." 11-3) Data collected on a one-year period indicated that 17 percent of the children admitted into the paediatric service at Baptist Hospital suffered from protein-calorie malnutrition. Realizing the necessity for education of the mothers for rehabilitation and long-lasting positive effects, the hospital sponsored a feeding program for under-5 children in a nearby village in which the hospital's Community Health Division was already working. Children received a daily supplemental feeding of a mixture of locally available grains and foods. Villagers took part by providing firewood and some of the grains; one of the village women assisted.

In April 1977 the Nutrition Rehabilitation Center (NRC) was dedicated. Located on the Baptist Hospital compound, the building, constructed in village style with brick walls and thatch roof, contained a kitchen, space to house 10 mothers and 10 children, and a large room for classes and other daily activities. Not only were children fed a supplement of cheap, locally available food, but the mothers took part in the daily operation of the center by cooking, cleaning, working in the garden, mixing the food supplement (a high-protein blend produced by hand), and attending teaching sessions daily. The mothers were taught about Jesus Christ and learned to sing songs about Jesus. By June 1978 the well-established program housed 14 children with their mothers.

Although useful and one way of meeting needs of mothers and children, this center moved out of the way for expanded Community Health Department outreach and education programs (March 16, 1990). In 1975 the IMB approved the request that a Community Health Department be added to Baptist Hospital programs. The purpose was to "provide health care for at least 2,000 persons in four villages the first year; it will expand to serve 5,000 villagers within four years" (*The Commission.* October 1975). In 1979 the outreach program broadened its scope of training and outreach again. This expansion gave formal training to village health workers. These village residents are the same people who hand out medication and take care of the minor medical problems in between the regularly scheduled visits of the Community Health Team. The village health workers are taught to treat minor wounds including cleaning and dressing them, to manage anemia with iron and vitamin supplements, to teach mothers how to make oral rehydration fluid for children with diarrhea, and even to send patients to the hospital rather than wait for the next visit of the team. When the team arrives, the village worker often identifies those who are ill and need a visit. One important function of the health worker is that of ensuring proper antenatal care for not only the new mother but also the baby. These workers play a vital role in motivating and encouraging care such as feeding and immunizations. (*The Commission*. August 1979. 42)

New training programs, departments, and facilities continued to be added. As Naylor recently observed, *The hospital has always been evolving, even today in 2008.* The gobar methane gas plant gives insight into the resourcefulness of Baptist Hospital administration ably directed by Naylor. Every effort has been made throughout the years to provide facilities as economically and environmentally friendly as possible. Even as the nutrition center had used locally available products; so did the gobar plant. Naylor writes: *This is a very economical way to produce fuel using cow dung. It is quite a big brick structure with a drum or dome on the top. You fill it up with cow dung and gas is produced which can be piped to your outlet and fuel burners or stoves. A few villages are starting to have these. But this will be an educational thing as well as save so much money on wood in Nutrition Rehabilitation Center.*

During 1985 Naylor struggled to learn another facet of administration—finances. By 1986, she learned to set salary scales in compliance with laws in India and according to each employee's longevity and position. The pension plan, avows Mr. Prasad, head of the laboratory, is directly attributable to Naylor. Certainly under her direction, a new policy of sending the pension to the surviving spouse of a deceased employee began. In 1986, another adjustment had to be made after India passed the minimum-wage law. Careful to ensure that Baptist Hospital stayed within the Indian law and God's commandments, Naylor struggled to understand the laws, the nuances of the wording, and the culture. The team of attorneys and the external auditors required by Indian regulation contributed their knowledge to Naylor. Without their wise counsel, her job would have been even more difficult. On July 17, 1989 Naylor handed the arduous responsibilities accompanying the position of medical superintendent to Dr. Stanley Macaden, with the change effective in 1990.

Thus the hospital continued to evolve and to expand its physical plant, its staff, its services, and its programs. Similarly, the chaplaincy effort emerged. Because one of the two purposes for Naylor and the other missionary personnel being in India was to have an active witness and evangelism program, some pushed diligently for a formal department within the hospital—that of hospital chaplaincy. (Initially Indian pastors and evangelists led in the evangelism and follow-up work.) By June 1981 the little department began. Jarrett Ragan, a missionary with pastoral-care training, acted as pastoral-care director on temporary basis. Pastor Anthony Jacob, hired full-time in 1983, had spent two months at CMC Vellore for its counseling program. A graduate of South India Biblical Seminary with a bachelor of theology degree and a committed evangelist and man of God, he fit right into the hospital program. In 1987 he moved to the position of director of pastoral care. The records for 1986 show 152 professions of faith among patients in the hospital and the formation of seven Bible-study groups. Currently the chaplaincy department has a U.S.-seminary trained and pastoral-care-certified director with a staff of 10 chaplains as well as young men and women in the certification and licensing program for hospital chaplains— one-year programs. Dr. Philip Thomas, ophthalmologist, is the administrative director of the department.

On a tapering schedule the FMB removed daily operation budget monies. That does not, however, indicate it severed all relationship or denied money to this burgeoning evangelical and healing entity. Money arrives regularly through Lottie Moon Christmas Offering funds for special projects and for the pastoral-care department. One use of IMB money has been for housing. Hunger Relief Funds have provided support for Community Health.

Housing presented problems. When the hospital was initially constructed in the 1970s, the property was far from the center of Bangalore. Initially Naylor and Linda Garner lived in a duplex at 15th and Main Road in Upper Palace Orchards, a lovely upper-class residential area of Bangalore. Construction of a building to be used as guest housing for the many volunteers, trustees, and missionaries from other parts of India began shortly after their arrival. A mission meeting decision changed the use of the building. In 1975 Naylor moved into one side of the duplex and Garner into the other; there Naylor lived until her return to the United States in 2002. The move had several advantages and effects. Naylor no longer had to drive an unreliable vehicle alone on the rural, deserted, unsafe roads. Valuable time was not lost in sending a messenger. Transportation and telephone service became non-issues. Expert medical staff immediately was available for the hospital. In retrospect Naylor sees the move as pivotal in her relationship to the hospital, to the activities, to the medical care, to her involvement with all operations of the hospital—the chaplaincy, the medical services, the administration.

[1]Estep, William R. *Whole Gospel Whole World: The Foreign Mission Board of the Southern Baptist Convention 1845-1995*. (Nashville: Broadman and Holman, 1994), 304-308.

Entrepreneur Builder

Above, Bangalore Baptist Hospital pictured in 1980;
below, BBH as it appears today

Above, Rebekah Ann Naylor School of Nursing sign;
below, Rebekah stands in front of School of Nursing plaque.

REBEKAH ANN NAYLOR
SCHOOL OF NURSING

IN HONOR OF

RUTH RAY HUNT

WITH OUR GRATITUDE TO GOD
FOR HER HEART'S DESIRE
TO SERVE THE LORD THROUGH OTHERS

For nothing is impossible with God
(Luke 1:37).

Entrepreneur Builder

The bed problem is very acute. There were almost 60 patients in Casualty on Saturday and Sunday. Beds completely ran out . . . It is becoming more evident that we are growing almost faster than we can keep up . . . The news that $250,000 is being given remains so incredible to me—I have to pinch myself to realize it. God has provided so miraculously time and time again . . . The most major decision concerns nursing school—we MUST START.

"Rebekah is quite the entrepreneur! The money she has raised for BBH!" Dr. Clyde Meador, currently IMB executive vice president, accurately observed. Indeed the term matches well her successful, enterprising endeavors. As medical superintendent, Naylor sought to secure income for adequate operational funds, equipment replacement, and special project funding. During the 1970s the hospital had a large garden as well as outbuildings for the various animals. The cows provided milk for the hospital dietary department needs; surplus milk was sold to employees, staff, missionaries, and people of the community. Naylor comments, "We always had some money-raising project going on, like those chickens, the broilers we were raising and selling." The exact number? 1,056! Jumble sales, bake sales, trinket sales, even patron groups—all brought revenue for special needs and often ongoing operation expenses. Without the many patron groups, individual patrons, one-time donors, U.S. churches, IMB support, and the various fundraising events, the Baptist Hospital would not have the physical plant nor be the facility it is today. Finding money, however, always followed countless discussions centered on building limitations, expansion of space, continued services for the poor patients, and increased services such as mammography and residency programs.

Chapel met in the hallway outside the Intensive Care Unit that Sunday morning. Dr. Alistair Walker, pastor of First Baptist Church, Spartanburg, South Carolina, attended but not as the preacher for the service. As customary Naylor led the chapel service. As Naylor and Walker left the area, she lingered a moment, looked wistfully out a window, and remarked, "Someday this will be our chapel—a chapel readily available to all." The seed planted that morning took root. Walker's congregation sent to the Foreign Mission Board money gifts earmarked for the chapel. The first major addition to the original structure, the chapel was begun in 1979. The Prayer Hall, a spacious room, stands at the end of the second floor of a two-floor addition to the original hospital building itself. Naylor describes the process by which supplies were moved from ground level to the roof of the existing building. Crews of both women and men formed a line that began on the ground, extended up the sides of the walls, and ended on the roof. The person nearest the cement mixer held his or her bowl out for cement. In turn the bowl was passed along the human chain, from person to person on the ground to those who stood on bamboo ladders, ultimately to those on the roof and to the one who poured the bowl contents into the forms. *This week they have been pouring the roof for the chapel. All by hand, of course. Their only equipment is a very small cement mixer. They had the usual assembly line up two floors.* (September 25, 1979) The Prayer Hall was only the first of many projects.

Baptist Hospital building and expansion ensued. By 1989 beds numbered too few to meet the patient load. The number of paying patients needed to be increased to supplement income. Yet no proper facilities such as semi-private or private rooms existed, nor was a clinical area designated for the private-paying clients. To maintain a competitive edge with developing hospitals within Bangalore and close proximity to BBH, the addition of services seemed prudent and essential. Underneath the space, income, and service needs lay the original purpose of the hospital—that of becoming a teaching hospital that included paraprofessional training, National Board residency programs, and a nursing school, all of which CMC Vellore wholeheartedly advocated.

By June 1989 the decision was made to construct a new wing to the hospital. No money, however, was available. The hospital operated on a tight budget; borrowing money at the relatively young age of the facility frightened the staff and might not have been possible.

Naylor flew home for her furlough with the usual speaking engagements planned as well as anticipation of spending time with her parents. Uppermost in her mind was ascertaining from her father, an extraordinary fundraiser, methods of securing the needed $400,000. A second contact was a dear friend, Dr. John Seelig, the vice president of public affairs at Southwestern Baptist Theological Seminary. She was sure her dad and Seelig would know how to gain this money. Both men told her this was impossible! People weren't giving; people didn't know her; people didn't know Bangalore. Seelig gave her a book with names of foundations that donated money to medical and charitable institutions. Many of the 30 to whom she mailed appeals never responded to her letters. Those who responded refused to entertain the requests. To raise money, she needed to have raised some money first. Having some money would make her and the hospital credible. If the hospital were just starting to raise money, how could it have money? The situation seemed impossible. July became August; the end of September arrived—no money. Before an October appointment with the missions committee of First Baptist Church, Dallas, Rankin called to tell Naylor that $200,000 in

Lottie Moon funds would be given to BBH if the hospital could raise the other $200,000. Now, when she made an appeal, she could say the hospital had money.

Naylor made her presentation to the committee, most of whom she had known since her residency days. She asked for no amount. Dismissed, she went to the office of Libby Reynolds, primary director at the church. This dear, close friend asked, "What happened?"

Naylor told her. Libby queried further, "How much did you ask for?"

"I didn't ask for anything. Wouldn't it be wonderful if they gave us $25,000?"

"No! No, it would not! We're praying for $100,000." With that, Libby sank to her knees and prayed for that $100,000. After the prayer and hugging Libby, Naylor left Dallas.

That night one of the committee members called Naylor and told her that the missions committee recommendation to the church was to be $150,000. Before her return to BBH, the church presented the check to Naylor. By the time the building began, $500,000 had been raised. This gave BBH adequate money to build not only the new private-patient wing but also the shell of the outpatient-department wing. God provided the impossible. At every building phase and every financial crisis, Naylor gives testimony to God's provisions. What appeared to her as impossible—even to authorities in the area of fund-raising as impossible—God gave.

Costing $425,000, the new wing added 25 beds, for a total of 143 beds. Enlarged clinical space for outpatients, an attractive, spacious lobby, and a portico were part of the construction which Naylor says was "a dream, a vision, a need." Donations from the Foreign Mission Board, First Baptist Church, Dallas, and other donors in both India and the United States made the immediate construction feasible (*Baptist Press*. September 18, 1991). Although Naylor herself was on site daily, she grew to rely on others, too. Nothing in medical school had prepared her for dealing with outfitting a hospital wing, let alone constructing one. How was she to know how many different contractors had to be hired—electrical, plumbing, concrete, steel, painting, landscaping—and how many items had to be located, selected, and delivered or retrieved—chairs, beds, bassinets, faucets, door knobs, light fixtures, paint color, flooring, curtains, linens, dishes, trays for dining service, light switches, dust bins, oxygen supply, generator, water supply? The list seemed endless. Groundbreaking was April 5, 1990, with dedication scheduled for August 31, 1991 and opening September 1991. Several letters echo the theme of frustration with the process:

> *The final aspects of the oxygen installation have not been done—can't find the engineers—could not call Bombay due to phone problem. The painters are hopelessly far behind. I asked to double the work force and it did not happen. The finishing work is poor—switch plates at different levels, putty needed here and there.* (August 22, 1991) *I am wondering if I will ever survive. My compulsive personality and finishing a building in India are in such direct conflict that much tension is created. My standards and thinking are so different.* (August 22, 1991)

The new wing significantly enlarged the hospital facilities; the means for income from private-paying patients also became possible. The wing, though in use, did present problems—unfinished work, non-delivered supplies such as sheets for the patient beds, unresolved equipment failures, and specifically two big essentials for operation of the entire facility, the solar water-heating system, and the generator. The problem of a non-functioning generator was solved much more quickly than were the problems with the hot-water system.

Today the solar water heating man, the architect, the consulting engineers, and I met regarding the solar water system. We are still facing some problems which they are trying to rectify. This entailed a trip to the roof. It seems our maintenance guys don't help the situation as they come along and change things the engineers set. What to do! (November 19, 1991) *Would you believe that 10 months since opening we still do not have hot water in our wards?* (June 23, 1992)

In 1995 Foreign Mission Board missionary Bobby Jones assigned to Indonesia was posted to BBH on temporary assignment. Jones, whose specialty was overseeing construction and physical plants and who was a much-needed expert in finding and correcting problems, provided guidance, knowledge, and support for Naylor. As needed, he traveled from Indonesia to Bangalore. Through his ingenious resourcefulness and minute inspection of facilities, he found a partial solution to lack of hot water in the private-pay patient wing: *For very little money Bobby Jones has solved the problem of no hot water in the private wing. He hit upon the idea of one-way valves. Result? HOT WATER!* (May 30, 1995)

The new wing with its modern facilities met approval from both staff and patients and has stayed in constant use from its opening on August 31, 1991.

Patients and staff continue to enjoy the facilities. I had my first experience in the birthing room. It was great! . . . a first baby. The husband was there and he was so excited. They could not afford to stay there for the entire stay but spent the one day there. The bed, the ease of it—all was great. I have had a patient in the VIP room more than a week. He enjoys the TV and the AC. (October 8, 1991)

The fact that, despite devoting much of her day to building concerns, Naylor had time to fulfill her role as surgeon and share the obstetric/gynaecology patient load seems unbelievable. Earl Goatcher, IMB (retired) missionary to Thailand and a hospital administrator, notes: "Some kind of construction, or planning for construction, has gone on at BBH much of the time. Again, as though by default, Rebekah ends up serving as almost a general superintendent. Her administrative and pragmatic skills have been honed by these projects. Dealing with architects, contractors, and the noise and confusion of construction projects while continuing with all her other work became rather routine. (Not that the setting [of India] ever made it easy.) In the past 15-20 years there has been the added concern about finding the financial resources for capital expansion. With little or no help from the IMB, loans become necessary. That is scary for a mission hospital." (February 11, 2007)

Subsequent to the 1991 additions, however, facilities proved inadequate; another major wing needed to be built. The building committee met to discuss and to plan phases of the project. Of prime consideration was ensuring minimal disruption of hospital function. The first phase, the completing of the outpatient department wing, began in January 1993. A second phase, the entrance block including the registration area, began March 12, 1993—truly according to Indian methods with no machinery and only human workers. *Friday morning we did turn the soil for the new entrance building—just a prayer and groundbreaking—no speeches. About 100 staff were gathered. Mr. P. and the architect were there. They are digging (by hand, of course).* (March 14, 1993)

The enthusiastic tone of mid-March letters evolved to that of frustration with lack of progress, despair from feeling alone, and gloomy pessimism about completion and quality. More than once the operation chugged to a standstill. The delays, the cessation of work, the absence of workers, the shipment of the wrong supplies or furnishings, the improper placement of pipes or outlets—many types of problems persisted.

Much of my day went for building related things. The electrical contractor has now delayed the civil work by 2 weeks—way behind. (March 30, 1993) *They are now about 45 days behind schedule on that block.* (April 21, 1993)

Despite the delays and negative reports, the building construction did move to the point the OPD could be used. *The building . . . has been a burden, even a nightmare. . . BUT today we used the building for patients. I just decided on Saturday that **today** was **the day**. I nearly despaired over the weekend. But despite some confusion and minor problems, all were happy today. There was much excitement. It will be even better when the connecting wing opens. Now we must concentrate on the new building.* (July 28, 1993) Finally the connecting block with medical records and pharmacy showed near readiness. *The building is looking good! Mr. Parama Shivan is pushing it right along. We are going to make it by October 9 except for some stone outside. We are down to planning internally how to make it functional—like signs for instructions to patients. Medical records staff have fairly well planned the move of the records on the night of October 9th and all day on 10th. Our plan is that 11th morning we are ready to function from there.* (September 19, 1993)

A subsequent letter chronicles details of the move—not an easy feat during busy hospital activities.

The big move was horrendous, but our staff were so organized. They are so proud and happy that they glad-

ly undertook the work. Supervisors, department staff, and other volunteers helped mid-afternoon. I am amazed we did not all end up in bed or at least requiring physiotherapy! There were over 200,000 charts. The racks we bought (only a portion of total that could be in the space) were more than enough. The space for the medical records department is fabulous. The lobby is magnificent. Our painting of Jesus at the Pool of Bethesda which hung over our old registration counter absolutely is incredible in this lobby. I get a fresh reward just thinking and writing about the building and the events of the weekend. Parallel to this, on Sunday the entire pharmacy moved across the hall to the old medical records. The cash counter is functioning at the registration counter. Again staff did it in such a well-planned way. (October 12, 1993)

Perhaps this project looked even grander and more ambitious in scope than the wing built in 1991 because the operation of the hospital had to continue in and around the newer portions and remodeled older sections of the extant facility. The 1991 wing was for a new, different function and service of the hospital—that of private-paying patient rooms. The 1993-1994 projects, which initially were the OPD (outpatient clinic), registration area, and pharmacy with its cash counter, also included a nursery, paediatric ICU, and Casualty (the equivalent of an emergency room)—each at a different stage of completion and each one essential to the daily operation of a medical facility. The construction and remodeling of the multiple areas overlapped with current services. Nonetheless the projects and plans continued under Naylor's scrutiny and vigilant leadership.

A month later Naylor comments on the constant unfinished state of projects.

*The cash counter-pharmacy area is finished
(almost!) I think nothing is ever quite finished. In the
next couple of days some details in the cash counter
have to be finished. They have done a major part of the
civil work for lab expansion. We did open the cash
counter-pharmacy counter yesterday. I had asked
Santosh Benjamin, as Director of Paramedical
Services, to read Scripture and Anita as Director of
Administrative Services to pray. Those cashiers now
have light and air which is marvelous!* (November 6,
1993)

The several phases of the planned expansion and improvements begun in 1993 saw completion—some in 1993 and others in 1994 and 1995. Two involved care for infants and children.

*A wonderful event was the opening of the nursery
on Tuesday afternoon at 2:00 [November 2] Nurses,
medical staff, administrative committee, maintenance
staff who had worked so hard . . . And it is really
nice—quite an upgrade from where we were! We sang
in the hallway, a nurse read Scripture, Pastor Jacob
prayed, and Victor [paediatrician] cut the ribbon.
NICE!* (November 6, 1993) Paediatric Intensive Care
Unit opened July 25, 1994.

*The compound has changed! The long awaited and
planned big lighted sign by the front gate is in place
and looks good. Should help the PR [public relations
and publicity]. A bulldozer cleared the land beyond the
tennis court over to the mission property and also
around the chicken shed. What an improvement!
Hopefully some snakes died in the course of it. The
chicken house is being converted to a sports hall with*

an outdoor stage also. We had planned this with some
special gift money we had ($2,000). The cow shed had
already been converted into a car and vehicle garage
for the staff houses—very cheap ($250).

Even with the private-patient wing and the additions and
renovations, Naylor notes the critical shortage of space and
beds. *We have been trying to think what to do. Obviously*
whatever we do means more floor space and money, more
staff. (June 25, 1995) Nine different maintenance projects
already were in progress, with Bobby Jones again as overseer.
The long-range plan for BBH made provisions for updating
facilities as well as expansion. New flooring and stainless
sinks were installed in the kitchen; the operation theatre had
major work. *The big event of the weekend was complete reno-*
vation of OT—new scrub sinks, linen washing area, new utility
area—all stainless steel. Bobby Jones had planned and
designed the whole thing. We had to close Surgery and in 48
hours day and night the work got done. Dr. Alex [Thomas]
was in charge and staff cooperated wonderfully. Mr. Parama
Shivan's people did a heroic job. For an entire project of that
magnitude to be completed satisfactorily in 48 hours must
have indeed seemed miraculous in light of the usual delays
and behind-schedule work. Included in the smaller projects for
1995 were the drilling of a new water well, a bore well,
replacement of the X-ray machine, and remodeling of the medical-staff area. Toilets added to two of the staff rooms gave
better facilities for night-duty physicians. Naylor's apartment
had the leaking pipes and the roof replaced.

Because of the bed shortage immediate discussions ensued,
even as the other projects were underway. During the August
1995 board meeting, the members decided to move maintenance to the old NRC (Nutrition Rehabilitation Center) and to
expand the laundry. Initially the board agreed to follow the
long-range plan for the kitchen and canteen. It would put them

together in a separate building to use that space for patient wards. Jones returned in July 1996. Using his design, contractors built a separate, small building at the back of the hospital for the oxygen supply and suction. This freed some space in the hospital itself. A new telephone system throughout the hospital and air-conditioning in operation theatres were installed. New equipment and power demands necessitated a generator and the building of a new generator facility.

Naylor narrates this saga well: *The generators. They are moving the main one presently in service and we have hired a generator temporarily. This evening it quit.* (December 16, 1996) *They were to connect the generator yesterday. There were major problems with some fuses blowing so it is delayed.* (February 16, 1997) What seemed simple to complete was not. Eventually the new generator functioned and was placed in the new exterior building. When the nutrition center became the new maintenance area, the laundry expanded into the vacated maintenance area.

The laundry project involved not only renovation of a different area of the hospital but also new machinery. All this was accomplished while the laundry remained functioning. New machines were ordered with expected delivery in mid-December 1996. Cables, a sewer line, and plumbing had to be moved. The new steam-powered washing machines necessitated the purchase and installation of a boiler. Once again Naylor clearly describes the situation, progress, and lack of progress:

> *In the midst of this [generator installation], is the laundry. The washing machine man missed 5 appointments and showed up at 1:30 Saturday. He only takes care of sewing machines. He brought the representative of the company making the washing machines . . . [who] services them and does not know how to install them. Is this not hopeless?* (December 16, 1996). *The laundry is not done—trouble in getting necessary peo-*

ple there. Our staff are doing a heroic job of the laundry. They are keeping up by working shifts. (January 31, 1997) *The electricity board commissioner said the boiler could generate steam for the laundry. The drains and water supply are about finished. The washing machine man is to arrive Friday.* (February 11, 1997) The anticipated day arrived: *The first major event of the day was the opening of the laundry. Those laundry men are so excited and so proud. The finishing work has to be completed, but the machines are all functioning and today the clothes were washed in the new machines.* (February 16, 1997) From August to February to install a boiler and washing machines!

While the laundry renovation and boiler and generator installation were under way, the administrative office area was being expanded. Stone had to be chipped off the outer side of the wall in preparation for making a connecting door. This project included built-in office furniture, new windows, and offices for the medical superintendent, associate medical superintendent, hospital administrator, and secretaries. These offices from 1997 remained in operation until 2006, when an entire administrative department complex was created.

Although several large projects had been completed from 1989 through 1996, another one began in 1997—that of staff housing. One of the original recommendations during the negotiation of terms for the Christian Medical College of Vellore and Bangalore Baptist Hospital management contract pointed to the necessity of staff housing. With donations and funds from the Foreign Mission Board, several units were built: Men's Hostel, Quarry View, Mays Quarters, Court View Quarters, and Richmond Quarters.

The building of these new quarters began. The end of June, tenders were let for the general contractor; ground was broken July 16, 1997. Overseeing this project differed from previous ones. Not only did the architects have an engineer at the site full time, but Mr. Keshavamurthy, the contractor, had five full-time management people, including three engineers. Because finding water on the hospital grounds and having adequate water supply always presented challenges, the contractor drilled a well to furnish water for the project. By October 17 Naylor observes

> *construction is incredible. The men's dorm [hostel] has a second floor and a roof was poured this week. They are starting to put window frames in the lower floor. The smaller apartments are having second floor wall. Roof slab will be poured by the last week of October. The bigger apartments are almost ready for the slab on top of ground floor.* A November 4 letter chronicles the progress: *Even in the darkness the concrete mixer is churning, the people are working, and the roof of the four smaller apartments is being poured. It is such a relief to have Bobby here.*

By Christmas Eve 1997 end phases of the work showed: external plastering, roof slabs, flooring laid, plumbing begun. Surely enough, by spring 1998 the men's hostel, the Mays Quarters, and the Richmond Quarters were dedicated and complete but just not usable. The problem involved electricity connections. The electric company indicated that the wait for a third transformer was one year. Naylor records an amazing story of God's provision: *Yesterday a high-up electric official came to Dr. Alex with some arm problem! He [the patient] will take care of the transformer problem! Mr. Suri the architect is following up immediately. Another one of those miracles!* (March 19, 1997)

The years of 1999 and 2002 brought other improvements such as expansion of the cycle stand, paving the back road, extending the operation theatre, and creating a third theatre—

adding a second floor above the private-patient wing. The most recent large project was the addition of two floors—second and third stories—above the outpatient clinics.

How did a charity hospital that received minimal fees from the majority of its patients and decreasing annual allotments from the Foreign Mission Board accomplish without loans and debt-free these many building projects and replacement of equipment? Naylor writes: *The building itself, free of debt, is cause for much gratitude.* (October 10, 1993) Naylor perhaps will first answer the question that this happened through sacrifice, fundraising activities, good advice, generous people, but she always will emphatically aver that the monies arrived because of the miraculous workings of God. Hospital staff, Goatcher, and Rankin, among others, credit Naylor for her unparalleled ability to secure funds from Stateside friends, supporters, churches, and organizations.

Goatcher refers to Naylor's "home base" and her far-reaching contacts: "Rebekah was totally immersed in the life of the hospital and in India, but she did not neglect her home base. She was a prolific letter writer (before the days of email and the Internet) maintaining contact with countless children, churches, individuals, and institutions through hand-written letters. As she became more widely known throughout the Southern Baptist Convention and in medical schools and medical organizations, correspondence requirements increased. This is one reason BBH has become so well-known and has had so many medical people come to visit and to work in the hospital. It is also why so many individuals and church groups have visited and worked in the Bangalore area. This cultivation of the home base was begun as a desire to let people know what the Lord was doing with the resources they had entrusted to her (and others). It was later made necessary when the FMB began to cut back on financial help to mission hospitals. Her wide range of contacts enabled her to enlist financial (and other) assistance from individuals, churches and organizations that the hospital desperately needed." (February 11, 2007)

Goatcher's observations accurately depict Naylor's activities throughout the 1990s. As early as April 6 and April 9, 1989 Naylor wrote her parents:

> *Every 6 months the lady who is the executive direc-*
> *tor of Vellore, New York board comes to Vellore for the*
> *Council meeting. Tomorrow she is coming here. The*
> *main purpose of that group is fund raising for CMC.*
> *Our capital requests also may go there. I intend to*
> *impress her tomorrow with potential and need which*
> *leads me to other things in my mind. Do you think I*
> *could get money for the hospital there at home from*
> *non-Baptist sources—one time grants that could be*
> *used for endowment or replacement equipment fund? If*
> *I could do that during my furlough, it would be a per-*
> *manent help to the hospital . . . I am gaining a strong*
> *impression that my new role here may be fund raising.*
> *I, of course, never had to worry so much about that*
> *before. It just seems so strange that Lottie Moon*
> *[Foreign Mission Board] won't help us in the future.*

Certainly during any furlough in the States, Naylor made contacts; she spoke frequently and passionately presented not only the medical work of BBH but also the evangelism outreach efforts and successes. Each trip home, through those whom she already knew and through others she met, she compiled a list of influential and corporate leaders who might be sympathetic and helpful to the financial need of BBH. The role her parents played in these efforts, beyond advice, seems paramount. With their wide circle of acquaintances, their contacts were invaluable. They oversaw the record-keeping in the States, coordinated with the Foreign Mission Board, and assisted with the correspondence and communication with the various people involved in the efforts. Because telephone service and mail service to and from India limited speedy communication, their assistance became even more valuable. The Bangalore architect, Mr. Thacker, recognized Naylor's ability to raise money and the critical need for funds. He suggested that Naylor "must make another trip to the USA soon so we can get the money to finish the clinic wing downstairs!" (October 5, 1990)

That "home base" Goatcher mentioned included First Baptist Church, Dallas—Naylor's home church during her tenure in India. As a first-year resident in 1968 Naylor joined that congregation and remained a member of the fellowship until she returned from India in 2002. (At that time she made Travis Avenue Baptist Church, Fort Worth her home church.) The connection between the Dallas congregation, Naylor, and BBH has consistently been one of great strength. Prayer groups pray daily for her. The women's organization relies on her to speak to it during furlough. Often she speaks during the primary Sunday worship services. Throughout the years this congregation contributed to specific building projects and to general upkeep of the hospital facility. Through First Baptist, Dallas, Naylor and FBC member Mrs. Ruth Ray Hunt became acquainted. Today plaques acknowledge Mrs. Hunt's generous gifts to BBH—the entrance building and the nursing-school building.

Other persons performed vital services in the acquisition of funds and equipment. Dr. Joel Gregory, pastor of First Baptist Church, Dallas (1990-1992) and a trustee for the Foreign Mission Board, secured approval for a group of people interested in BBH who had connections with organizations that either could donate or secure donations. This group formed a Dallas-based advisory council, Samaritan Medical Outreach Ministries. Among the membership were Dr. Sam Law, John Thomas, JoAnne McCullough, Dr. John Seelig, Norman Roberts, Dr. Terrell Mays, and Dr. Bruce Leitch. Separate from the Samaritan Outreach Ministries group, Mays spearheaded efforts in Kentucky. A volunteer physician at BBH and mission-minded, Mays contacted Baptist Hospital Systems in Kentucky; the possibility of a five-year partnership ensued. Mays himself donated generously, a $20,000 gift once and $2,000 in 1992 to fund Dr. Joy's salary for one year. Mays' will provided $50,000 which funded one set of staff quarters, the Mays Quarters. Recently, his widow gave $100,000 for a radiotherapy unit. Norman Roberts effectively arranged an agreement with the Baptist Medical System in Little Rock and gave the BBH administrators ways in which the Little Rock group could help during 1993-4. Sam Law assisted with vigorous, fruitful efforts that sent to the FMB for BBH many donations, one of which totaled $14,175 (January 24, 1999).

Naylor sought corporate funding and grants. She visited both Indian and U.S.-owned plants, factories, and businesses in India. One such event, a gathering of 11 multinational firms, Naylor attended with Dr. Stan Macaden. Naylor reported on the meeting: *During the BBH presentation, Dr. Macaden said that as they use our services, that also helps us in caring for the poor. At that point, one man asked what other help we needed! I explained that we are trying to generate income for operation but that all capital funding—equipment and buildings—depends on donations. I told about the outpatient wing need—not an amount.* Visits to other large international companies and their factories followed. Naylor's presentations stressed to management the availability of top-quality health care at competitive prices for employees. Insurance coverage and company payment for the employees' medical and dental care allowed the national worker access to facilities such as BBH. Such visits to large firms and corporations occurred several times during a period of years. Naylor revisited IBM, Texas Instruments, General Electric, Digital, Wrigley Gum, and Vera Fone Software Systems. At least two companies, Wrigley and Vera Fone Software Systems, did award healthcare contracts to BBH. Naylor notes Vera Fone *gave us company's health care business—at least all checkups for 100 employees—500 rupees each.* (December 12, 1994)

Unfortunately and frequently the contacts proved discouraging. Naylor assesses the difficulty of persuading corporations to give: *I am glad to know about Texas Instruments. I am not too surprised but am very disappointed. It tells me that the corporations will be difficult if not impossible to crack. Where do we get money in future?* (April 4, 1993) Today Naylor notes that "these efforts in those years formed the pattern. Today corporate clients produce about 30% of the hospital's income."

As a Foreign Mission Board missionary Naylor could not make trips to the States to solicit money nor could she during her speaking engagements directly ask for money. Under FMB policy she could speak about the hospital and the work of the hospital; nationals, however, could go to the U.S. at any time and make direct appeals for financial help. Through Dr. Macaden's connection with Wake Forest University, that institution has underwritten projects including the palliative care department. Administrative personnel and physicians began to search for ways to seek more local support. *Dr. Alex made contact with a Dutch organization thinking of nursing scholarships. Santosh Benjamin contacted a well-to-do businessman in his church.* (February 4, 6, 1995)

Publicity in the Bangalore area seemed prudent. Always the pragmatist, Naylor enlisted the assistance of Mr. Calla, a hospital attorney and a trusted advisor. The meeting dealt with public-relations efforts such as with companies, increase of patients, and raising money. Calla suggested updating the hospital brochure, forming a local organized group called the Friends of BBH, and generating a list of potential hospital users and supporters. With these ideas, a plan emerged: the hospital's 20th anniversary in January 1993 might provide a platform for much publicity and opportunity for fundraising. Such an endeavor could add money to the poor-patient fund.

The anniversary on January 15, 1993 involved far more than merely a staff thanksgiving service and tea marking 20 years of operation and care for the poor.

We hope to raise money. On 15 January it will be just staff—thanksgiving, tea. On Jan. 16-17 we will have a "fête" as they call it—entertainment and selling things here at the hospital compound. Jan. 23 evening we will plan a big program in town—some name singer. The key is to get sponsors for every aspect—the hall, the artist, the tickets. We spend nothing but receive the ticket money. We are trying to organize our efforts with companies, PR in service clubs. (July 12 #2, 1992)

The planning proved fruitful. Naylor exuberantly writes reports of the concert and the fête.

Our concert Saturday night was successful. We sold more tickets at the hall. We had exhibits about the hospital. The singer is an excellent performer. We had about 750-800 people. The staff again did a marvelous job of organization and so many worked so hard. We began with prayer. Stan welcomed them; Clyde [Meador] spoke. I concluded with expression of thanks, so everyone knew our position and what we believed. (February 2, 1993)

Since I last wrote, the big event was the fête. Another success!! The opening function was Saturday at 11:30, mostly staff, some of our "friends." The chief guest was retired chief of naval staff, Admiral Dawson. To preside we invited Dr. Devaraj from the Agricultural College—longtime friend and patient—now the Vice Chancellor. We launched a program of school health

checkups for needy children in city schools. We are
starting with 3 schools. The head mistresses were there.
We announced the start of our residency program. One
of the big newspapers had a reporter there and a great
article came out in Sunday's paper. We submitted
another article to Times of India *paper. The fête*
included games stalls, food stalls, a big health exhibit,
a hospital exhibit, and a number of outsiders took
stalls. We have taken in over Rs 32,000 plus the sale in
November (almost Rs 15,000), the gifts of a day's
salary by employees, and the two big programs in
January. They have worked so hard. We definitely want
to make the fête an annual event and have already
begun to talk about "next time." I stayed around all
the time both days as did Stan, Santosh Benjamin,
Michael, Pastor Jacob.

Similarly the 1994 and 1995 fêtes Naylor pronounced successful:

The fête on day 1 was a success. I am sure there
were more people than last year . . . The stalls are all
better: food, plants, handicrafts, games. Health educa-
tion exhibit is very good. The food stalls did big busi-
ness. All of my Saturday baked goods and a cake from
Ted Swanson and cookies and a cake from Florence
were gone by 2 P.M. I then sold all of my Sunday cakes
and Usha B. brought a big chocolate cake and it sold.
Once again the staff worked so hard. I worked in the
food stall 9 hours (February 6, 1994). The income for
the poor patient endowed fund amounted to 167,000
Rupees. Likewise the 1995 fête netted a sizable amount
for the poor patient fund: *Tomorrow is the FÊTE! We*
have received over Rs 14,000 in donations so hopefully
we will take in a good amount in sale of items. Mary

has baked 3 recipes of cookies, 48 brownies, chocolate
cupcakes, and carrot cake. Linda Beck and I are split-
ting that cost. Stan has worked extremely hard visiting
people and inviting people. Sarojini has worked end-
lessly in planning, organizing, and carrying through.
(May 5, 1995)

Letters of the 1990s record donations of equipment and money. Each is a significant testimony to God's faithfulness accompanied by fervent gratefulness to generous, concerned people. Occasionally a letter reports phenomenal gifts.

We had the wonderful news that the FMB has allo-
cated $15,000 towards annual capital budget for med-
ical equipment and a new ambulance and upgrading of
telephone system (November 15 #2, 1994) *That is so*
terrific about the lady's gift of $10,000. (April 23,*
1996) *One wonderful thing happened. A man in*
Kentucky named George Manley, a Baptist was of
Indian origin but lived most of his life in America. He
had a strong relationship with CMC and gave money.
He had also put a little money in the Kentucky
Foundation for medical student scholarships at CMC
to be administered through us . . . He died at 94. The
money he left was to CMC . . . But it seems that all
know that he had much interest in BBH. The CMC
board in New York (Bob Carman) sent us $30,000 to
establish the George and Florence Manley Endowment
Fund for nursing and paramedical students. This is
enough to support about 4 students per year. Isn't that
fantastic! They sent us a check directly and we already
have it in the bank. God is so good to us continually.
(September 3, 1996) *Several weeks ago before the pag-*
eant we had approached Ingersoll Rand about a dona-
tion . . . Today the man we were dealing with brought a

check for Rs 50,000 for scholarships. He wants to talk to our top level about quality assurance, how to deal with the customer in health-care industry. Over the next few months we will be talking with him and planning this. I was excited and impressed. (September 20, 1996) *Big news is about Caterpillar. Friday they called and asked for an appointment Saturday. Mr. Dillon, the American, came with three Indian men representing their dealers and service people. Caterpillar is going to provide a 180 KVA generator (we were buying 100 KVA) for Rs 220,000. It would cost 750,000. He wanted it to be free, but the maker of the alternator would not give that part. These men all went out back and spent time looking at our present space. They did figure out how to fit the big new generator into our present building. They have saved us a huge sum of money and have given us a much bigger generator than we dared dream of. The Caterpillar engine is said to be one of the finest in the world. God is so good to us. Over and over again these miracles.*

Aside from fundraising during the 1990s Naylor continued to serve as a physician and associate medical superintendent—both full-time positions. Another mandated project generated a need for funds. Perhaps the biggest challenge of all the other programs and other building projects she undertook and saw to completion was The Rebekah Ann Naylor School of Nursing. The 1973 dedicatory address for BBH and the legal deeds to the property stated that a nursing school must be included in the hospital as part of the training and teaching programs. Part of the CMC Vellore management takeover addressed the need for quality nursing care through a nursing school. The BBH Governing Board minutes for April 1994 indicate the time had arrived to begin this school. *The most major decision concerns the nursing school—we MUST START!* How appropriate the capital letters punctuated by an exclamation point. Naylor must have been eager for a school, but certainly nothing in her previous years gave her the information needed to secure permission to open a nursing school, to write a curriculum, to staff a school, and to prepare facilities including an adequate library.

Naylor, others on the administrative committee, and the governing board worked together to form initial plans. Sister Sarojini Mirajkar, a registered nurse with a master's degree in nursing from Christian Medical College in Vellore and a long-time nursing-staff member of BBH, was selected as first principal. She and a volunteer nurse (Anna) prepared a catalog including criteria for selection, admission, purpose, and goals of the school. By September 1994 the inspection for the nursing school occurred and yielded a positive report. BBH should raise money so that the construction could begin in 1995. Further affirmation arrived from the Christian Medical Association of India (CMAI), which wished the program could open in 1995! Adequate funding as well as approval from legal entities in India and the FMB allowed school construction to begin in 1995. The largest donation was unsolicited and a complete surprise.

First Baptist, Dallas member Mrs. Ruth Ray Hunt and Naylor share at least three commonalities. Both had memberships at the same church. Both were vitally interested in the work at BBH. Beyond that they shared a connection that dates back to when Mrs. Hunt was 12 or 13. G. R. Naylor, Rebekah Naylor's paternal grandfather, led a revival in southeastern Oklahoma. Naylor tells the story: "Mrs. Hunt was in that little town in that revival meeting and was saved at one of the evening services. I first met Mrs. Hunt in maybe 1990 or 1991. Mrs. Hunt became such a friend, of our hospital and me. She did help with the private wing and gave a larger gift for the connecting wing and indeed her name is on the stone of the entrance block. So far as the nursing school, I never specifically presented that project to Mrs. Hunt. She got my newsletters. She kept up. The $250,000 she gave us for the nursing school was a complete surprise. I was informed by Richmond [FMB]. They received a check in the mail. That morning when Richmond called to tell me, I called up Mr. Parama Shivan. We had the plans ready for ages.

"I called him up and said, 'You can start collecting materials. This money has come. You need to be sure that you understand where this money came from.'

"He was so excited. 'Oh, yes, this wonderful lady gave this money.'

"Oh, yes, she did. But the money came from God. He just used Mrs. Hunt. God does that.'

"And that was just one more opportunity to witness to Mr. Parama Shivan."

During the endeavor to start the building of the nursing school, letters heralded joyful news of funds and the groundbreaking ceremony.

Isn't that marvelous and wonderful—God gives exactly enough. We have over $80,000 in our building fund. (February 5, 1995) The news that Mrs. Hunt is giving $250,000 remains so incredible to me—I have to pinch myself to realize it. God has provided so miraculously time and time again. (April 14, 1995) Today I have checked all of our balances of funds in hand as best I know—around $420,000. Two local Christian organizations are interested in providing full scholarship plus room and board for underprivileged Christian nursing students. The verse that I have repeatedly seen in the last 2-3 months is Proverbs 16:3. God has again fulfilled His promise. (April 26, 1995)

Thus the largest project of all commenced. As with other building projects various delays, improper procedures, and miscommunication ensued. Each of these required general meetings with Naylor, Macaden, Bobby Jones, the site engineer, the contractor, and the architects in attendance. Delays relative to supplies and workers ensued. No bricks were available. No cement could be purchased. No power or limited power raised costs. By February the cost of the nursing school had risen to be 35-40 percent more than the original projections. Bricks arrived, but the workers didn't because of a festival. Letters chronicle the tiny steps toward completion as well as the meetings and lists of unfinished or improperly done pieces of work—toilet placement, use of space, plugs, electrical outlets, door handles improperly placed, bad laying of ceramic tile, uneven steps, walls not straight. Shoddy work often went without attention because of lack of inspection and constant presence of an engineer on site with the workers. Had Naylor herself not visited the building site daily, the delays and quality could have been irreparable. Hear the tension and frustration in Naylor's words:

> *I have good days and bad days so far as the construction. Today was bad . . . all coordination breaks down—one contractor does not carry through on what he said yesterday—the electrical contractor does not follow up pending supplies—the site engineer is missing at critical times-and I am overloaded with other work!! What to do!!* (May 28, 1996)

Naylor's vigilance proved wise. On one inspection she noted round ceiling fittings not the type for fluorescent tubes which gave better light and were more efficient and more economical. The June 2 letter tells a story that is difficult to conceive:

Construction is lagging. The engineer disappeared. It never ceases to amaze me how they do things. They had made this fine wall on top of the building. Now they are chipping huge holes in it for drain pipes. Why not make the holes to start with? I was going up the stairs to the third floor. I saw this large wood pole coming through the wall of the building—they had even plastered around it. Surely enough, when I investigated it was one of the big bamboo poles that was a part of the outside scaffolding which was still up. They just raised the wall around the pole and left it. Now they have removed the pole and there is a hole in the wall!
Finally June 5, the ominous, dreaded word arrived: *Yesterday all admitted the building was not going to be ready and even all previously set targets would not be achieved. I am now concerned about July 1 date [beginning of the nursing school classes for the first class of students]. I am so disappointed.*

The sadness, the frustration, the grief emerge through the words of the letter; the June 14, 1996 dedication plans were set and already in motion. Students were to arrive July 1! As the Indian nationals wryly say, "What to do!"

Naylor followed the contractors, called the architects, and dogged the workers. She became the supervisor herself. The workers seemed to respond to her direct supervision. The buildings are another story. *There are too few painters. As of last night they had not started the final coat. They have not put the screens in. The furniture man was not finished. Disaster!!! We all now see that they may not finish by June 30. I am upset but what to do.* (June 12, 1996)

Without a doubt Naylor had problems untold with the construction of the buildings and furnishing them. She had the responsibility of fundraising and building construction while she served as a physician with a large private-patient load. The aloneness and the emotional drain must have been even a greater burden. Millicent Kohn, a close friend and confidante, avers that Naylor never outwardly showed her anxiety, frustration, or hurt. Many of the hospital employees concur. According to other American missionaries who served with Naylor, employees frequently were terrified of Naylor because of her position of authority, her forthright manner, and her many successes, yet these very same people loyally followed her. Staff members, though, seemed to produce within Naylor a feeling of isolation and thoughts that they resented her. Almost lost amidst the dramatic fundraising, the step-by-step construction incessantly interrupted, the often faulty renovations, the building of nursing school, yet equally important, was the completion of those initial aims set forth for a complete medical institution that gave quality, first-rate care to all including the poor and operated as a first-rate training institution with a nursing school.

The Rebekah Ann Naylor School of Nursing did receive full approval and accreditation from the Indian Nursing Council, Karnataka Nursing Council, and Christian Medical Association of India. The first class graduated in August 1999; this ensured quality nursing care and thereby satisfied another goal the founders and administrators of the hospital set. Naylor's duties did not end with the construction of all these buildings; indeed in her missionary capacity and IMB designation, she served as a surgeon in conjunction with holding the position of associate medical superintendent; as a member of the nursing-student selection committee; and as a Bible-study leader.

Equally as important, she became the Rebekah Ann Naylor School of Nursing professor of anatomy and physiology.

The Anatomy Madam

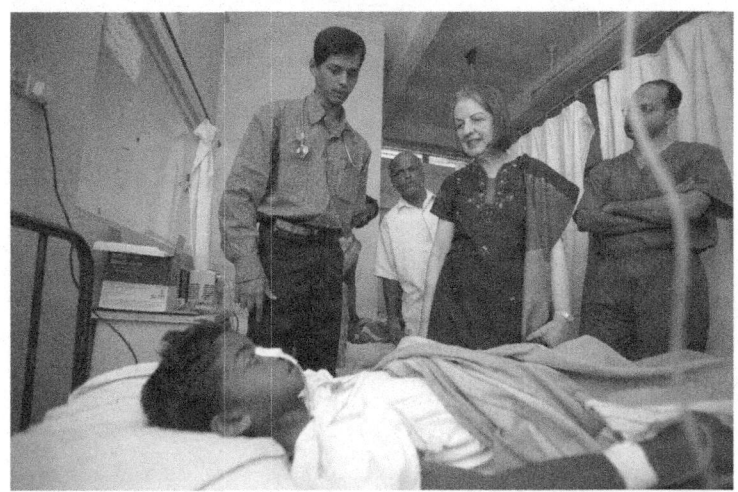

Rebekah at a patient bedside at Bangalore Baptist Hospital

In her office at University of Texas Southwestern Medical School

Teaching BBH medical students, January 2008

Teaching in the Rebekah Ann Naylor School of Nursing in Bangalore

To another, the message of knowledge . . .
some to be . . . teachers . . .
(1 Cor. 12:8 and Eph. 4:11).

The Anatomy Madam

The big thing in the last two days is my debut as a teacher.
Yesterday and today I have had sessions with the dietetic
interns . . . The difficulty is that my three-days' lectures got
over in two days! Next week I start some in-service training
for our own nurses twice monthly. (July 4, 1991)

Even though Naylor speaks of her debut as a teacher, she might have added "in an academic setting or within accredited certification programs" to provide clarification. Since her time as a student in Baylor University and Vanderbilt University School of Medicine, she frequently served as a Sunday-school teacher, for which she prepared each lesson as carefully as she would for an organic chemistry problem or in presenting a case during Grand Rounds.

While in her surgical residency and a member of First Baptist Church, Dallas, Naylor gave part of her summer vacation, June 1972, to serve as a counselor for a cabin full of 7-year-old girls attending children's camp. Naylor herself had never attended camp. She preferred home, five-star hotels, and country-club dinners and had limited experience with children; yet, all that aside, she went—partially to extend her training in witnessing to children and partially to use her abilities. Her letter on the following page notes her positive experience regardless of the need for flexibility and despite the less-than-ideal environment.

June 1972
Rest time—Wednesday

Dearest Mama and Daddy,

I managed a scrap of paper and purchased an envelope and stamp from one of my dear little campers. The week is about half over and am I ever glad! But I wouldn't take anything for the experience. My girls are very sweet and we are getting along well. I have been able to control them with just quiet reprimands.

Monday was the worst day. The heat was unbearable. And we were all having a hard time to get going. It was hard to get them settled Monday night and they were awake and ready to go at 5 Tuesday morning. Late yesterday afternoon we had an awful storm, eliminating some of our recreation. But they were real good and we sang and played games. By last night they were just dead and I had to shake them awake this morning.

Two of the girls are unsaved. One of them came to me after devotionals Monday and we talked together. She went forward in the service last night. Another girl with whom I had not talked went forward. Both need more counseling. I spent time with both of them last night. Both girls will receive no encouragement at home. In fact, one has parents who are not even nominal Christians. (A few minutes later). One of them just came and we talked. Her understanding is much clearer now. In our devotional last night one of them told us (this was another little girl) that she felt God was calling her to be a missionary.

I am surviving well other than oodles of bites and one serious attack of hay fever. Fortunately I have my pills. Oh, one of my kids got sick and went home.

Rest period is about over. Time to start recreating.

All my love,
Rebekah

Being a camp counselor and teaching Sunday-school lessons served only as initial experiences, for Naylor sought other
teaching venues. Her first teaching endeavors centered on
Bible studies, retreats, and other service-related places not
unusual for a missionary or full-time worker on the mission
field. During her early years in Bangalore, the '70s and '80s,
the missionaries had Bible studies which she occasionally led,
but generally she preferred to remain quiet and noncommittal.
Somewhat enigmatic, given her zeal for sharing Christ and her
commitment to Bible study, is that often she wrote letters
home or read books during the Bible studies she attended! *For
the most part I have sat quietly and if I got too lost in thought,
I read a book inconspicuously* (March 2, 1978). *I am sitting in
the session . . . a little letter writing is going on!* (August 31,
2000) Naylor agreed to speak at retreats and Christian medical
groups. These teaching endeavors stemmed from her desire to
share the Gospel story of Christ's redemption and were well
within her role as missionary. From the beginning of her time
at Bangalore Baptist Hospital, Naylor gave the Bible story and
Bible message during hospital chapel services. She utilized a
flannel graph to tell the stories.

After a visit to BBH Dr. Scott Middleton remarked: "And
there she was, Dr. Rebekah Naylor, surgeon, using a flannel
graph to tell Bible stories to the audience. For pity's sake, flannel graph hadn't been used in American churches for two or
three decades, maybe longer. I became acutely aware of limitations of a third-world country and Naylor's amazing work.
Those Indian people sat intently listening to her and watching
her every move." Movies and film strips (though in limited use
in America in the early '70s), and videos simply were not

available in India. The flannel graph, bridging the gaps created by language, culture, and religious background, gave effective visuals to the stories. The flannel-backed scenery and paper doll-like figures for the story were packaged in a kit. Two different types of boards exist: a lightweight wood covered in flannel, which sat on an artist's easel, and a smaller folding board with carrying handles. Naylor used both: the large one in chapel and the folding one during visits to the villages. With the narration, the storyteller placed the scenery and figures on the board and made those characters spring to life. The more accomplished narrators changed their voices for the various characters. This was quite thrilling to the young child! David's diminutive size in comparison to the Philistine giant, Goliath, the pieces of Saul's armor, the five smooth stones from the brook, and even the brook itself no longer were words merely heard but were lifelike parts of an exciting story. One Easter Sunday Naylor told the story of the resurrection of Jesus and emphasized the open tomb. With the pronouncement of the words "appeared a great light," the flannel graph centurion guarding the tomb slipped into supine position and eventually fell off the board. The audience had firsthand a demonstration of God's power and the blinding light! During the telling of the story of Zaccheus from Luke 19:2-10, Naylor faced another near-mishap. The Bible tells that Zaccheus, the short Jewish man who served as a tax collector for the Roman government, was too short to see Jesus during Jesus' visit to Jericho; therefore, Zaccheus climbed a tree. Unfortunately, the figure of Zaccheus was missing. Naylor dismissed his absence with the comment that Zaccheus was too short to be seen amidst the trees. She moved to the main point that Jesus had ignored Zaccheus's governmental position and social status but looked at the person of Zaccheus and chose to dine at Zaccheus's house. Generally, however, the narrations were not accompanied by dramatic interpretation or mishaps but with straightforward recounting of the events. Millicent Kohn, long-time friend of Naylor's, remembers that on a visit with Naylor to Bangalore, Kohn cut out the figures and scenery for new sets of flannel graph stories.

In October 1982 Naylor began a long-term Bible study, *MasterLife*, with a group of women associated with the hospital. Each of the two 13-week sets of lessons focused on Christian growth. Some of the topics of study included spending time with God, studying the Word, praying, fellowshiping with believers, witnessing, ministering to others, developing prayer lives, gaining skills in using God's Word, witnessing through relationships, nurturing new Christians, and maturing as a disciple. Those in the study learned how to share their personal testimonies and participated in a prayer retreat. Because Naylor knew the *MasterLife* program through her personal study with other missionaries in the Bangalore station, she believed it might be the perfect one for the women who asked her to lead a group.

Systematically studying the 26 lessons, the group also participated in the prayer retreats, testimony sessions, and reflection/meditation times incorporated into the study materials.

I had my MasterLife group meeting Tuesday. Their interest and participation has remained very high. We finished 11 sessions. They are coming almost every week and sharing witnessing experiences. They pray with great concern. Tuesday's session began a week-long effort to write a full testimony of their Christian experience. They each shared the outline. Glory has worked for us almost three years. She comes from a Christian background. But God started speaking to her exactly three years ago that day when she came for an interview at our hospital. Dem Ward asked her [during the interview] how long she had been a Christian. She answered she was born one, to which he only smiled. But she started thinking—for over two years she exam-

ined herself. One night in bed last January she commit-
ted her life to Christ. How about that! Priya comes
from a Hindu background. Of course, her testimony
was interesting. She held off for years in fear of her
family's response. (December 17, 1982)

During a prayer time this same group of young women expressed concern that the five medical schools in Bangalore had no Christian group—no activities. They averred they should pray about that and that God could use them. Naylor's first thoughts? "We're single women in a male-dominated culture; I'm a foreigner. What can we do? How can God use us?" Yet she prayed with them. She comments today that "my students' faith outshone mine." The very next week the women reported they had identified in each of the five schools a Christian who willingly and enthusiastically agreed to begin a Bible study in his or her dormitory room on campus. From those five initial gatherings evolved Bible studies. The local chapter of Evangelical Medical Fellowship of India emerged and became a vibrant group of professional and student members that provides strong Christian influence, support, and encouragement to the students and a strong evangelical witness to other students in these five medical schools. Naylor says this group is "evangelizing Bangalore and had its start in this first *MasterLife* group."

The enthusiasm from this first group and the requests from other women encouraged Naylor to continue the study with at least three different groups of women.

MasterLife group got started on Part II—week 14.
They are very excited. I had asked a girl who comes
from Hindu background to lead the Bible Study. She
was frightened but did fine. Last Saturday at the testi-
mony workshop, Dr. Ruby told me about three visits to
witness to patients. She said the first time she was

scared and confused and felt she did poorly. The second time was better and the patient got excited and interested and asked for a Bible. The third patient was also interested and wanted to pray. Ruby was thrilled that she could communicate and share. (July 11, 1985)

Saturday . . . afternoon was wonderful. My MasterLife group had its half day prayer retreat. We prayed individually almost three hours and then had a sharing time. They all were there; all were excited and gave positive testimony as to what happened. I myself again found it a fine time. The disciplined plan of time and coming to a different place (we met at the student centre) really helps. I was excited as so many Scriptures came to mind as I prayed for different things. God has given me renewed peace about being here and even peace about the job I am doing now. I have realized that whatever administrative gifts I have, God gave them so I should not feel guilty about doing less surgery. Nor can we say surgical skills are wasted when I think of the thousands I have operated on and the teaching I have done. Well, it was a good time. (August 18, 1985)

Saturday morning was one of my most thrilling experiences. My MasterLife group had been asked to have the Saturday chapel service, and they had agreed. I did not know what they had planned. All 12 participated. They had a song, Scriptures, and three spoke. One girl, the telephone operator, talked about a quiet time — well done. One of the doctors gave the message based on the story about the wedding feast — very clearly outlined the Gospel. The third talked about fruit bearing and witnessing. All spoke with authority and conviction. I was really overcome and in tears by the

*time they finished. Thursday in our session they shared
such burdens about witnessing. Oh, when I think what
this kind of concern could do for our hospital staff!
And patients!* (September 8, 1985)

After the group studying the *MasterLife* materials completed the last of the prescribed sessions the end of October,
Naylor led the members in a study of spiritual gifts.

During an EMFI (Evangelical Medical Fellowship of
India) spiritual retreat for medical students Naylor met a
young woman who had many questions about Christianity, the
Bible, and living the Christian life. Not unusual for her, Naylor
invited the student to her home.

*We visited about two hours. She is still confused . . .
I hope that I helped. But I really got a taste of counseling cross-culturally. She said she had done something
awful. I talked to her about confession and forgiveness
in I John. But she wanted to tell me also but could not
find words. Finally it all came out—she was feeling
attracted to a single man. She is 17 years old! I barely
kept a straight face. I had expected something really
awful. Cultural standards are so different. I was able to
help her understand what our standards [as believers]
are, no matter the culture.* (November 11, 1985)

Simultaneously with the *MasterLife* study, which met
weekly for women connected with the hospital, Naylor began
a Bible study in the ladies' hostel on the hospital compound.
Both met on Thursdays but at different times. *My MasterLife
group was good on Thursday—all were there. I had 18 in my
ladies' hostel Bible Study Thursday night.* (August 25, 1985)
These studies she often wrote herself and based her broad
topic and/or weekly lessons on the January Bible studies
taught annually within the Southern Baptist Convention

churches or sermon series written and preached by her father. For the women from the hostel, Naylor led studies on books of the Bible: James, 1 and 2 Peter, Hebrews, and John; on topics such as women of the Bible, the patriarchs, David, and Jesus; on Christian growth principles—prayer, Bible study, personal quiet time with God. Eventually Naylor was instrumental in the inauguration of a weekly doctors' community Bible study, which the physicians continue today. Because the staff physicians moved into housing constructed in the compound in the '90s, such studies were more feasible. Transportation, location, call duty for the hospital, and small children—all large issues—no longer were a problem.

The evangelism arm of the mission and hospital plans staff retreats—integral activities promoting not only the story of Jesus as Savior but also opportunities for Christian growth for both mission and hospital personnel. In the '70s and '80s when missionaries also were the physicians and nurses on BBH staff, the retreats were for all. Often Naylor was instrumental in planning these retreats. *I have had a busy but very focused weekend. Out next staff retreat is April 10-11. Our theme is vision. I have prepared five Bible studies . . . This afternoon Jo, Bobby, and I did the 42 days of Bible readings and thoughts for morning prayers during the six-week emphasis. I just now have to organize all of the readings into a proper order.*

When the chaplaincy-certification program at BBH began, Naylor and others organized and planned the program. Naylor has taught in that group both before and after she left BBH in 2002. "I do about 6-8 hours in teaching sessions on personal evangelism with those students. I also teach them medical terminology. These are non-medical people. I take a [patient] chart and show them parts of the chart that they would be reading in the chart, called the *progress notes,* which tell what was happening to the patient."

Leading Bible studies, speaking at retreats, participating in

Bible studies led by others, or even teaching these sessions appeared as an extension of Naylor's commitment to God and desire to share His message. The idea of being a teacher as a profession, however, was not one Naylor often considered after she made her decision to attend medical school and not to pursue a graduate degree in order to teach piano. Dr. Tom Shires, Naylor's mentor and professor of surgery, talked with her in the fall of 1973. *Dr. Shires asked me if I had changed my mind about teaching. For the first time I seriously questioned teaching.*

Throughout her tenure in India Naylor did indeed teach. Although she frequently presented physician in-service and continuing education, rotating through the cycle of lunchtime presentations with other physicians and consultants on staff at BBH, these sessions were one-time lectures and discussions among fellow doctors, many of whom were in the same specialty. As the hospital sought postgraduate courses and formal training programs that led to certification or National Board Examinations, qualified instructors, curricula, classroom instruction, and hands-on experience had to be developed and in many cases incorporated into the work load for various doctors on staff. Naylor remarked: *I am excited about potential teaching opportunities . . . I so hope we can do these programs.* Other paramedical programs were also being sought. Dietetic intern training and medical records-technician training began that same year—1991. Naylor wrote of the medical records curriculum: *There is a heavy lecture schedule required including 50 hours of anatomy and physiology and another 15 hours of other basic science. I am planning likely to do a big part of that.* Thus by the middle of the summer Naylor was teaching not only biochemistry to the dietitian interns but also anatomy and physiology to the records technicians, giving in-service twice monthly to BBH nurses, and presenting surgery continuing education. Her subjects more often than not remained anatomy and physiology or biochemistry.

In an August 14, 1991 letter Naylor compares her teaching to that of full-time professors: *Here I am supposed to teach 10 hours a week plus my weekly Bible study and the chapel services and any extras. I have thought of the seminary faculty for whom I guess that is a work week—10 hours plus some preaching. And this teaching for me is just incidental to my real job. Hilarious, isn't it!*

Although Naylor served as a lecturer in many of the programs, other physicians shared the work load. Physicians on staff at CMC Vellore assisted by serving as faculty lecturers. Dr. LBM Joseph, retired surgeon and retired director of Christian Medical College and Hospital, Vellore, was one of these. Joseph did much to help BBH in planning and guiding the postgraduate programs. Naylor's *curriculum vitae* reads that she founded these programs and taught in them.

Teaching the residents brought new challenges, learning experiences, and skills for Naylor.

We [physicians at BBH] have been involved in teaching. Dr. LBM Joseph is here for four days teaching surgery. Actually he is trying to get our program organized. Saturday the surgeon from CMC came. The plan is that Dr. Joseph will come monthly and the CMC person monthly so that about every 2 weeks we will have surgical teaching help. (February 12, 1994) *One of the special things this week is real initiation into teaching. Yesterday I led a seminar for Fred Job on gallstone disease—all the surgical aspects. The seminar took three nights of preparation, but I really enjoyed doing it. We spent over an hour Wednesday afternoon—all of us. The teaching is going to help me so much. Santosh [Benjamin] is working with Fred on basic science; Naveen and I are doing lectures. Fred is motivated. He is studying very hard and looks happy. Santosh and I are determined to try to get him through this residency successfully.* (August 11, 1994) *Monday afternoon we had a surgery teaching session—Naveen as teacher. Fred [residency student] remains very interested and motivated. The medicine residents have been coming to our sessions, too. My next turn is in 2 weeks. The 3 of us—Santosh, Naveen, and I—rotate. A CMC surgeon will come again on 29th. Dr. [Robert] McClelland [UT Southwestern surgery professor] sent us 4 bags of books and hundreds of teaching slides. The slides are in sets with guides to read as you see them. We used them yesterday afternoon to supplement Naveen's lecture and we used them today at lunch. This is such a marvelous gift.* (October 18, 1994)

Dr. McClelland's gift of teaching slides and books used on those two occasions represent only a fraction of the extensive library in the hospital and the one in the nursing school. McClelland has furnished far more than merely slides. He tells of the genesis of the library: "When new textbooks were printed and furnished by the publisher and the ones in use became out-of-date, I, through my secretary Barbara McKenney, sent these out-of-date texts to Becky [Rebekah]. Becky has sent me pictures of the hospital library. From pictures she sent me, I could recognize every title and realized each book was one we had used here." Naylor explained the acquisition of books for the hospital medical library: "I was really kind of responsible . . . in getting books, either donations of money or books." Sister Sarojini, retired principal of Rebekah Ann Naylor School of Nursing, credits the large nursing-school library to Naylor. Several nursing schools in the U.S. donated books, which nurses in Mississippi shipped to BBH. Thus, Naylor secured for her colleagues and students reference material, an essential source for teaching and training.

Although excerpts from letters do not record the exact number of lectures or the precise hours spent in preparation that occurred for more than 25 years, they do indicate that Naylor served as a teacher in various training programs of the hospital. Perhaps her favorite, and the one for which she had the most training, was that of a lecturer/surgeon within the surgery theatre. The letter for January 13, 2000 notes that she spent a morning in the theatre teaching to the surgical residents the procedures for a mastectomy. Since 2002 Naylor has made twice-yearly trips back to Bangalore. During each one she teaches at BBH. As she planned the January 2008 trip, she outlined the instruction presentations. "Not only will I teach residents. We've just begun to have medical students in the hospital [BBH]. I have 5 hours of lecture with medical students. I will be doing faculty development. I will do four hours of teacher training. One session will be with the residents. I'm going to do basic things such as how to do bedside teaching — always take someone with you to teach, ask questions, give students feedback, introduce the residents to the adult learning theory. With the medical staff I will do some of the same things. I will meet with the core leadership in our education programs to talk to them about graduate medical education in America which is based on six competencies. I'm going to spend some time with them about those six [domains] about development, needs assessment, and how to write evaluations in both directions, the evaluation of the students by faculty and the need to be evaluated by the students. Also with students I'll be doing clinical studies such as abdominal pain, breast malignancies — symptoms, exams, work-ups, evaluations. One session I'll teach how to do presentations — how to present a patient, how to tell the patient's story during rounds or even at Grand Rounds. The teaching at BBH just goes on."

Apart from teaching students and fellow physicians, while Naylor was on staff at BBH, she also taught patients. She prepared for use in the hospital educational materials such as post-mastectomy care and exercises. She herself drew the diagrams and had the materials translated into multiple Indian languages and then photocopied for distribution. Naylor elaborates: "[The materials weren't] fancy like patients get in America, but they served the same purpose." A major educational tool revolved around breast-cancer awareness. Naylor created materials that were used for the women and trained the nurses to do the education. Breast camps, an outreach of the hospital community-health program and a focus for Naylor, already were in operation. When Naylor, who perennially looked for methods and materials to make any program more effective, was asked by a journalist, a former patient, Meera Pillai, to meet the president of Cancer Patients Aid Association, a voluntary cancer-aid organization in Bangalore in February 2000, Naylor went along. This group wanted to make a film on breast self-examination. Pillai was doing the technical part—the shoot—and needed a professional consultant to be sure the exam was done correctly. Naylor explained how she used the video for a teaching vehicle in the village breast camps: "I took the video—someone helped me—and took the still shots out of the video and created the flip-charts for non-literate women. No writing at all appeared on the charts. The flip chart could take the women through breast self-exam, breast lumps. Our nursing staff and people like Beulah I taught how to use the chart and teach it. The nurses then took over that breast-cancer awareness program. That all happened at the same time we were getting the mammogram machine at the hospital, so the breast camps and the machine all dovetailed."

Naylor speaks of mentoring and investing in three young doctors:

"Prior to the 15 years of teaching at BBH, I had invested in three physicians: John Anand ('70s), Fred Job ('80s), and Joy Thomas. John, the first one, did complete a general surgery residency away from BBH and therefore had formal training as well as the training

148

I had given him and he had gained as a surgeon at BBH. For 25-plus years, he served in mission hospitals across southern India, holding positions of chief surgeon and medical superintendent of several hospitals. Fred Job, the second physician, came without his residency but chose to complete a surgery residency at BBH. He is reliable, skilled, consistent. He has a special ability to know what he can do and do competently and does that well. I was totally comfortable with Fred because he knew what he could do. He called if he needed help from one of us. As a result, he took primary surgical call. Joy Thomas was one of the students BBH sponsored at CMC Vellore. When he came to BBH for his compulsory two years, we assigned him to OB/GYN, which I was running at the time. We worked like fury and would think we'd never finish. Joy's residency at CMC Vellore was in OB/GYN. I taught and trained him in basic general surgery such as treating a perforated ulcer and appendicitis. While Joy was in medical school, with three or four of his classmates he covenanted to establish a mission hospital in an area that had no medical or missionary presence. Joy's wife, Grace, a teacher, pursued graduate training in public health administration; she completed the medical team of the four classmates and Joy who went to the state of Orissa in the jungle with lions, tigers, and bears and people who were almost cannibalistic they were so primitive. In that mission hospital they established, Joy did not only all the OB/GYN but also functioned when necessary as a general surgeon. Joy and Grace stayed until the children needed different schooling. Currently he is completing during 2008 a fellowship in Australia."

With the opening of the nursing school, Naylor found herself in an academic classroom. This program, not unlike the paramedical and residency programs, also presented a required course of study to meet accreditation criteria. Unfortunately for the instructor the daily lesson plans and the individual lectures and exams were not written. Instead, Naylor, like teachers in other areas of academia, found herself with only a textbook, the required number of lecture hours, and prospects of an external certification exam as the final test of her teaching expertise. First-year nursing students entered the program on July 1, with the academic year beginning the same month. Requiring 80 hours of classroom lecture, anatomy, and physiology, Naylor's course ran from July to March. As early as July 1996 letters describe her experiences and record her thoughts on not only being in front of a class of students but also on other aspects of teaching such as facing student failure to grasp concepts, devoting hours to preparation, and writing different exams.

The next big event is the launching of my teaching career in the nursing school. The material I planned for the week is going to finish by tomorrow. What to do!! I teach Monday, Tuesday, Wednesday, Friday, Saturday. Tomorrow they have a little quiz and one on Friday. I was so worried about their understanding. I am having trouble remembering names. That will take time. (July 16, 1996) I have finished 5 sessions. We have gone faster than scheduled. We finished the first 2 units which were introductory units. I gave 2 tests. They were quite wide ranging in their performance. One girl made 100 both times. Yesterday we started the skeleton. They are so eager and look happy. (July 20, 1996) We have studied the anatomy of the heart this week. So far I have made it every day, 5 days per week. Tomorrow finishes 4 weeks. My hard work on it in July

will run out in another week, so I must really start
studying. (August 9, 1996)

Additionally Naylor discovered frequent modification and
adjustment of methods and lecture content—a necessity when
her students didn't grasp concepts:

I have fallen behind on the [physiology] studying.
So have they! I gave a big exam on Tuesday. Last night
I graded them. Even basic concepts they have not
understood. I must revamp everything. (August 22,
1996) *I will only teach 3 hours per week since the girls*
are having so much trouble keeping up. I have to give
another exam this week to replace the disastrous
grades they made last time. (August 26, 1996)

Often letters record only the remaining number of lectures,
the hours of study, the preparation of a second test. Surely as
Naylor looked at the lengthy list of chores for each day, she
must have been overwhelmed.

We are studying the nervous system. I have worked
hard on lectures this week. (December 6, 1996) *I*
taught anatomy and the students were so glad to see
me. Just another 4 or 5 lectures! (February 14, 1997)
Wednesday night I finally finished my anatomy lecture
preparations. I will have to plan their review sessions,
but the lectures are prepared. I still have to prepare a
major exam. Saturday I gave my last anatomy lecture.
That is an accomplishment to be sure! Next Sat. I give
the last major exam. There will be review. Their big
external exams begin May 27. (March 2, 1997)

Amidst the discouraging test grades and prodigious preparation were humorous and bright spots. During the study of the

skeleton one young student asked in sincerity and respect a question about the numbers of ribs in men and women. Basing her knowledge of the rib count on the story of Adam's and Eve's creation from the Book of Genesis, she deduced that men have one fewer rib on one side than the other side, or 11 on one side and 12 on the other. Her thought process evolved thusly: God took a rib from Adam to form woman; therefore the number must be one fewer for men; women have 12 ribs on both sides. Naylor chuckles today about the experience of fielding the question and supplying the answer in such a way the student understood the biblical text as well as the anatomical reality that men and women have the exact number of ribs—12 per side.

Yesterday morning all 20 nursing students were lined up by 7:30 with big smiles. They presented me a red rose and a card they made—Happy Teacher's Day!! What a nice way to start the day. (September 6, 1996) Sometimes the joy was in passing grades, other times a party. *On the exam I gave Wednesday, only one failed. The girl who has always made the lowest passed with a roaring 63—I am so proud. She has studied so hard!* (August 26, 1996) *One of their terms for me is the **anatomy madam**. Just hilarious.* (December 13, 1996)

For the next five years, Naylor taught A and P to new classes of nursing students. Her lectures tested, refined, and revised, Naylor with confidence embarked July 1997 with the second class of nursing students. What a difference in the tone of the letters of years two, three, and four from that first year!

The teaching is going smoothly. Having all of my notes and visuals ready from last year has made a lot of difference. I still do some study, but not so bad.

Writing the exams does take time. Next Wednesday I give the first big exam. (July 27, 1997) *I taught my first classes on Friday and Saturday. One girl joined late only on Saturday. They are now all here.* (July 7, 1998) *All the girls passed anatomy and physiology national end-of-the-year exams, even the girl who had to repeat year one. My teaching is going on. Four or five girls in the class are consistently doing well on every quiz. But some are struggling . . . I am repeating every lecture twice and give them fully written notes plus their text books.* (July 24, 1998) *I completed my anatomy teaching Friday! I have to write a big exam today and that will be given this week. For me the school year is then over.* (March 28, 1999)

Although some letters indicate Naylor received satisfaction and fulfillment from the teaching and realized she could teach, one letter stands apart from those carrying a litany of hours, remaining class sessions, exams, and reviews. Naylor wrote that she was teaching anatomy and physiology and that she enjoyed the teaching—both the subject and the girls. (January 7, 2001) When the principal assumed the teaching of the course, Naylor commented: *I hope I can get it back in the future!* Much to her delight, Naylor did learn that she would teach the A and P course for the next class of students. (July 5, 2001) No doubt she thought that with all lectures, exams, notes, and syllabus ready, the course should run the most smoothly of all the other years. Didn't she receive notice that the textbook had been changed for that year's course? Textbook change—so often the bane of a teacher's life! Teaching two groups of students—those who entered in January 2001 as well as the group which entered July 2001—added to teaching the residency and paramedical (allied health programs) students, practicing surgery, and seeing patients made for a full calendar. A new text extended the work load.

Finally January 24, 2002 she writes: *I have finished the anatomy teaching for the year. I have now taught six classes of students. These girls have done very well.* Little did she know as she penned those words that she had taught her very last class of Rebekah Ann Naylor School of Nursing students at BBH. She did know, however, that the nursing-school teaching was an invaluable learning experience and gave her the experience of writing course syllabi, exams, and lectures as well as being in the formal classroom for several semesters.

She reflects on those students and those years of teaching them:

> "Many were from a weak socio-economic background and . . . also from a weak educational background. They were required to have completed 12 years of schooling, high school. They excelled at the science emphasis they had to have in the 11th and 12th grades. For some girls, especially those from the rural areas, [education] wasn't anything like the girls in Bangalore had. There's that background. There were the language issues. They had to take an English comprehension exam for entry. The interviews were theoretically to be in English but usually they had to lapse into their mother language. They gave rote answers. 'Tell us about your family.' 'I have one father. I have one mother. I have brothers two. I have sisters one.' And then if I asked a follow-up question, they were lost. I'm sure that some of those girls had never seen a bed before they arrived in the dorm much less slept in one. I can't even imagine those kinds of adjustments that they had to make. Very shy as young Indian girls are, afraid, but so incredibly motivated. I think these were the most motivated students I've ever taught at any level in any program anywhere in the world. Their whole future, their family's livelihood, their own liveli-

hood, the future of their families depended on success. They were very disciplined and they worked very hard. I think that was part of the reason it was such a joy to teach them. They were so motivated. It was always so remarkable to me to see even pretty quickly how much poise they managed to acquire. One little cultural thing—every day when I walked into the classroom, they stood up, as a group, to their feet. They would not sit down until I remembered to tell them to sit down. I let them sit wherever they chose to in the beginning of the year and I told them to stay in those places. I took down their names. Well, I don't remember which year it was, but I'd done that. One fine day, I arrived and started to check the attendance and very quickly realized they were out of place. They had purposefully mixed themselves up before I got there to see if they could really confuse me. We had such a big laugh. In three years, those girls are just transformed. They are totally competent professionally but they are self-confident. They are poised; they are mature. At the same time, they have a good time."

After Naylor returned to Fort Worth the spring of 2002, she assumed other teaching positions, one of which was at Southwestern Baptist Theological Seminary. Dr. Kenneth Hemphill (no relation to Andrew Hemphill, the music professor when Rebekah's mother was a student) was the president.

"Dr. Hemphill had talked to me even earlier than 2002, maybe when Daddy died in 1999. 'You know, we'd be happy to have you teach in the Seminary.' When I finally did come home, I went to talk to him. By then fall term was already set with professors and classes. He proposed that I team teach with Dr. Mike Barnett in the Missions Department. I didn't know Dr.

Barnett. He and I met. I was introduced to the book, the reading, the syllabus. Through the fall I sat and heard Mike teach, except for the unit Mike gave me. I have laughed about this ever since. He thought it was just so appropriate, but for me, that semester and every semester since, it was the unit I dreaded and hated. It was the unit on culture and cross-cultural communication. I loved teaching about the history of missions, the biblical basis of missions, even the strategy of missions. Starting in January 2003 I had my own class. I taught five semesters on my own—had to totally prepare all my lectures, a major undertaking, do a lot of reading. The funny part of it is I had never had a missions course. This was really learning for me. I enjoyed what I learned. I found teaching seminary students was quite different from the medical world. I'm used to black and white of science and found the thinking and discussion they talked about [interesting]. Students enjoyed the idea of having a doctor as a teacher. I used to tell them: 'If I get confused which day of the week it is, I will teach you surgery and go teach missions in Dallas.' Those three years were very valuable. I learned a lot about teaching, I'm sure. I learned a whole lot about missions that I've used in other settings. I very much enjoyed relating to the seminary students. I always had a few in my class who were looking at missions long-term, usually had a few in the class that were considering Journeyman responsibility. I consider that a very positive time."

Without a doubt, the teaching responsibilities Naylor assumed and experiences she encountered laid groundwork for her current position at University of Texas Southwestern Medical School, Dallas. Shires' query about her teaching became more than just a question to contemplate. On staff as a part-time faculty member of the surgery department, Naylor acknowledges her responsibilities have continued to increase since her initial employment in 2002. Currently she holds several positions, jobs, and titles. She is associate clinical professor of surgery, a position to which she was promoted September 1, 2007. This post involves teaching patient care and clinical responsibility in the operating room to residents assigned to Parkland Hospital. As director of student education for the Department of Surgery, an administrative position, Naylor directs the eight-week surgery course for third-year students, oversees electives in surgery for fourth-year students, teaches second-year students in lecture situations, and counsels and guides into residencies those students who decide to enter the medical specialty of surgery. The third major position is developer of the web curriculum project for surgery. Although other faculty have read and approved the lessons, Naylor has done all the writing, all the editing, all the assembly, all the revision. Currently several institutions have signed a license agreement to have the product. As an educator Naylor has been asked to participate in a research study relative to pedagogical techniques within the purview of medical education. Her paneled reports have been accepted for presentations at major conferences and for publication. In 2007 she accepted appointment as a mentor for first-year students. She will follow this initial group of students weekly through their four years of medical school and annually will add another group of such students. Thus in 2008 she will have both first- and second-year students; in 2009, first-, second-, and third-year students, and 2010 the four groups from first year, second year, third year, and fourth year! When asked why she undertook another responsibility, she retorted, "How could I refuse? What a compliment as part-time faculty to be asked to do this!"

From children's camp in Dallas and Sunday-school teacher in Nashville to surgery professor at Bangalore Baptist Hospital and Parkland Hospital to anatomy and physiology instructor for the Rebekah Ann Naylor School of Nursing, Naylor has, despite lack of formal study of teacher techniques, practiced and taken advantage of every opportunity to develop the gift of teaching. In doing this she has added one more career, several more lines to her lengthy *curriculum vitae,* and one more title: *The Anatomy Madam.*

Missionary Doctor
and Strategy Coordinator

New missionary to India, 1974

After six months on the field

At left, at Petro Church
with Pastor Anthony Jacob, as he
translates Rebekah's message for a
Sunday-morning service in 2004

Below, Rebekah speaks
at Hope Church.

Pastor Jacob, Rebekah, and a woman believer
near Petro Church

But whatever was to my profit I now consider loss for the sake
of Christ. What is more, I consider everything a loss compared
to the surpassing greatness of knowing Christ Jesus my Lord,
for whose sake I have lost all things. I consider them rubbish,
that I may gain Christ and be found in him, not having a right-
eousness of my own that comes from the law, but that which is
through faith in Christ—the righteousness that comes from
God and is by faith. I want to know Christ and the power of
his resurrection and the fellowship of sharing in his sufferings,
becoming like him in his death, and so, somehow, to attain to
the resurrection from the dead
(Phil. 3:7-10).

Missionary Doctor
and Strategy Coordinator

Primrose is making trips over Karnataka with the
women's convention and work. She has asked me to go
with her to the Telugu Camps in August. I will be lead-
ing the Bible study . . . Saturday I sat on the porch of
the hut during one of Primrose's sessions—surrounded
by a dozen staring children, a group of baby chickens,
a buffalo. You should have seen it—hilarious!

The young seminary student absorbed the words of
the introduction for the professor of missiology and
blurted aloud, "Gee, I've never met a bulletin insert
before!"

Missionaries have varied experiences. Their witnessing to
people groups takes on various forms—retreats, camps, conversations in the market, services in huts, the treatment of disease. Some missionaries remain on the field longer than others

or have a unique position. Some become spokespersons for the area in which they serve. Frequently Naylor found herself not only amongst the villagers in either medical or evangelical events but also being photographed in India for focus on prayer for missions in India. One mission-emphasis publication—part of his church's worship folder—made a big impression on the young seminary student enroute to the mission field himself. Imagine his awe at meeting Dr. Rebekah Naylor, missionary to India, about whom he'd heard much, and learning she was his professor of missiology!

Missionary denotes the role and title by which Naylor defines her life. Yes, she is a highly trained general surgeon, an administrator, a teacher. She is foremost a missionary. When asked about her role, Naylor quickly replies, "Sharing my faith in Jesus is a part of who I am. I very much see myself as a missionary. Missions is my life, my passion." The 14 years of preparation provided valuable, essential education, and the means to equip and facilitate placing Naylor on the mission field. Medicine served as the avenue through which she could enter India, while general surgery furnished a practical specialty that allowed the best skill for attending the greatest number of physical needs of patients; mission orientation gave practical advice such as cultural and evangelism instruction, while the seminary training provided in-depth study of the Bible. Naylor has held several International Mission Board positions, the first of which was that of missionary surgeon assigned to Bangalore Baptist Hospital, a position she held from 1973 until 1999, the year her role became IMB consultant to BBH. In 1999 she was appointed strategy coordinator for Karnataka, with BBH as the hub of the area in which she worked. From 2002 Naylor has been on special assignment as she continues both of these roles and mobilizes personnel for South Asia.

As a medical missionary Naylor's primary work remained within the hospital and through the various programs of the hospital. Because she was in a Christian hospital on a mission field and because of her zeal to share the love of Christ, she moved beyond mere medical care. Before each and every surgical procedure, she prayed with her patient. Sister Flora, longtime chief theatre nurse and now director of nursing, says that never once did Naylor fail to pray. She prayed with families of her patients. If the patient spoke a language other than English, she asked one of the theatre nurses to voice the prayer. Sometimes Naylor specifically named a nurse to pray; other times she allowed the nurses to volunteer. Often Flora prayed and eagerly did so. According to Sister Flora and other staff, the prayer before surgery and prayer with patients strengthened and encouraged the staff. They saw Naylor's strong commitment to Jesus put into action. Additionally Naylor led the hospital service on Sundays in the Prayer Hall (chapel). She invited the patients to the hospital chapel service. She walked with them or pushed them in wheelchairs to the place of prayer. The hospital staff has its own chapel service each Friday morning. Naylor frequently presents the main address and always uses a biblical story to challenge each participant to be a more active witness, to commit more wholly to Christ, and to lead by example others to Christ. Naylor did not confine her missionary activities to the hospital.

One of her memorable experiences was a trip with Primrose Vasa into the far rural areas of the state of Karnataka.

We left at 7:30 Friday morning and were in Davangere by 12:45. The driver from the hospital was excellent. We had lunch. Primrose and I ate some sandwiches we took and fruit and got a cold drink . . . We stayed at the usual place—roaches about 4 inches long and flying, bathroom unbelievably filthy. We had taken our own sheets and towels! We did survive! I had taken cheese and some real Premium crackers given to me by visitors . . . That, fruit, and tea (I had my water heater) were quite fine. Friday we left at 2:30 for the village—

Thimmappa Camp. All thatched mud huts except one tile-roofed house that was white washed. We have a church in that village with a building (like the huts) and that is where we met. We finally had 24 widows and about 8-9 other ladies. The 3 pastors and 3 Bible women who work in the Telugu Camps had promoted the retreat and were there and involved. The ladies were so attentive and very responsive. A few could read (Telugu). I had an hour Friday afternoon followed by 3 small groups, a pastor with each. Much singing and fellowship. We came back into town to eat—Indian food, of course. In our room by 9 and Primrose and I played UNO. Saturday we were on the way at 8 and returned only at 9:30 p.m., a full day. We went again to Thimmappa Camp—my session, small groups and discussion, and a session by Primrose. We did this routine again all afternoon. We ate lunch on banana leaves with all of those ladies. They each had paid their transport and had brought their rice from home. Primrose provided all other food. Several of these ladies had been won by Pastor Ranga Rao [Primrose's husband]. They spoke of him with such evident love and fondness and gratitude. All weekend Primrose recalled experiences they had together in those camps. We left there a little after 5 and went to see where one of our pastors lives and a storeroom built for agricultural project equipments. We drove a fair distance to see the one granary David had built. Finally by 7 we ended up with Pastor Carey—we ate dinner in his little hut—he has electricity (other pastors do not) but the same type of hut. His church people gathered in the house. I brought a message. Sunday we again went to Thimmappa camp for service and Lord's Supper. Then an hour's drive to another place—again a service and lunch. I managed a different message all 6 times! Back

to Davangere by 2:30 and on the road by 2:45.
Bangalore a little after 8. (September 3, 1984)

During Naylor's several terms as chair of the IMB mission group in Bangalore and always as a member of the Bangalore mission, she pushed for money to support and to fund evangelism and church planting. She strived for a balance of funds between the teaching and the healing functions of the mission and the hospital. This put emphasis on both medical care and evangelism.

In the years since 2002 Naylor has been instrumental in presentations about evangelism and medical missions. Her contention is that the hospital allows and fosters evangelism. Followup visits to the family of the patient as well as to the patient make contacts in the community. Eventually as a group of believers emerges, a believers' group forms.

Outside the hospital medical function Naylor served in various capacities; all were within her role of missionary. She led Bible studies for young women associated with the hospital, a weekly Bible study for administrators and physicians and their spouses, and Bible studies for the women staff members living on the compound. During the late '80s and early '90s she was a participant in Baptist Fairs.

Sunday was quite a day . . . a special experience. I had been invited to speak at a Baptist Fair in a village almost 55 kilometers from here up north. Almost 15 years ago scattered believers were out there, mostly from hospital contacts. Brother Solomon worked there so long churches came. And it spread. I had been to this particular village about 5 or 6 years ago one night—met in the house of Mr. Gowda. Today they have a church building. This fair had called Baptists together—from several villages—a 2.5 day thing. They brought some relations with them. Services, film show.

*It is a place where there has been opposition before—
this time threats but no trouble. I had arranged coverage so that Dr. Mays could go with me. Grace
[Solomon] went. Pastor Ramaiah was running this
whole affair. His wife and little daughter and a lady
friend all came also. We reached there—already just
burning up—by 10. The people were gathered—about a
100 in a small room—singing. The first service had
started. The man who preached seemed good. Much
singing. Then baptisms. They had built a baptistry in
the floor of the little platform. It was the deepest I had
ever seen—very steep steps—and dry! Would you
believe, one water pot at a time, over 45 minutes, they
put almost 2 feet of water. It was also very narrow.
Somehow Ramaiah managed—15 people—3 teenage
boys, and adults including 3 men. For many there it
was their first time [to see a baptism]—I am sure that I
have never been hotter—people so pressed together, no
air. They swept the church—great clouds of dust.
Finally we were ready to start the next service at nearly 1. I thought he would keep it short—but no. Special
songs, congregational songs, offering. At 1:30 it came
my turn to speak (it was to have been 2 hours earlier).
Mine became shorter and shorter as the morning wore
on. Then Lord's supper. Just terrific. Four common
cups amongst us served by these villagers. Just so
thrilling to see so many. Ramaiah had to give a vote of
thanks, as we say here, to everyone. At 2:30 the service
got over. Those people had been 5 hours in there—no
food or water—heat—yet so attentive. They swept the
church again. Mats were laid out—then banana leaves
placed. They apologized because they were too poor to
have any meat—vegetable, rice, and dhal only. I felt
bad just to eat that. Finally left there after 3. Home
after 4. Terrell Mays really took it in—I was so glad he*

*went. As he kept saying—people at home wouldn't
believe it and there is no way to describe it.* (April
17, 1989)

Frequently, Naylor accompanied Grace and Pastor
Solomon on their visits into the rural villages. One particular
Sunday afternoon, they were invited to enter into the believers'
tiny hut topped with thatched roof. As guest of honor Naylor
was shown to her seat, a box on which she gingerly perched.
The others sat on the dirt floor. The host family began to prepare tea for their guests. They indicated Naylor was to stand;
she did. From the box the lady removed chunks of dung, the
fuel source for boiling the water for tea!

Another village trip Naylor describes:

*Pastor K. Jacob was working at the hospital when I
first came. He would go out with Pastor Solomon and
ultimately was called to preach. We sent him and his
wife to seminary in Andhra since they needed to study
in Telugu medium. Now for over 10 years they have
been working in villages about 45 KM away to the
north. Some of this work dates back to Pastor Solomon.
It all had its beginning with hospital contacts. Today
they were opening their building, the first in that area.
Jacob, Diwakar, others, Florence, Clyde and Elaine
Meador, and Harry Bush went. I was driving, one hour
each way. We reached there at 11:30 for the baptism,
but it started late. The story of the building is terrific.
The KBSS has not put in any money. A lady named
Pillamma was said to be possessed by demons. Jesus
healed her and she became a believer. Through her, her
elderly parents believed. The father gave the land and
built the building. He is a thin, stooped farmer who
obviously loves the Lord. He also has 4 sons and at*

167

least the eldest has become a believer and has put all idols out of the house. Just outside the building is the baptistry, a small rectangular tank. Getting in and out of it was a feat. He baptized 8 people, 7 of them women. I cut the ribbon. We entered the one-room church. In this room which was about 20 by 25 feet were crammed 130 people (counted by Clyde). I spoke about new things. Our Jacob presided. Diwakar had the dedicatory prayer. There were many welcomes and garlands and thanksgivings. It was after 2 when the service was over. There was to be lunch for all. We were taken to the home of this eldest son who has become a Christian. The rice they brought from the church, but they had prepared chicken curry and several other things for us. We had plates instead of banana leaves; however, this was a typical village home. The small entry room was for the cow and other animals and just inside we sat. They moved tables from somewhere for us. It was a dirt floor. The people are so hospitable. It was another great experience.
(August 28, 1994)

Experiences such as these may fit with a person's concept of a missionary in a foreign land. Naylor's evangelism efforts covered other venues also. With the pastoral-care department of the hospital, Naylor planned retreats. Those labeled *seekers' retreats* focused on individuals who wished to know more about Jesus. Some retreats were for the nurturing and spiritual growth of staff. Twice yearly the hospital-staff members participate in a 24-hour prayer chain, with personnel taking 30- to 60-minute intervals around the clock. Specific prayer requests and needs compiled before the vigil are made available to the participants. During the 1970s and early 1980s, Naylor, Grace Solomon, and perhaps one or two chaplains carried the brunt of the responsibility of the weekly worship service, retreats, prayer days, and visitation. Since the creation of the pastoral-care department and the chaplaincy certification and diploma programs in 1999, additional chaplains are available to undertake more evangelistic work. Hospital staff continues to participate and support the varied efforts. When chaplaincy students indicated they believed they could talk about Jesus only if they were asked, Naylor and others quickly assured them that direct contact and speaking boldly about Jesus were needed. The philosophy of open evangelism continues to be in place within the department.

No program, even one that introduces people to Christ, runs without problems. As the pastoral-care department grew, more chaplains increased the instances of interaction with patients, their families, and their visitors. When individuals responded positively to the Gospel presentation or indicated they wanted to discuss the Gospel more, personnel were needed for these follow-up visits.

> Some staff think the follow-up should be handed over to churches. Maybe we should reduce chaplains as they have too much free time and without proper teachers, the training program should not continue. I was stunned . . . I must prayerfully and carefully defend our ministry. This has been disturbing! Yet I realize that it will give me opportunity to make clear to the [BBH] Administrative Committee my view and the IMB view of why the hospital is here. (January 24, 2001) Another issue arose concerning the chaplaincy students, their supervisors, and the hospital staff chaplains. The chaplains have been having a heated time with the training supervisors because the wards assigned to the students cannot be visited by a staff chaplain. The students do not share Jesus in the same way. Professions of faith are fewer. The staff chaplains, very upset, asked Dr. George [and me] to meet with them. We heard what they had to say. I

appreciated their zeal and concern. I kept trying to see how to solve the problem. Suddenly I so felt the Lord gave me an answer. I told them that the students may not have a vision for lost people and burden like they do and also may not know how to share their faith. I challenged the chaplains to give the students the vision and train them how to do it, that this investment might win more people over the next years than their own evangelism in those particular rooms. Furthermore there is more than enough work to go around. We gave them lots of ideas for what to do. I think it was a good time. The Lord really helped me. (October 27, 2001)

As always, sharing the saving grace of Jesus was uppermost in Naylor's comments during the discussion and finding the most practical and effective way to do so remained paramount.

A role change for Naylor happened, in part, as a result of Dr. Clyde Meador's January 1999 visit to BBH. Meador, BBH governing board member and area director for India from 1989-2001 as well as Naylor's immediate supervisor and personal friend, met with a committee of trustees to determine administrative leadership roles for the hospital. The four persons at the higher end of hospital administration would work as a team. Stan Macaden was named director (60 percent administrator, 40 percent medical). Santosh Benjamin was named associate director, with 10-50 percent administration. Alex Thomas was named chief of medical staff, while Naylor was IMB consultant—a new role. Meador's concern for Naylor's continuing presence in Bangalore and at BBH in face of license and visa problems was evident. *I was shocked and grateful and said so,* she wrote. Meador returned to Bangalore for the Bangalore Baptist Hospital governing board meeting March 24-29, 1999, during which he announced Naylor's new role and her responsibilities: participate in pastoral care, teach in the nursing school, teach in the residency-training program, coordinate the volunteer program, relate to the IMB, represent the IMB, and serve as a fundraiser. The position change necessitated an office change to the back office near the library area with the other medical-staff consultants. Ever the realist, she wrote: *I admit it is not easy to be out of the mainstream.* (March 28, 1999)

As IMB consultant Naylor has worked on-site from her hospital office (1999-2002), from her home in Fort Worth (2002-present) through email and telephone, and during twice-yearly visits to BBH. Because of her roles as administrator, surgeon, and teacher and her long relationship with BBH, Naylor has needed, useful skills. Two large areas of responsibility are hospital administration and hospital-training programs. In July 2007 the hospital added a new program—that of medical-school level students rotating through the hospital for their clinical training. Naylor gives input on administration and materials for these programs. Occasionally she has provided input on new policies or issues such as the revision of the vision and mission statement for BBH and the 10-year plan. Along with the nursing-school administrators Naylor has been instrumental in fundraising, giving educational support through teaching and curriculum development, and facilitating the creation of current and long-term goals. Apart from various medical programs Naylor assists the pastoral-care department (IMB-supported) in personnel matters, strategies for evangelism and follow-up, supervision of the consultant to the pastoral-care department, and the relationship the BBH pastoral-care department has to the India Baptist Society and the relationship the India Baptist Society has with BBH. A significant contribution, vital to the ongoing operation of the hospital and the emphasis on evangelism, is facilitating and evaluating the IMB, CMC Vellore, and BBH relationship, ensuring and strengthening IMB interest and support of the hospital, and making the three-way relationship a true partnership.

Naylor's desire to share her belief in Jesus led her into an aspect of mission work she never imagined for herself. Dr. Clyde Meador traveled to Bangalore in January 1999. As customary when friends and other missionaries visited, Naylor planned a dinner outing.

As she drove, Meador said, "I'd like for you to consider becoming a strategy coordinator and taking the training." Naylor laughed and concentrated on driving—no small chore given Bangalore traffic and roads.

On the drive back, Meador asked, "Did you hear me when I asked you to consider becoming a strategy coordinator?"

Said Naylor flippantly, "Yes, and I laughed."

Meador, sincerely, candidly, continued the conversation. He recognized her unique qualifications to fill this role: fervent desire to share her faith to the people throughout India, administrative and organizational skills, involvement in South Asian mission work as well as her well-known presence among other missionaries in the area, knowledge of the culture and the geography, and her tenuous situation with renewal of her Indian medical license. Becoming a strategy coordinator as an alternative for practicing medicine would allow Naylor to remain on the mission field. Naylor listened cordially but firmly declined! Meador relates that although reluctantly she did attend the training.

She described the training proposal.

Clyde is very supportive of me (and patient!). He talked to me about attending a training (4 weeks) in Istanbul in September for strategy coordinators—a term they use to describe team leaders in their new structure. I thought it was funny, but I would like to do it. He said I could know what terms and all are being used. It is a way to get the hospital back on the map of what the new approach is. I might have to have a people group but he said to find out in the hospital what is

our main unreached people group among patients. He
also said I would discover that some things I have been
doing for years are what they do. I want to do it but 4
weeks seems such a long time to sit in something.
(February 27, 2000).

Naylor made plans to be away from the hospital. Changes
occurred: the location—Izmir, Turkey; the time—three weeks.
Naylor packed her medical journals and letter-writing and
Bible-study materials along with the surveys of people groups
and areas for church-planting focus. She says, "I went with my
normal attitude of reading journals, skipping sessions as I saw
fit, and soaking up the culture, eating good food, enjoying
myself."
Several letters chronicle the training sessions.

Our meetings are 8:30-4:30 daily—a very nice
meeting room area . . . The leader lives in Singapore
but mainly works in India. Other leaders will come in
and out to do their part, but he is here throughout. My
biggest problem is seeing how this applies to my situa-
tion or why should I develop this big master plan
which is not realistic. I am trying to work on things
related to the conference that I can take back and use.
(August 23, 2000) *I have been here a week. Some I just*
can't think I will ever use. Some may be relevant, but I
wonder how to implement anything given my present
circumstances. I do know God can take care of that.
Thursday the whole day was spent on communications,
much of it computer related, how to set up prayer and
support network. Friday we had our discussion of
Joshua. As a model the afternoon was spent discussing
and reviewing a church planting movement in
Cambodia. That was interesting. We are to be working
on the master plan of reaching our people. I have

started doing that in the format they want. It is no problem to do but seems to me to be unrealistic. Maybe the need is for my attitude to improve! (August 26, 2000) *We have discussed partnerships with other groups, precision harvesting, use of volunteers, Acts, the Gospel we read. We have each presented our people whom we are targeting. I had come prepared about the people we care for in the hospital—people groups, religions. I had also looked at our state, the people groups our church planters work with. Tuesday morning I had the devotional for the group—Romans 12:1-2.* (August 31, 2000) *Today we are talking about church planting principles and methodologies. I think I have helped these young folks to see that it can happen.* (September 4, 2000) *Monday was on church planting. Yesterday and today are on platforms, ways we get into places. I have completed the writing of my master plan. I have worked on some volunteer orientation and procedures.* (September 7, 2000) *I skipped out after lunch, a long walk, a swim, surgery journals, packing. . . a good way to finish my stay. In small groups we shared some things about our master plans that we projected for winning our people group. The funniest thing was that my little group thought the answer to doing everything lay in requesting more IMB personnel. Such a thing never entered my mind. I thought all of the workers would be nationals. They began a time of praying for each other—the person or couple would share prayer needs. The group would gather round them, lay hands on them, and pray for them. That was a pretty emotional thing.* (September 10, 2000)

When Naylor returned to Bangalore, the training proved more useful than Naylor first imagined. Her attitude did change—not only about the concept of becoming a strategy

174

coordinator but also about filling the role. Meador averred that she became "enthused and took on the role wholeheartedly." Shortly after her return from Izmir, she initiated her plan.

> *I met with the pastor and five deacons of Hope Church. I shared with them my vision and the role of local churches to achieve them. Very specifically I talked about their involvement—prayer, 10 percent of budget to outreach, personal witness, supporting a church planter . . . prayer walking . . . following up hospital contacts on this side of the city. They were very responsive and interested. We are all praying to see what may happen.* (October 29, 2000)

Naylor explains her strategy-coordinator position with the IMB and relationship to IBS:

> *A strategy coordinator assumes responsibility for a geographical or people group, developing a strategy to reach the people and to facilitate a church planting movement (CPM) which is a rapid multiplication of indigenous churches planting churches within a population segment. The SC produces strategies and forms a team to reach the people. The work of the strategy coordinator includes research and knowing the people, prayer, partnership, proclamation, planting, and preserving. The work moves from initial access to whatever it takes to plant churches and lead people to become believers. A Master Plan, a document that states clearly the goal (end vision) and the means for accomplishing the goal, or where will you go and how will you get there, addresses specific action plans as well as a built-in review of strategies, plans, and success. Regular modification occurs since some activities work; some do not. (The Master Plan developed for Karnataka has*

been revised three times.) My people group is
Karnataka with BBH at the center of the strategy. The
end vision is a church within walking distance of every
person in the state by 2025 and every patient at BBH
introduced to Jesus resulting in 10,000 churches in
three districts served by the hospital. Karnataka has
more than 300 Unreached People Groups in 33,000
towns and villages. Of the 53 million, 1.9% are
Christian; the predominant religion is Hinduism with
12% Muslim. The majority of the population (more
than 70%) is rural.

Naylor describes her specific role.

"My role is to cast the vision, then plan and coordinate all activity. My team is the nationals through
Indian Baptist Society, the Director of Church
Development, and church planters and trainers. An
ongoing activity is reaching the people groups in our
state, developing profiles and looking for bridges over
which the Gospel can enter that group and travel. Our
sources for information are the Internet, government
population statistics, materials prepared by various
mission agencies in India. Seminary students have
occasionally taken one of the Unreached People
Groups (UPG's) and written the profile and proposed a
strategy. Prayer involves developing a prayer network
in the USA and in India. Another major activity is
mobilization of personnel and financial resources. All
potential volunteers to be involved in our work contact
me; I shepherd them through the process of preparation
and then hand them over to BBH and IBS. I have
planned multiple team trips such as the South Carolina
Singing Churchmen; First Baptist Church, Dallas trips;
youth mission team as well as others teams from Travis

Avenue Baptist Church, Fort Worth; and a vision trip for women through the IMB. I do mobilization for long term. A pastor contacted me about a personnel request I placed at the IMB for a person to work with chaplains. For over nine months I prepared this couple, then did field orientation once they were on site. I continue supervision through emails once or twice per week and during site visits. I mentored a young woman from 2003-2007 who is now appointed by the IMB to Middle America and the Caribbean. For a few years we have had diminishing funds. Our plan was 50 church planters (two per district). We reached just over 30 planters when funds began to diminish. We are now down to 12 planters. We have known the funding might end anytime, but we moved forward in faith. God has provided. A role I had at the Southwestern Baptist Theological Seminary on behalf of South Asia was mobilizing students for South Asia and representing our region on campus. The other resource to be mobilized is financial. The IMB, through Lottie Moon (World Missions) offerings, has continued church planter support to some degree by providing training through the Leadership Equipping and Developing Program, which is carried out by itinerant missionaries in South Asia, training pastors and church planters. Annually I plan a budget that I submit to IMB. The portion not funded has until now been covered by special gifts as I make people aware of needs. I do monitor expenditures and budget and am also involved in managing our invested savings (special money gifts).

The big part of the job is planting churches and proclaiming the Good News. I interact with other IMB personnel whenever possible to gain ideas, information, strategies, and methods that might work. I stay up-to-date on what is happening in India herself—political, economic, Christian community, persecution.

I communicate regularly with national partners and colleagues, initially Pastor Jacob and since 2007 Pastor Subba Rao, about our church planters. I am responsible for our IBS staff in the IBS office as well as church planters. When we need new church planters, I partici-pate in interviews and selection. I receive reports regu-larly from church planters and from BBH Pastoral Care Department. I communicate regularly with hospital administrative people and chaplains about integrating our church planting strategies. Much of my email com-munication is to follow up on details of work, share new ideas, make plans. My regular visits allow us to plan work for the ensuing five to seven months.

A major activity of mobilization (people and money) is church partnerships. An ongoing part of mobilization, securing resources and partnership is reporting to churches in USA, personalizing the mis-sions, telling churches about South Asia and India par-ticularly. In January 2008 I initiated a partnership rela-tionship with another megachurch. Travis Avenue Baptist Church, where I work with the pastor, staff and India mission core team, arranging trips, equipping and training church people, keeping the vision before the church, built a partnership in 2005."

Dr. Michael Dean, senior pastor of Travis Avenue Baptist Church, describes Naylor's contributions to the partnership project:

"When we established the partnership with India as a church, and specifically with Karnataka, we were able to plug in through the program called Project Thessalonica where essentially a church becomes strategy coordinator rather than an individual missionary. This [program] permits the church to do that. We assumed that role under the umbrella of Rebekah's role as SC for state of Karnataka so we focused on [and] became the Strategy Coordinator church for the district of Mandya, working under her, working with her . . . tremendous help to us because here she sits on the team that works on the partnership. She's a tremendous resource as a church member and as a missionary—a missionary that develops strategy to reach [people groups]."

Currently Travis supports four church planters.

Naylor also has an official relationship with India Baptist Society. A member of the governing board and until 2002 the treasurer, Naylor explains that she still *takes responsibility for overall finance since the money is IMB money in origin. Of as great significance to the program is personnel, such as Pastor Jacob's replacement and interviewing prospective church planters.*

The search for Pastor Jacob's replacement as director of church development had been an ongoing concern and the subject of many emails. Pastor Subba Rao, a church planter, emerged as the most likely successor. After Naylor and Pastor Jacob talked with him, he prayed about his decision. After an October 2006 meeting Naylor had with the planters and Pastor Jacob, Subba Rao with the greatest of sincerity, said, "Dr. Naylor, I am afraiding."

"Good!" Naylor's immediately responded. She assured him he should be afraid, for that meant he was not taking the position or the work lightly. She continues to mentor him and ensures that he understands the work and the goals.

Naylor currently oversees the preparation of the annual report to the IMB and fills the strategy coordinator job of networking with two or three other IMB strategy coordinators in Karnataka as well as networking with other Great Commission Christian groups such as Campus Crusade. She remarks: "Essentially I function as a non-residential missionary."

Speaking engagements occupy much of an active missionary's Stateside assignment. As Naylor and her parents together planned their holidays, visits with other family members, vacation, and medical appointments during her leave, she worked into the calendar various mission emphases in churches, colleges, seminaries, and camps, as well as Southern Baptist Convention-related events. A willing guest speaker and a high-profile missionary, she has found herself in demand as a speaker. She often receives invitations a full year before she returns Stateside. Jamie Walker Erwin, a medical student, tells that as a 7-year-old girl she first met Naylor at Travis Avenue Baptist Church when Naylor spoke to a children's group. Naylor's testimony so inspired Jamie that she gave herself to medical missions. At least two missionaries in India today are missionaries because of Naylor: one because she heard Naylor speak in Mobile, Alabama, at the first IMB missionary-appointment service outside Richmond, the other because as a young boy he heard her speak at his church. Generally when Naylor speaks, she wears one of her beautiful Indian sarees, with the ensemble accented by gold bangles, earrings, and necklace. With her black hair and perfectly wrapped saree, she looks the part of the dignified Indian woman. Her Indian friends say she is perfect in appearance. Her dress combined with her powerful message impacts those who hear her.

Dr. Dean avers that Naylor is a valuable resource to the church as a missionary. She "is a poster child for missions. Having that person—that real, live person—who is connected to our church, makes missions alive. On that level, we've really benefited from her raising awareness of missions in our church, raising awareness of India . . . She has done so much just for the cause of Christ in India but [also the] cause of missions in our church."

One presentation she makes stands apart from others—her characterization of Lottie Moon. Dressed in a long black skirt and high-necked blouse as Lottie Moon, she begins her monologue:

Oh, my. I feel so cold and lonely. My old bones are complaining. In my heart I feel so sad—my people are starving and suffering in this famine. So many are dying without Jesus . . . You know as I sit here in my familiar bungalow in Tengchow, home for so many years, I think back over all that God has done for me and in this country of China. My full name is Charlotte Diggs Moon. I was always a prankster and even told people that my middle initial of D stood for devil. Little did I realize that years later in China I would be taunted with hostility as a foreign devil. One night I finally consented to go to a church revival with my friends. I really went to make fun. But that night I was faced with my sin and need for Christ. Later that night alone in prayer I gave my life to Jesus. Oh, what a difference it made. Almost immediately I felt God calling me to be a missionary. I am ashamed to say that there have been times in the years when I felt that Southern Baptists back home were almost callous. Why, they even said that missionaries did not have any hardships any more. I wrote back: Living in native houses with dirt or brick floors, sleeping on native beds, and eating only food prepared in the native style most people would consider a hardship. People at home have no idea the psychological isolation felt by a missionary. Money is so short. On bad days I wonder if the people in the

*churches at home prayed or even remembered that we
missionaries existed. At this last stage of my life, I am
tired—so tired. Now famine has struck China. It is time
for furlough, but my family back home are all gone. I
have spent my last penny buying food for people and
books for the children and medicines for the suffering.
Yet there is still so much to do. I have a firm conviction
that I am immortal until my work is done.*

Quickly Naylor loosens her hair from a bun at the nape of
her neck and dons her lab coat before she finishes the presentation.

*Lottie Moon, one of my real heroines. When she
said that she was immortal until her work was done,
she was thinking about her vision for work in China.
Today almost 100 years later she is immortal in spirit
as Southern Baptists reach out to win a lost world to
Christ. Exactly 100 years after Lottie Moon was
appointed a missionary to China by the Foreign
Mission Board, I was privileged to be appointed by
that same Mission Board to India. My, our world has
really changed in these years. Lottie traveled four
months to China. Today we can go anywhere in our
world in hours, just one or two days. As I look back
over more than 30 years of missionary service, I realize
that some things have changed very little. The lostness
of our world and God's love for the lost are still the
same. God still is calling out His people just like He
called Lottie to go and tell others about Jesus.*

What a powerful, impassioned speech—heartfelt and perfectly bespeaking the vision held by Naylor, the missionary
surgeon, strategy coordinator!

Legalities, Laws, and License

Labor union outside Bangalore Baptist Hospital gate

Effigy of Naylor hung outside the hospital gate

Legalities, Laws, and License

*Consider it pure joy, my brothers, whenever you face trials of
many kinds, because you know that the testing of your faith
develops perseverance
(Jas. 1:2-3).*

Legalities, Laws, and License

*Ignorance of the law doesn't make you innocent; Doctor, you
are still guilty.*

Harsh words? True words? Applicable words? Mr. K.G.
Raghavan, senior attorney, gravely summarized correctly the
reality of being unaware of the laws. Regardless of whether
one is a civilian worker, a military member, or a tourist in a
foreign country, certain laws apply to that individual. The
visa—the legal document attached to the passport that allows
one to visit or to live in the country—spells out specific regulations that must be followed, such as registering with the local
police or paying taxes to exit and re-enter the country. Dr.
Rebekah Naylor entered India as an American citizen on a
one-year missionary residential visa; her occupation listed on
the visa was that of missionary surgeon at Bangalore Baptist
Hospital. She therefore was subject to Indian laws. Bangalore
Baptist Hospital, even though supported financially by the
FMB and staffed by doctors from the United States, was subject to the laws of India. Throughout Naylor's tenure in India,
she dealt with local, state, and national law in matters relating
to building permits, labor unions, visa, and medical license.
Compounding the situation created by government laws and
regulations were Indian cultural practices, Foreign Mission
Board policies, and Christian ethics.

A major hurdle in each and every building project concerned the issue of building permits. Sometimes both the city

of Bangalore and the community of Hebbal assumed authority over BBH property. BBH, a Christian institution which operated in a system in which some officials asked for personal payment, adhered strictly to the codes and laws. Often not complying with an individual's demands created delay tactics and harassment; nonetheless, led by Naylor, the staff and hospital board remained firm. The building permit for the new wing built in 1990 was not granted until June 10, 1990—four months after local authorities received the application and three months after the groundbreaking. Similarly, issuance of the building permit delayed the staff housing project. Not unlike securing building permits for other projects, the wait for the necessary permission documents lengthened to four months. This saga differing somewhat from other situations presented a unique set of problems.

> *A patient related to a city official complained that we were not a charitable hospital because he had to pay for his care. He had demanded concession that was not given because he could afford [the charge]. He filed a complaint. Bangalore property tax on our hospital building itself has always been exempt . . . We are not sure why a relatively minor complaint went to the top level of the state. We will appeal to the Secretary of Housing.* (February 5, 1997) *Mrs. Chandavarkar [architect] went with me to meet a high-up official to seek his advice how to go about this [building permit problem]. He suggested we go to the Bangalore Development Authority top lady. Today Mrs. Chandavarkar and I went there. She did not know anything about the situation. She immediately said the permit should not be withheld if we had paid the amount of tax we were told to pay. She said that [the patient's filed complaint] should be totally separate from the issue of the amount of tax. She called in a lower*

official to find the full story, clarify, report back
(February 19, 1997) *BIG NEWS!! We have in hand*
building permits for the staff housing and dining room.
(April 29, 1997)

As plans moved forward for the building of the nursing
school, similar to problems encountered on other building
projects, legal documents allowing construction proved difficult to secure. Tax authorities moved forward with more taxes
levied, disputes over which agency had authority over BBH,
delays, and confusion over amounts. BBH never paid bribes; it
remained firm this instance. Harassment followed. A retired
government officer who had in the past helped BBH met with
Naylor and Dr. Macaden. He gave them a letter to the
Secretary of Housing for the state of Karnataka and advised
securing a definite ruling on the authority to which BBH is
subject—Hebbal or Bangalore. To meet the Secretary of
Housing for Karnataka was not simple. He was out; he was
busy; the next day was a holiday. Finally Dr. Macaden spoke
with the secretary on the telephone and made the appointment.
This official, realizing the problem, gave Macaden a letter to
the Bangalore Development Authority about jurisdiction and
building permit application. The Hebbal office also received
the letter. *Stan and I so clearly felt that God had gone before*
us. The man told us that if there were further trouble to come
to him. (May 16, 1995) When the permit application was submitted, however, more taxes were assessed—this one a tax for
a water scheme—4 rupees per square foot of land. For BBH
that would be 2.5 or 3 million rupees. As Naylor writes, *It is*
one thing after another. (June 1, 1995) In January 1996, six
months after the initial application, the building permits were
issued; construction of the nursing-school facility began.
    A significant complication—one that crossed cultural prac-
tices—revolved around the naming of the nursing school.
Because Mrs. Ruth Ray Hunt had given the bulk of the money

for the building and furnishing of the nursing school, the decision was made to name the school for her. Letterhead, publicity, brochures, and dedication stone had been ordered for The Ruth Ray Hunt School of Nursing. Imagine the surprise and furor that occurred when a fax arrived from Mrs. Hunt directing that the school be named the Rebekah Ann Naylor School of Nursing! Naylor herself could not have been more surprised and shocked. The board of trustees insisted naming a building for a living person was not proper; perhaps after Naylor retired then the school could be renamed for Naylor. The staff indicated that such a naming should not occur. Naylor's letters reveal the emotional turmoil:

> *Mrs. Hunt sent what she wants read at the dedication. The bombshell was that she wants the name changed to the Rebekah Naylor School of Nursing. What to do!! Everything printed, the logo done. I presumed Stan and the AC and the Board would need to decide and respond. Stan said I must give my opinion and he presumed I would decline. Well, that would be the simplest way out. But I felt I should not be put in that position. I have asked him that the others decide— even if I decide to decline, I felt it was not right that they be let off the responsibility. We did not need this crisis now. I only wish it could have been dealt with earlier . . . We shall see what he does with it.* (May 18, 1996) *To my amazement, Stan called a meeting of the Administrative Committee without me at 9:30 Saturday. Apparently there was no objection raised to changing the name—after the dedication since so much printing is already done. He then sent a fax to Vellore to get board approval and we may know tomorrow . . . We purposely printed enough copies of the prospectus for next year to save money. Invitations had just been printed. The plaques are in process.* (May 19, 1996)

*To my utter astonishment the CMC board members are
holding it up. Their position is that it is culture and
tradition in India to do this only when someone dies or
retires, so we cannot violate this. I was rather stunned.
Clyde, of course, gave his hearty approval. Now Stan
has been trying to talk to Clyde. We want Clyde to talk
to Dr. Mathan. I have tried endlessly and patiently to
explain about wishes and donors. I have pointed out
that the donor is of another culture in which this is
done. I have told him that the support base in USA is
because of me, not just the institution, and that this
decision affects all of our donors. The CMC folks say
the school can be named for me when I leave. They are
happy that it be done but not now. Stan is now caught
in the middle between all parties. I so wish it had never
come up. (May 24, 1996) Clyde Meador called about
10 p.m. last night. All is settled to go ahead . . . He
reached Dr. Mathan Friday night India time.
Apparently it had been decided to go ahead even by the
time Clyde talked to him. Clyde felt Stan was very
much for it. Clyde had the impression that Dr. Mathan
had already told Stan that it was to be done . . . I just
wish all could be proud, happy, and grateful. I will
admit that I had a tough week dealing with all this.*
(May 26, 1996)

*The naming of the nursing school matter is now
concluded . . . but there were many negative feelings. I
was asked to meet with the group and some bad things
were said. Based on the fact that those I must work
with and on whom I depend for everything were so
upset, I decided finally it was best not to do it. That
decision also upset them and more anger happened.
But yesterday we agreed and they said they were all ok
about it. I pray so. We had some discussion about the*

189

program. We will put the dedication stone honoring
Mrs. Hunt. Just above it will be a stone—Rebekah Ann
Naylor School of Nursing. (June 8, 1996)

Twelve years later when Naylor recounted this experience, her agitation and anguish showed.

Although labor unions are not part of the government, they can have a strong effect on employers and employees. India, after colonial rule ended, began to develop as a nation with its own economy. Labor unions emerged. A labor department became part of both national and state governments. Hospitals generally had few interactions with unions. The mid-'80s brought a change. Little did anyone know the impact unions would have on both BBH and Naylor. A letter dated June 23, 1985, portends the ominous events:

Wednesday evening (June 19) at 5 was the hospital
administrators meeting at St. John's Hospital. Easho
Jacob and Mr. Daniels went with me. These are from
charitable hospitals in town: 3 Catholic hospitals, 3
Hindu charitable hospitals, CSI (they never come), and
ours. This was a special program with the Karnataka
Labor Minister there and the Labor Commissioner. All
of the hospitals except ours are having terrible trou-
bles—demonstrations, work stoppages being instigated
from outside. The various administrators really tried to
make these men see the terrible problems created,
pointing out that a hospital cannot be an industry or
factory. I listened carefully and came away more deter-
mined than ever that it must not happen to us—careful
hiring practices, good communication with our
employees, being sure we are in the law at every
point—all so important. (June 23, 1985)

Regardless of Naylor's resolve and the desire of the majority of the hospital employees, union and labor problems emerged. At the end of August 1985 government labor office personnel appeared at BBH to inspect attendance records and to ascertain whether employees received holidays. The attendance registers (record-keeping system for employee hours and days at work) did not meet standards. A new system had to be devised and instituted immediately. In March 1986 at least three labor problems caused Naylor to seek legal advice. She writes: *Only six employees are known to have signed an agreement to join a union. But there is some coercion going on* (March 9, 1986). Rumors of strikes, walkouts, and rallies made their way to Naylor and staff. Tension grew. A staff welfare committee was formed; this gave employees a way to be heard if proper channels failed. On some days several employees in dietary, on the driving staff, and in the security force failed to report to work. The union made demands on the hospital which involved discussions, arbitration, legal consultation, and court appearances. In November 1986 a settlement for a two-year period was granted with the hospital meeting the union's 19 demands, one of which involved salary. A new salary schedule and back pay to adjust salaries for acceptable wages went into effect with the November 29, 1986 payday. Union members stood at the bank and required the employees to give to the union when employees went in to cash their paychecks. Union activity and demands lessened for a few months and began anew in March 1987. The complaints? Shoes and uniforms! Someone didn't like the shoes; one shirt wasn't delivered as quickly as the contractor promised. Shortly thereafter a long list of complaints appeared on Naylor's desk. She writes: *The union is really giving us trouble. As I was upset about that yesterday, Stan matter-of-factly said that we had to live with it from now on. It is like a chronic painful illness from which you know you will never be free or recovered.* (April 4, 1987).

The symptoms of the illness, as Naylor aptly described the labor union activity, worsened. Just outside the front gate along the wall of the hospital compound, union members set up banners, posted signs, and stood there banging on drums and chanting. Simultaneously the hospital was undergoing equally serious and far-reaching situations in other areas. Income was short; this necessitated a retrenchment plan. Building programs were under way. The agreement between BBH and CMC was in progress.

Earl Goatcher, at BBH on loan from Thailand to help with construction and administrative issues, comments: "She had to deal with agitating labor unions and labor issues. Often at the instigation of a small segment of the population there would be noisy picketing at the hospital, with allegations and demands that were ridiculous. Still very vivid in my memory is coming through the hospital gate one day and seeing an effigy of Rebekah hanging from a gallows near the gate. I can only imagine the hurt and anguish it caused for Rebekah. The accusations and allegations against her were so totally opposite of who she was and what she was doing. She was a compassionate, very capable physician giving her life to help, to heal, to give hope, and to share the love of Christ with a people who were hurting and had no hope. She had brought healing to thousands of people who otherwise would have received no help whatsoever. Now this was the response—totally false accusation on public display on the main highway leading out of the city. Rebekah was hurt; I was angry. It took great restraint for me not to go amongst them, tear the effigy down, and flog them with it. It would have been a foolish act, but it was tempting. It was at this time, just as in hundreds of other similar times, that God answered prayer and provided the grace that picked her up and carried her through the work God called her to do."

The effigy was burned late one night the week of November 15, 1987; new hope arose that the other displays and activities at the front gate soon would be cleared away. The effigy and picketing, however, were minor in comparison to the next event. Cases against the hospital made their way through the legal system. Naylor was summoned to appear in court. In a letter dated December 21, 1987 to Millicent Kohn, Naylor summarizes the account of her court appearances:

I think I last wrote to you just after my first trip to criminal court on the 5th of December. This is in reference to the government's case against me for failing to obey the Factory Act since they allege that our hospital is a factory. I am personally the accused in the case. I went on the 5th with a junior lawyer and at the time I felt things were not done properly—we did not get done what my primary lawyer said should happen. On the 12th, the police sent for one of our doctors. At noon on that Saturday, he returned from the police station saying that the police had a warrant for my arrest. Because the local sub-inspector is our friend, he did not want to arrest me nor tell us on the telephone. He agreed to do nothing over the weekend and instructed us as to what our lawyer should do on Monday. Can you believe it! It was into that tension that my folks arrived! So on the 14th my lawyer, our labor consultant (also a lawyer), the junior lawyer, and Dr. Stan Macaden, my closest friend and support at the hospital, went with me to court. Stan stood personally surety for me, having to document his income, property. I felt very secure and supported, but it was traumatic. To top it off, I was running a temp. of 101 that day and not feeling too swift. I found out only after the fact that the warrant for arrest was without bail. Incredible! Otherwise the labor scene is totally calm. Just our legal battles are before us. The spirit in the hospital seems good in all of our Christmas activities.

The court system moves slowly. Mr. Raghavan and Mr. Calla, attorneys for the hospital and for the labor issue who continued to work with Naylor and hospital staff and board in all legal matters, provided the liaison between the court and Naylor. In her January 26, 1993 letter to her parents, Naylor writes:

> *Today I had an appointment with Mr. Raghavan about several items, mission and hospital . . . I found out the factory case is to come up in high court tomorrow. He said the judge now is very reasonable. If he wins the decision, the criminal court will dismiss the case against me.*

Hope that the matter might be resolved emerged. That hope became reality. The unmistakable joy rings through the February 1, 1993 letter:

> *I am no longer a criminal. On Friday Mr. Raghavan argued our petition in the High Court of Karnataka that the hospital is not a factory and that the case was filed with ulterior motives. The prosecutor got mad and the judge told him that if he uttered another word, he would make an even stronger statement. Since there is no factory, I did not violate the Factories Act and the case is dismissed. PRAISE BE!*

Labor-union agitations were not the only reasons for visiting government offices. Naylor and other foreign missionaries—not only those from the FMB but also those from other missionary groups—entered India in the 1970s with residential visas. These often were for a one-year period and some for five. Some visas were for multiple exit and re-entry; some were for single entry. All visa holders were required to register with the police and pay income tax. Naylor's initial visa issued in 1974 was a one-year residence visa; she had to apply for and secure an exit permit and return visa any time she desired to leave the country. Each year she applied for a renewal of the visa which Indian officials attached to her U.S. passport. Some years she would be told to do all this in person; other years the hospital business manager or the mission business manager could carry the paperwork from office to office. No records were computerized; every item was written in triplicate by hand. Governmental offices operating hours were often arbitrarily kept and set. The frequent government holidays and religious days complicated matters. But the visa was just a part of living in India. For several years the renewals were rather automatic.

Shifts in Indian policies surfaced by the mid 1980s. Not one new missionary, whether teacher, physician, or nurse, was given a visa to enter India. (The last two FMB couples assigned to the Bangalore mission entered the country in 1980.) When Dr. Van Williams, the pediatrician, returned with his family to the U.S. because of education needs for his children, an appeal was made for a replacement for him. All such appeals for replacement personnel were denied. As people returned to the U.S., their positions went unfilled by Americans until finally all the denominational groups in India had only one or two missionaries remaining. Renewals became a problem. Delays in renewal of visas occurred; some delays were as long as eight months. One missionary couple was deported. The mission boards of the various denominations were helpless in face of Indian policy. The deportment, the delays for renewal, the variances from year to year in forms and paperwork to be submitted, the necessity of repeated visits to more than one government office fomented disquietude until paranoia set in. *Is this my year to be deported? Is this the year my visa will not be renewed? What if I can't return to India? What about my work? Didn't I receive a call by God?*

Naylor was exempt from neither the government policy and attitude shifts nor the tension. By the mid-1980s delays were the norm. Generally her application needed to be submitted in December. Often when she took the paperwork, officials sent her away and told her to return at a later date. More than once the official announced that her paperwork was lost. These tactics created problems with Stateside assignments and travel to Malaysia for the medical-missions conferences held in January as well as for holiday travel. The 1991 application for renewal wasn't acted on until March 1992. In the meantime her prayer letters; her home church, FBC, Dallas; and her parents' church, TABC, requested prayer support and Divine intervention.

A more dramatic experience occurred during the 1997 process. Doctor Louis and Anne Carter describe that trying time:

"Then in 1998, we had the opportunity to work with Becky at Bangalore Baptist Hospital for two months. At the time she was experiencing some major stresses—not the least of them her parents' failing health and not having a visa to even be in India. People kept assuring her that the visa would eventually come through, but she was on a time limit. A friend had graciously paid for Becky to take a Bible Lands tour and she couldn't leave India without her resident's visa. Without a visa, she would not be allowed to leave and re-enter India.

"As we talked to her about this dilemma as the day of departure for her trip was drawing near, Anne asked her a tough question. 'What is the worst thing that could happen?'

"Becky replied, 'I would have to go back home.'

"Anne said, 'What's the worst thing about that?'

"Becky said, 'I would have nothing to do—no one would hire me.'

"Anne became prophetic and said, 'Surely they would be glad to use you in the residency program at UT Southwestern.'

"Becky was not so sure of this—neither was Louis.

"Anne added, 'But your parents also need you. Your time would not be wasted in caring for them.'

"As it turned out, Becky got her five-year resident's visa . . .."

Surely enough, Naylor's letter of April 14, 1998 reports that she had her temporary extension of the visa for return as well as the residential permit in her passport. Both arrived just in time for her trip. The flight for Israel left Friday, April 17.

In August, Naylor was given a five-year multiple-entry visa with a December 13, 2002 expiration date—exactly five years from the date of expiration, December 13, 1997. When Naylor's father died in February 1999, she was able to arrange air travel, pack her bag, and pay her income tax—just to leave the country without the extra hassle of securing the official permit. God provided.

The visa granted in 1998 did expire in 2002. By this time Naylor had returned to Fort Worth to care for her mother, who was ill. She applied for the visa before she left India in March and scheduled a return to India for December. The request for a three-month extension to allow the visa to arrive from Delhi was waved off—"Signature is required and no one is available to give it." Word arrived February 2003 at BBH that a five-year visa was granted. Doctors and administrators from BBH pled with officials that the visa be placed within Naylor's passport, but their efforts were rebuffed. She herself must be physically present for the visa to be issued. Her visa had expired; therefore, she had no re-entry provision. Even that piece of information had no effect. To return to India, Naylor applied for a 10-year tourist visa through the Indian Consulate in Houston and had no problem in gaining the visa. In India Naylor visited the Office of Home Affairs in Karnataka and asked that the visa be placed in her passport. The blunt refusal "not possible; passport has tourist visa" defeated hopes for the residential visa. Since 2002 Naylor has used her tourist visa for the trips to and from India.

Not only did Naylor have problems with visa renewal but also with her medical license. To practice, physicians are required to pass exams for license. Countries often have recip-rocal agreements with other countries; they recognize degrees and licenses. Certainly Naylor held degrees and certifications; unfortunately, Vanderbilt and India have no reciprocal agree-ment. From 1974 until 1990 Naylor and her FMB colleagues served as full-fledged physicians at BBH; thoughts of a license never entered anyone's mind, not even at the FMB. A well-known orthopedist from Mississippi planned a trip to BBH to perform hip-replacement surgeries. An article published in the local paper concerned the upcoming visit and surgeries. Health ministry officials must have read the newspaper article. Shortly thereafter BBH administrators were notified that this orthopedist had no license to practice medicine in India and therefore could not perform the surgeries. Naylor quickly real-ized the implications of the communication: she herself had no legal permission to practice. Discussions with her parents, her colleagues, and administrators at CMC Vellore ensued. She sought counsel from the hospital attorney and her friend, Mr. Raghavan, who commented sadly, "Ignorance of the law doesn't make you innocent; Doctor, you are still guilty." Cold facts to face seized her.

The right thing to do was to apply for registration with the Indian Health Ministry and the Medical Council of India. The application began in 1990; two letters of refusal arrived February 6 and June 7, 1991. For almost eight months Naylor saw no patients and worked entirely as an administrator. Finally in September her parents called that a two-year renewable license had been granted. The FMB had been notified but Naylor hadn't been! Just like the renewal applications for the visa, renewal applications for the registration ensued. Each application required visits to Delhi and not to the local government offices or the state offices in Bangalore. The 1993 extension was for one year, 1994 for two years until October 3, 1996; thus the pattern continued. Frighteningly close to expiration the renewal in 1998 arrived two days before expiration, but in 1999 the letter to practice did not appear. From October 22 through November 11, 1999, Naylor could not practice. She was very careful not to go into the surgery area, not to do any medical procedures, not to see patients or be in the wards; instead she occupied herself with administrative tasks. What rejoicing went on when the permission letter was delivered November 11! Another interruption occurred—this one connected to the October 22, 2001 expiration date. Approval did not arrive until March 18, 2002; Naylor had not been allowed to practice medicine from October 22, 2001 until that March day. This renewal, however, extended her license only until October 2002. No more requests for registration or license were requested; the license was allowed to lapse.

Naylor despised having to go into Indian government offices and submit herself to their questions and attitudes toward her as a foreign woman physician. She felt humiliated, demeaned, and harassed. Her letters describe the exhausting trips, the miserable travel, the small neighborhood hotels with a scarcity of English spoken by the staff, the heat, the traffic, the time away from her practice. Various male staff members as well as missionaries accompanied Naylor on each visit for the renewal. Colleagues aver that the Indian government was not singling out Naylor. Dr. Santosh Benjamin, when asked about the energy required of Naylor during these trips, bristled and retorted, "Her license took all our energies—administrators, Karnataka people, even Embassy people!" He explained matter-of-factly: "The Medical Council of India is in charge of medical licensing. Not one foreigner was practicing long-term in India since the 1970s. They were not getting paid, doing charity or volunteer work or mission work. Vanderbilt is not on the reciprocal list. There's red tape. The government was bending rules to let her practice. It wasn't humiliating, just a long process through many steps."

At least two different times intervention in the process occurred. A good friend of Naylor's contacted his U.S. senator, who went through the Indian Embassy in Washington, D.C. to appeal Naylor's case. The license was granted for two years with a verbal admonishment. In 1992 Naylor was Stateside on a short furlough (four months) during which she gave a Lottie Moon World Mission Offering Emphasis talk at Immanuel Baptist Church, Little Rock, Arkansas, on the first Sunday of December. President-elect Bill Clinton attended that service; he arrived in time to hear Naylor's presentation. In 1993 a member of the U.S. Embassy staff in Delhi, a diplomat who had assisted her on multiple trips, went with Naylor to ask for renewal and stated, "It is important for us and the White House that Dr. Naylor be here and be allowed to work." The renewal was granted. Naylor does not know the hows of the interventions but remains grateful for them.

At one point in the uncertainty, the turmoil, the tension, and the exhaustion, Naylor returned home to Fort Worth to help her parents move into a new home. During the spring 1991 visit, she went to University of Texas Southwestern Medical School to apply for a job. In the interview, as she realized she had to go back to India, she left the interview. Praying, she suddenly knew that she had always submitted her skills as a physician to the Lord; perhaps she also had to submit to Him not having use of those skills. Within 10 days, the licenses arrived.

Earl Goatcher summarizes the situation succinctly: "An ongoing frustrating issue concerned her visa and Indian medical license. The struggle to obtain and keep those consumed untold hundreds if not thousands of hours. I have gone to New Delhi with her as have others and walked the halls of various bureaucracies, talked with many officials (Indian and American) only to hear, 'Maybe next week . . . Come back later.' Bribes might have brought it about, but we don't do bribes . . . much wasted time and money. "

No longer was Naylor ignorant of the law. She was, however, the dignified survivor of legal battles, whether in the courts, in municipal, state, or national government offices, with her honor and integrity intact.

Maestro

Rebekah, wearing pink saree, at piano

Choir chimes in a performance

Medichoir performs at the hospital's silver jubilee in 1998.

Ron Owens leads the choir at the silver jubilee. The saree is the choir uniform for the women.

Sing to the Lord, praise his name; proclaim his salvation
day after day
(Ps. 96:2).

Maestro

Today I practiced while listening to the World Series. The
Yankees did just barely pull it out in the seventh . . . And to
think, were I not here I would have a Master's in piano and be
drumming up students for piano lessons . . . Her comment
about my piano playing was how much I obviously enjoyed it!

Music has always played a large part in Naylor's life.
Exposed to beautiful music in her childhood both at home and
church, she moved beyond merely the enjoyment of music. By
the time the family relocated to Fort Worth, Rebekah was formally studying piano as a pupil of Mrs. Jeffus, playing recitals,
and competing in National Guild annual auditions. At Baylor
she chose a degree in science but continued her piano studies
under Dr. McKamie, music professor. As a freshman and as a
non-music major she was assigned a practice room—a tribute
to her capabilities and serious attitude toward honing her ability to play and to perform. Normally practice rooms were
reserved for piano majors and junior and senior students.
McKamie frequently entered Naylor into competitions, which
involved recorded performances before a jury panel and travel
to live competitions. As an upperclassmember she was on the
program of Wednesday-afternoon recitals at Roxy Grove Hall,
the concert venue for the Baylor School of Music. Such a slot
was a coveted one; not every piano student was asked to perform for these recitals.

The crowning achievement of her Baylor music experience, however, must have been the recital she gave during her

senior year, January 1964, at Southwestern Baptist Theological Seminary's Cowden Hall. According to Linda Dunlap, Naylor's Baylor roommate, Rebekah "played a very demanding classical piece with her well-known teacher. She got a very good review in the *Fort Worth Star-Telegram* with the performance. This piano recital put a lot of pressure on her to perform while she was doing grueling pre-med work." Beethoven's *Third Piano Concerto* definitely satisfies the adjective *demanding*.

Close friend and colleague Clyde Meador avers that Naylor easily could have been a concert pianist. She had to choose between music and medicine; she chose medicine because she found medicine to be a better avenue through which to serve God. Yes, she did choose medicine for her life's work, but music played a large part in her ministry and evangelistic efforts.

The hours of practice, the many lessons, and the competitions did not diminish Naylor's love of the piano. She had a piano during her residency. The piano became her solace in her isolation and loneliness and refreshment amidst long work hours and difficult living conditions. Many evenings after work she sat at her piano and played hymns and classical pieces into the darkness of night, even before her evening meal. This "piano-playing," as she refers to her time at the keyboard, relaxed and soothed. Beyond the personal benefits the daily playing kept her skills and technique perfected and her sight-reading sharp.

Accompanying congregational singing in church services is one way Naylor uses her musical training. From her earliest days in India Naylor played the piano for worship services at Calvary Baptist Church and later at Hope Baptist Church and at the hospital. Even on her visits to India she slips out of her chair and onto the piano bench as if she's been there every Sunday. She tells of an incident that occurred January 10,

1982: *I was to play the piano at Hope Church. I got there and was merrily playing my prelude when I realized there was no hymnbook. Their books have only words and the regular pianist has the book with notes. I forgot that. Finally they dug up an old Broadman hymnal.* At Travis Avenue Baptist Church she goes beyond playing a hymn for the assembly time in the Crossroads Sunday School Department, her department; she plays several difficult arrangements of sacred music as preludes. Each time she plays, the care with which she chooses the pieces and the time spent in practice are evident.

Because of Naylor's training and ability to play the piano, her knowledge of recitals and concert protocol, and her diligence in rehearsing, she had a unique experience in India. One of the missionaries, Sarah Williams, a classical pianist with a master of music degree in performance piano, and the Maharani Vijaya Devi, sister of the last Maharaja, planned a concert in Bangalore. The Maharani had a huge home totally furnished in Western-style furniture and décor. The immense living room, unusual for a house in India, at one end held two grand pianos that faced each other and looked out over her lovely garden. The Rani frequently hostessed recitals and performances in her home or in conjunction with the International Music and Arts Society or the American Women's Club of Bangalore. Although both Sarah and Rebekah knew the Maharani from those organizations, the first contact Rebekah had with her was through the hospital. Rebekah delivered the Maharani's first grandchild in 1974 just after Rebekah arrived at BBH.

Sarah tells the story of the concert. "The Maharani had studied piano performance at the Juilliard School of Music in New York. When she met me and realized that I also had a piano-performance degree, she invited me to come over one afternoon to sight read two-piano music and then have tea. This event turned into a once-a-week practice that grew a strong friendship. Both of us were glad to be able to use our music. After about a year, she casually said, 'We should give a concert and charge an entry but give the proceeds to charity. We could each choose which charity our half would be given to.' As a member of the International Women's Club I was aware of many worthy charities, so my portion was donated through that club."

The Maharani and Sarah selected their music and began practicing. Sarah continues her story. "I had reservations about spending so much of my missionary time preparing for this recital. It demanded up to four or five hours a day of practice for several months. After much prayer the recital seemed to be an open door to make contact with people who would otherwise never know what we were doing in Bangalore. This proved to be so true.

"Rebekah entered the picture because I needed a friend to turn pages for me at the recital. I knew she could read music. With her skills and patience as a surgeon, I knew she could stay on task and focus all the way through and not get distracted. She and I were prayer partners, friends, and travel buddies. All in all she was THE one to do this task for me. She was so consistent and never let me down. I could not have had the confidence at the performance without her willingly giving her time and ability to help me with the concert both in preparation, practice, and performance."

Rebekah practiced with Sarah in the Williams' home and at the Maharani's house. The dress rehearsal was in the concert hall: *I went to the big practice in the hall, the auditorium of a private (Catholic) high school. There were two grand pianos, one obviously old with beautiful carved legs, the one in the palace for so many years and is still owned by the Maharani's niece, the actual daughter of the last maharaja. The piano tuner from Madras had spent about 6 hours on the pianos Thursday and more time on Friday.*

Sarah remembers that at the recital the "governor sat in a raised gilded chair upholstered in red velvet. The chair was positioned in the middle of the aisle almost touching the edge of the stage. I could see him every time I looked left with my peripheral vision as I played the piano. He was enthusiastic but it was nervewracking for me!"

Rebekah's report of the concert follows the account of the rehearsal:

> Sarah was amazingly together. She looked very nice. I wore the new dark green silk with a print border saree I had bought for the occasion and fixed my hair as nicely as possible . . . The hall was filled—more than 400 people. They had never played better. The music was exciting. They were perfectly blended. Sarah and the Rani were very controlled. Most important from my side was that I did not make any mistakes. The governor of Karnataka was the chief guest. He arrived at exactly 7 in cars with flashing lights. What an event to remember! The actual playing time was about 1 hour 35 minutes so a little over 2 hours with applause and bonus and intermission. (October 17, 1982 #2)

The ambitious program featured *Sheep May Safely Graze* by J. S. Bach; *Sonata K. V. 448* by W. A. Mozart; *Variations on a Theme* by Joseph Haydn, *Opus 56 B* by Johaness Brahms; *Scaramouche* by Darius Milhaud; *Suite No. 2 for Two Pianos,* and *Opus 17* by Sergei Rachmaninoff. The encore piece was *Ritmo* from *Danses Andalouses* by Manuel Infante.

Sarah finished the story by telling of Rebekah's party and the positive result the recital effort produced. "After the recital Rebekah hosted an open house to include many people from the upper echelons of Indian life and society who had attended the concert. Since her home was on the hospital compound, it was the first time many of these people had ever visited the hospital compound to see what was there. They were very complimentary and much goodwill from the community resulted from this social gesture by Rebekah. Contacts were made that later turned into friendships."

Although that performance was the only one the two pianists gave, the memories linger. Rebekah, the Rani, her daughters, and her granddaughters have continued their friendships in the ensuing years.

Sarah had organized an English choir at BBH in the fall of 1980 and taught a Christmas cantata. *People are still saying how much they enjoyed doing last year's cantata. This year Sarah has compiled miniseries from three or four sources. I look forward to sharing in this and appreciate her doing it.* (September 17, 1981) Unfortunately Sarah returned to the States in 1983; the choir no longer met.

Five years passed before another choir began. In 1987 Joe Ann Shelton and Loeen Bushman, two fantastic performers and mission volunteers, went to Bangalore at the request of Naylor. They organized a choir at the hospital, with Loeen accompanist and Joe Ann director. A gifted singer and choral director with a powerful voice, Joe Ann loved the people of Asia and South Asia. She knew exactly how to reach them and what music to teach. Those who chose to sing in the choir blossomed under her tutelage. Naylor writes these accounts:

Everyone is working so hard. To do a major work with folks who cannot read music is quite a task. They learn the parts by going over and over. Some days we divide up. Glenda Travis and I work with the ladies, Joe Ann with the men. Jason has taken charge of the drama part and will do great with that. Joe Ann is trying to adapt, giving voice lessons. I am so glad that you all will be here to see it. (November 11, 1987) . . . At lunch Saturday Joe Ann and Loeen hosted the whole choir at home. We had choir rehearsal at my house, a long session in which she taught us. We are coming along beyond anything I thought we could do. The group is holding faithful and working so hard. There are about 26 or 27 in the choir. Saturday morning I spoke in chapel, an original sermon and those are rare! Joe Ann sang at the end and that added so much. (November 15, 1987) . . . *On the 12th Joe Ann will be leading a workshop with the pastors on music in worship and as a part of ministry.* (November 29, 1987)

Surely enough the choir did progress and performed the cantata *Paid in Full* in January in conjunction with the 15th anniversary of the hospital's opening. The four months Shelton and Bushman remained at BBH left a rich legacy and a strong musical influence. Even though Joe Ann and Loeen did not remain in Bangalore, Medichoir continued its rehearsals. Page-turner, church pianist, piano student, choir member—not one of those roles matches that of conductor/accompanist/concert mistress! And that is exactly what Rebekah's role became. Continuing to hold weekly practices, the men and women of the choir enthusiastically undertook performances in a variety of venues. A CSI hospital issued an invitation for the choir to sing for the 75th anniversary. The BBH pastoral-care department asked the choir to present special music for the staff retreat. The choir not only sang for the biannual BBH Board meeting but also chapel. By this time Naylor was both directing and accompanying. She grew bolder and taught the choir members new songs and the voice parts. Confidence and repertoire increased. The choir could sing the entire score of *Paid in Full* as well as many familiar hymns—"Christ the Lord is Risen Today," "How Great thou Art," "I Will Sing of My Redeemer"—a medley of songs centered on the theme of trust, another on the Cross. Several larger events were scheduled. On Good Friday 1988 the Medichoir in conjunction with a sermon series on the *Seven Last Words of Christ* sang nine numbers. They sang in April at an interdenominational city-wide revival meeting before 2,000 people.

During the spring of 1989 Carolyn Lee and Elaine Meador helped with the choir, as they taught parts, conducted, and held section rehearsals. Naylor writes May 19: *Elaine Meador has had training and experience. They responded to her and we accomplished so much. I even enjoyed it, played the piano more properly.* Each concert drew applause and frequently suggestions that the choir be recorded. An agreement to record a performance in July was made. The Medichoir, women in green sarees and gents in ties and white shirts, went from a group of hospital-staff members to a cohesive choir.

Realizing that a recording required not only a conductor but also a pianist and a trained choral musician, Naylor called Dr. Gnanamuthu, director of the choirs at the big Methodist Church in Bangalore. He had experience in leading choirs and had made recordings. He agreed to help with practices and the recording sessions July 8 and 9. Naylor wrote that she had to *practice quite a bit too, but my part is improving.* After hearing the tape, she marveled: I *am amazed at how well we did. If I do say so the piano was okay—I had really practiced.* With her standards, no doubt the piano part was perfect.

When Naylor returned from furlough in the spring of 1990, she found a new doctor playing the piano at chapel. Dr. Meera also sang alto. She became a valuable asset to the choir's efforts to renew itself. That spring Naylor brought from the U.S. choir chimes. She explains: "Choir chimes, similar to hand bells, are played the same way. The chimes are tuning forks perfectly pitched. They are more durable than hand bells, thus often used with children. I first saw them at Oak Grove Baptist Church, a rural congregation near Fort Worth. I was excited because I saw possibilities. The church helped to make that dream a reality." Initially people were shy about playing such an instrument. Few read music. Naylor devised a system by which each chimer knew when to play the chime; the chimes accompanied the voices. The chimers needed to look at their music scores not at Rebekah. They counted and played. They learned the notes to the "Doxology" but *plowed ahead, 1, 2, 3, 4. How to teach them? One of the chimers solved it by saying they would put an extra count after each pause. Now they have it.* (August 11, 1990) Eventually the chimers taught themselves two carols and a chord accompaniment to one of the cantata songs. Naylor wrote out the music which they learned.

December 1990 provided many opportunities not only for the choir but also the chimes to perform. The first program was December 15 for the hospital-staff Christmas dinner, the second at a Christmas concert put on by Campus Crusade in its convention center, and the third at Basel Mission. The chimes, according to Naylor's December 20, 1990 letter *were the hit of both performances—WHAT are those? A hospital making music out of medical instruments?*

Christmas 1991 presented more opportunities for the choir to perform: BBH hospital Christmas dinner and program, Indiranagar Methodist Church choir festival, a choir festival in the big auditorium for the Basel Mission Choir Festival, and a festival at another church. Dr. Gnanamuthu once again helped with directing the group. In the midst of the scheduling, Paul Dass managed to contact a programming director of the government television station. Stan Macaden, Dass, and Naylor went to the television station. When asked why the Medichoir was unique, Rebekah opened the box of chimes. With eyes wide the director agreed to hear the choir sing and chimes play. Not only did the television crews listen, but they recorded and showed performances two different times—December 25 at 6:15 and December 31st. The unmistakable excitement rings through the story.

Let me first tell about the TV—I still cannot believe it happened—absolutely unreal. The chapel was beautiful and elegant. The chimes "tables" were benches one on the other, draped with green bedspreads from the new wing. The choir was arranged on risers on either side of the cross. In front of the tables were beautiful green plants and many red plants. The back of the piano also had its green bedspread and a beautiful arrangement on top. Two of our doctors made up all the ladies. We had red rosebuds on our pink sarees. The television producer came at 12—plus three crewmen—lights, camera. Many staff were in the chapel. The whole hospital was so excited. The chimes were done first—5 songs—they just stood up there and played, the choir likewise. She recorded everything we had prepared and will use of it what she wants. By 2:20 it was over. I thanked her and made my excuses to leave quickly—and she said we now had to do the piano. I had to do one whole song with the camera 2 feet from me—my! We are to be on 25th at 6:15. (December 22, 1991)

I spent Christmas evening with the Swansons. We went downstairs to their landlord's to watch the choir. At 6:20 there was the Medichoir. I was so pleased. Friday the television woman called me to come to the station. Paul Dass went with me. She played the tape to be shown on 31st evening—good. Chimes, choir, piano (!!) choir, chimes. Her comment about my piano playing was how much I obviously enjoyed it! Sometime between 7:45 and 8:20 we will be shown. She could not name the hospital. Friday she told me we would be paid Rs 5000! Isn't it wonderful. I still cannot believe it. I want to send a write-up to Richmond right away. (December 28, 1991)

Although for the recording in the hospital stacked benches made tables for the chimes, performances away from BBH demanded other arrangements. The problem was solved when someone suggested using ironing boards. The day of the performance chimers gathered ironing boards from all the guest houses and clean hospital sheets monogrammed with BBH. The men in the choir willingly carried all the necessary equipment, chimes, music, and stands but never touched an ironing board; the women always carried those.

The next recording occurred May 9-10, 1992. This time Dr. Bob Carman, who directed the choir in Vellore for many years, willingly assumed that responsibility. Naylor returned to the piano, which she preferred. Dr. Gnanamuthu augmented the bass section. Medichoir's 23 singers recorded their songs and used the sales proceeds for hospital needs.

In 1993 another unusual opportunity arose. Medichoir joined with Bangalore School of Music. At the first rehearsal, the Medichoir sang the first song—one members already knew. As customary Naylor accompanied them. The director asked her to continue playing for the entire rehearsal. She also was asked to play for the performance on Jan. 23. During rehearsals at the School of Music, she played a grand piano. The evening of the performance, however, the piano from the hospital had to be transported to the concert hall.

Naylor's training and expertise was with the piano. Growing up she had a baby-grand piano—a family treasure. When Goldia married Robert Naylor, Goldia's mother gave Goldia the piano as a wedding gift. The same piano still sits in the family living room. During Rebekah's residency she had an ancient, used upright in her apartment. When she moved to India, however, she bought a new Baldwin studio upright, which she shipped in her crate. On the docks of Madras all her possessions lay exposed to all who cared to look. In the process of assessing duty on her furniture, books, clothing, kitchen utensils, and washer, the customs official looked at the obviously new piano and said, "This is just a used piano, not worth anything." Thus, the piano entered into India, free of customs duty!—totally unheard of on the docks of Madras!

Although she played on a fine Baldwin in her home, the instruments for the various performances were not the same caliber.

> *The instrument is an electronic organ—small thing. I never could figure out how to make it right octave—I have to play an octave higher to make it where every-one sings. Being an organ, how do I hold a note while I am conducting? It may be a total disaster. (March 12) They will have no instrument! They agreed to hire a Casio—one of those little electronic jobs. (March 29) The instrument was . . . a little Casio—it sat on a table. I played it a little and I thought it would be manage-able. Time came to sing. The first introduction sound just came and went. I never knew when it would play and when it would not. I was never so proud of the choir. Half of them could not even see me. They heard just enough notes to stay on pitch. They did magnifi-cently under those circumstances. I think they really sensed each other to stay together at all! And they sang well. It was a 22-minute concert. I was about a wreck!* (April 12, 1988)

The 1999 Basel Choir Festival organizers promised a piano for the program. When the choir arrived, no piano was in the hall—only a two-octave keyboard that belonged to another choir and an electric piano brought by a school. The school would not let Medichoir use the piano. Dr. Benjamin announced to the festival organizers that if no piano were there, Medichoir would go home. Medichoir was allowed to use the electric piano! Despite deficiencies in quality or type of available musical instruments, the choir performed amazingly well each and every time.

The choir continued when Naylor was not on furlough. But not until 1994 did it again perform. Dr. Carlos Welch from United Theological College directed. The chimes and the choir learned four songs and a cantata. That year they participated in the Basel Mission Choir Festival, the mission office party, and the hospital program. Then arose an incredible opportunity. In July 1995 Dr. Gnanamuthu invited Medichoir to join his choir of young adults to perform *Emmanuel Has Come*, a fantastic pageant, as a benefit for the Rebekah Ann Naylor School of Nursing scholarship fund. Medichoir practices began the end of January. The pageant required 12 songs plus "The Hallelujah Chorus" and actors. Naylor comments that *This is exciting, challenging, and frightening. We figure we will be ready for New York or Hollywood after this!!* (January 26, 1996)

Combined practices commenced May 2. Unfortunately for Naylor Dr. Gnanamuthu asked her to run the practice, since he would be out of town! Fortunately, however, the two choirs blended as if they'd always been one choir and responded well to Naylor's direction. She also began to practice in earnest because the closing piece, "The Hallelujah Chorus," is exciting to hear but difficult to play. The letters from January through August gave reports of actors, costumes, ticket sales, ads, donors, practices, time involved in each aspect, and the video recording sessions. The choir members, excited about the upcoming performance, the publicity for BBH, and the money-raising opportunity, enthusiastically learned their parts. Choir members had big adjustments to make during the process. Totally interdependent, choir members panicked when they learned they'd be separated and not be standing as customary during performances. The announcement that they'd be moving about the stage and doing some acting not unlike a chorus during an opera brought more anxiety than did any other facet of performing! Realizing music had to be memorized and the men could no longer pin the words of the numbers on the backs of the women who stood in front of them sent them into a tailspin. As the time for performance neared, practices were more frequent; they often stretched from 5 or 6 until after 10 in the evening. Naylor always drove her vehicle as one of the transports. One evening, in conversation with her women passengers, all as sapped of energy as she, she remarked that doing such a pageant was a "once-in-a-lifetime opportunity." From the back seat droned a tired voice: "I surely hope so; I'd never survive another!" The remarkable thing about the number and the length of rehearsals is that many of the choir members were medical staff on call. Not once during a rehearsal did a pager ring. Not once was a physician or nurse called from a rehearsal. They may have been called afterward and may have spent much of the rest of the night at the hospital but not during a rehearsal. The recording required both a Friday and Saturday in late July. Rehearsals continued through the first weekend of August and culminated in three nights of full rehearsal followed by the dress rehearsal from 2-10 p.m. August 9. The three performances ensued. BBH students served as ushers. The concert hall was filled with people of Bangalore. All the medical staff, the architects, and contractors involved with building at BBH were present. The performances "went without a hitch—absolutely fabulous!" according to Naylor's report home.

Ever thoughtful, gracious, and appreciative, Naylor, BBH staff, and choir members hosted a thanksgiving and appreciation dinner for all the people related to the pageant. During the evening Dr. Macaden, CEO, and Naylor both thanked the 170 guests and supporters. They reported that the scholarship fund gained about 4,000,000 rupees, or $10,000, even after the huge expenses. To close the evening, those involved shared the meaning of the experience.

The pageant remained alive and active beyond that dinner and the live performances. The video seemed an excellent opportunity to present a Christian message on Indian television stations and to do a bit of PR work for the hospital. Naylor, aided by other administrators, took up the challenge of seeking backing, endorsement, and public airing of the performance. With her usual vigor and relentless pursuit, Naylor eventually gained the required official endorsement from the Minister of Information from Delhi. A television contact from Delhi, Mr. Churchill, suggested the video be edited to 30 minutes. Success! Part 1, the first 30-minute video, was aired on the main government television station December 26 at 5 p.m. Naylor reports the *picture was great—sound excellent*. The second 30-minute segment which the television people titled *An Easter Pageant* was broadcast during the Easter season, March 30, 12:30 p.m. from Delhi. Imagine that the Christian hospital staff—nurses, secretaries, technicians, physicians, chaplains—sang about the risen Jesus on television—national television! A once-in-a-lifetime opportunity to be sure!

In the ensuing years Medichoir "waxed and waned," as Naylor aptly says. When Jo Jones returned to Bangalore in 1997, she picked up leadership. Eventually Dr. Benjamin directed. In August 1997 Medichoir hosted a choir festival, with 11 choirs participating—nine including Medichoir competed and two performed. The hall was oversold for both nights of the festivals, which raised more than $6,000 for hospital causes.

Later in 1997 the choir performed with four other choirs at Chowdaiah Hall as part of Voices for Hospice. The Hospice Trust sponsored a worldwide emphasis for hospice care. All choral groups performed the same day. In Bangalore only Medichoir sang sacred songs; the others sang secular numbers. The performance concluded with the five choirs combined singing "The Hallelujah Chorus"! BBH had just launched its own palliative care department. What a grand opportunity!

Christmas 1997 had the usual appearance at the Basel Mission festival, an appearance in Chowdaiah Hall, and the program at the hospital-staff dinner.

In conjunction with the hospital's Silver Jubilee celebration and a revival emphasis in Bangalore led by Ron and Pat Owens, renowned sacred musicians, song writers, and performers, Medichoir undertook another monumental concert on January 17, 1998.

THE CONCERT. What an evening! We had about 26 singers and had rehearsed every day this week except Thursday. The arrangements in the hall were very nice. We used the backdrop decorations from the August choir festival. An American had given all of the fresh flowers and arranged them. We hired a good sound system. The choir sat on the stage throughout the performance. Our singing was in the first half. We did well. Several said it was the best we had done and that we sang with inspiration and feeling. I so enjoyed participating as a choir member. Jo directed the choir but it was blended into Ron's program. He led right from one song to another. Pat's piano playing is so terrific. The audience initially treated it as performance but very soon it was evident that they had really entered [into] the worship of the occasion. One of the main [English] papers was there and interviewed the Owens after the performance. I said a few words in the beginning and then thanked Ron and Pat at the end. We presented a beautiful bouquet of roses and a gift, a silver tray engraved. We are just so thankful to God for it all. Though we had focused on the Christian community, inevitably there were lost people there. The music message was powerful. (January 13, 1998)

For the next four years the choir, at the urging and strong leadership by Santosh Benjamin, continued to rehearse and perform. Naylor assumed the role of accompanist but continued to select and annotate music for the singers. Medichoir performed at the Christmas Basel Mission Festival, for chapel, at BBH Board meetings and anniversaries, and in Bangalore churches. In 2000 the choir learned an Easter cantata which it sang at Dr. Macaden's church and a Christmas cantata which it performed at the hospital-staff Christmas dinner. The chimes weren't revived until 2001. The chimers played "Go Tell It on the Mountain" as people left the chapel the evening of the staff Christmas service and dinner. Appropriately, the chimers rang "Now Thank We All Our God" at the 2002 BBH anniversary thanksgiving service.

What a fitting song to play at what would be Naylor's last anniversary as a resident missionary and BBH physician! Truly these various experiences, performances, and occasions provided through Medichoir stand as highlights of her time in India and underscore her tremendous talent and use of her training. Not only did she journey across the world, she also transformed from piano student to maestro!

Celebrations and Occasions

Rebekah's
50th birthday
celebration
given in India
by her parents

Presiding over her Christmas tea

Greeting the president
of India

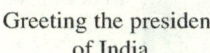

Receiving her 25-year
service pin
from IMB President
Jerry Rankin

Receiving tray
given her
at a citywide
function

Rotary Club of
Bangalore honors
Rebekah Naylor.

The boundary lines have fallen for me in pleasant places;
surely I have a delightful inheritance
(Ps. 16:6).

Celebrations and Occasions

One of our best strengths is planning occasions . . . We do
occasions well and right . . . I believe everything connected to
the 25th anniversary is going to be the biggest thing we have
brought off yet.

The combination of Indian culture and Rebekah's personality produces phenomenal festivities. *Occasion*, a term she uses frequently, may be an engagement party, a baby's 1st birthday, a mission meeting, or a holiday observance. Naylor revels in the myriad details of guest lists, décor, food, and the program. Bangalore Baptist Hospital also hosts multiple celebrations. Some revolve around construction of new facilities and equipment—others around anniversaries, graduations, and holidays. Naylor herself has led in these dedications and celebrations with as much vigor as she has devoted to the completion of the building projects themselves. A gracious hostess, she thrives on involvement in programs, festivities, occasions—celebrations.

The first significant celebration relating to new facilities Naylor observed was the Prayer Hall dedication. She narrates the account in her May 10 and 12, 1980 letters:

Our new chapel is . . . truly beautiful. We had the
first service at 9—unveiling of the plaque, cutting of
the ribbon, processional inside . . . Bill Wakefield
brought a very good message. At the front is a rose-
wood cross set forward from a glass panel behind

*which there is a light. Wood panels radiate out from the
cross. There is a low marble shelf at the foot of the
cross on which sits two large brass oil lamps—they
were burning. In corners of the room are four elegant
huge brass pots with plants. The light fixtures are
inverted domes of varying sizes and colors hanging at
different levels. Benches are there—plain. On each side
under windows are two covered benches with backs
fixed to the wall covered with a print sort of brocaded
material. Even the ceiling is attractive. Sunday morning having our service there was so great—good light,
space, comfort. Oh, the acoustics are also good. No
sound system will be needed at all. I believe you can
see my enthusiasm.*

The dedication of the private-patient wing marked the first
one in which Naylor had personal involvement in the planning.
The dedication on August 31, 1991 had an impressive guest
list that bespoke the importance and the dignity of the occa-
sion. Dr. Joel Gregory, his wife, Linda, and their sons, Grant
and Garrett, represented First Baptist Church, Dallas. Dr.
Clyde Meador represented the IMB; Dr. Pulimood, CMC
Vellore; Dr. Stanley Macaden, chief of medical staff; Dr.
Shirin Singh, and Naylor from Bangalore Baptist Hospital.
The Honorable Governor of Karnataka, Shri Khurshed Alam
Khan, and Mrs. Ernestine Heck, Consul General for the United
States stationed in Madras, were honored guests and speakers.
    Simultaneously with the appointment of a building com-
mittee, the selection of a separate committee, a steering committee that plans and orchestrates the dedication for the facility, often occurs. The outpatient-department wing involved
more people and more ceremony; thus the committee had a
greater responsibility. The building was first dedicated and
opened for use in June. Naylor's June 11, 1993 letter presents
a step-by-step description of that day:

*This morning our staff went in at 6:30 and started
cleaning while workmen were painting . . . We moved
furniture like mad all day. At 2 o'clock nurses, aides,
supervisors just descended with linens, pillows, stationery supplies, blood pressure cuffs. The potted
plants appeared. Flower arrangements appeared. The
lobby became just lovely. I would have never believed
it was possible even this morning. At 4 everyone gathered in the little road [outside the hospital and inside
the compound], senior architects, 14 Friends of BBH,
and employees. Stan made a brief speech; Pastor
Jacob said a few words, read a Psalm and prayed. I
said very few words and cut the ribbon . . . We served
tea and one kind of cookie.*

The formal dedication, a grand celebration, was not quite
as low-key. Preparations required keen oversight, much of
which Naylor did. *We went Friday morning to see the dedication stone. I hope Mrs. Hunt is pleased. I will now get the program finalized and ready for printing. The invitations will be
ready this week.* (September 19, 1993)

*The big day is at hand! The programs for Saturday
came from the printer and look very nice. Mrs. Hunt's
picture turned out very well. The curtain is all ready
from the unveiling of the plaque. Mr. Huskey, the chief
guest from Madras, sounds so nice on the phone. I am
having a small dinner party here at home afterwards.
Mr. Huskey and the CMC representative, Stan and
Rajini Macaden, Norman and Kay Roberts, and our 2
volunteers [are invited]. The menu is Chinese food.*
(October 7, 1993)

The ceremony itself—well-planned, dignified, and elaborate—occurred October 9. The letter dated October 10, 1993 completes the description:

> *In summary it was wonderful—I am so thankful. We had about 400 counting staff. The program lasted 40 minutes which was exactly as I planned it. The retired Chief Justice of India presided over the function. His remarks were appropriate and it was so good to know him and for him to see the hospital. All thanks to Mr. Raghavan. Mr. Jim Huskey from Madras was extremely nice . . . and his remarks also were fine. The chimes played first—three hymns. They did well. "Amazing Grace" missed a few notes though we had practiced. One of the ladies had her music upside down! Hilarious! Norman had the opening prayer. Stan welcomed and introduced. Mr. Huskey cut the ribbon— symbolic as we were already seated in the building. I spoke about the donors. Mr. Huskey unveiled the stone. The choir sang—it was wonderful. Scripture was read by the head of our medical records department. Pastor Jacob had the dedicatory prayer. A choral benediction [followed].*

As grand as earlier celebrations of groundbreaking and dedications were, those surrounding the Rebekah Ann Naylor School of Nursing eclipsed all others. The first, the groundbreaking, is described in the June 11, 1995 letter:

> *The groundbreaking ceremony was everything we had hoped for and more. We had quite a few friends and a large number of staff. We started at the hostel site and turned the soil. We walked to the Training Center, turned the soil and sat down. Sarojini presented*

the project. I appreciated the donors. Dr. Samraj from CMC was the chief guest and made a speech [which explained that] the Magna Carta was signed on June 15, 1215 giving freedom. This school will give freedom to girls bound down by poverty. Stan presented a challenge to staff and friends. Finally Dr. Sukant Singh from Christian Medical Association brought an excellent speech. The choir sang "To God Be the Glory" and "All Creatures of Our God and King"—did so well—13 voices. Bobby Jones, representing FMB, prayed. We had tea—displays of plans. We feel such a sense of God's working—I have rarely felt it so keenly in so many ways at once.

A year later, in the midst of the building project and other duties, Naylor and other hospital personnel had a press conference to announce the building and the opening of the nursing school. A young journalist, Stephen David, the husband of one of the BBH physicians, Dr. Shanthini, arranged and paid for a press conference held June 11 followed by lunch at the Bangalore Press Club. Naylor wrote: *Stephen said he is doing this because of me. He wants me to make the presentation.* (May 31, 1996) A subsequent letter of June 12, 1996 reports on the press conference:

The press conference was yesterday and a big success. There were 22 organizations represented including all of the major English and Kannada dailies, All India Radio, the South India reporter for BBC, and a few others. It went off very well. We will see now if they print anything . . . We had excellent news coverage. All four of the English dailies had articles near the front of the paper. All of the language papers had articles. Today we followed up on the instructions of the radio man on how to approach the TV station. It seems likely

that the TV people will attend on Friday. Is that not
wonderful? Everyone is so excited.

June 14, 1996, the day of the dedication, dawned.

The weather could not have been worse. Never
have I seen so much rain. It started noon on Thursday
and lasted until last night!!! There was a cyclone off
the Madras coast and it did not move. The wind was
relentless. The rain was continuous. Mud was knee
deep. We had put a shamyana between the student cen-
ter and the new school over the concreted verandah. It
was leaking like a sieve. We crowded chairs together
inside the center.

The spirit of the people, the dignity of the dedication ceremony, the impact of the culmination of a project envisioned in
1968 triumphed over the weather.

A number of good friends braved the weather to
come. Trees were down all over town and roads were
flooded. The staff were there. We think we had at least
300. I know many more would have come if the weath-
er had not been so bad . . . The program started at 4
PM. First, the chimes played 3 songs . . . The choir
sang. Sister Sarojini read the Scripture, and the Dean
from the Nursing School at CMC prayed. Stan wel-
comed and recognized everyone. I recognized the
donors. Mr. Handley (from U.S. Embassy in Delhi)
spoke—very appropriate, included Christian values,
and brief. Fred had the dedicatory prayer. Stan did a
gracious job of the announcement of the name. He read
Mrs. Hunt's fax. When he reached the paragraph with
the request for the renaming, the crowd broke into
spontaneous applause. He finished the reading and

said that according to her wishes, the school was renamed the Rebekah Ann Naylor School of Nursing. There was long applause. We moved outside. The rain had slowed to a heavy drizzle. We cut the ribbon and unveiled the stones, one on top of the other. The TV people had meanwhile come. People went through both buildings. We transported people to the hostel. For that unveiling the rain was very light so we were able to pray and unveil the stone with some reasonable calm. Sister Rosy Albert, Mr. Mohan's Auntie, unveiled the stone and cut the ribbon. She is such a nice lady and was so thrilled with everything . . . Everyone went inside. We had the ground floor all set up and decorated. Tea (high) was served in the two hostels. It was all wonderful. I wore my blue and pink saree that the employees gave me and all of my gold. I thought I looked very nice. (June 16, 1996)

If a school were opened with these grand occasions, certainly the graduation exercise would be spectacular. The first graduating class had a lovely formal ceremony. It was preceded by an elegant tea hostessed by Naylor. She describes the events.

I had the tea on Friday afternoon at 4:30 at home. Florence insisted on making the sandwiches as we had planned. Sheelamma reappeared on Thursday afternoon and was able to make the 2 apple cakes that I needed. Our dietitian bought one Indian sweet and made samosas, a non sweet. I made the punch. I had Principal Sarojini, the vice principal, the teachers, the 20 girls, Christabel and Mary from the hospital, Primrose, and Kimberly and her friend. I used votive candles and elephants on the table. Sheela had plants in the house. My punch bowl looked so nice. Kim, Mrs.

Hunt's granddaughter, had brought a book for each
girl and I gave them the Bible. The whole affair was
very special.

The formal ceremony celebrated the graduation.

The nursing school was decorated nicely with white
flowers and greenery for the graduation. We had to be
there at 3 for the photo—the class picture, students and
faculty. Sarojini had it organized to the nth degree and
[it] ran like clockwork. For the processional I played
"Joyful, Joyful We Adore Thee." The present seniors
were in their student uniforms. They held beautiful
ropes of jasmine flowers and greenery. The graduates
marched in between these. The graduates wore their
nursing uniforms. The service was lovely. I am enclos-
ing the program. Stan and George had planned out
their prayers. We received so many greetings. Mrs.
Hunt wrote a lovely letter, Clyde Meador, John Thomas
for our group, Vellore, two other friends, two other
hospitals. The red ribbons with the gifted pins and our
own pin on the graduates were pinned. I had gotten a
white rose for each. They did well with the song "O
Master, Let Me Walk With Thee." My other job was to
give the prizes. Dr. Khan had given the two top student
awards. Mr. Parama Shivan had given the two best
bedside clinical nurse awards. Our Dr. Michael gave a
community health award. I could recognize the donors.
The girls were so excited. After the service pictures
were taken with the donor and the winners. The student
speech was given by the top student. She did so well.
Confident, bold. She is so small. When she came she
could barely speak English. Her parents were there and
were obviously out of the village and could not speak a
word of English. They were so proud. She also received

an award from Christian Medical Association as their
top student in all of their accredited schools. Terrific.
Our school ranked first academically this year amongst
all of their schools. Just incredible. For the recessional
I played "A Mighty Fortress Is Our God." They
marched out between the jasmine ropes. They stood as
a receiving line outside. For over an hour the guests
and families stayed and visited and had a grand time
. . . There was endless picture taking. I don't think that
I ever had my picture taken so many times by so many
people. It was beautiful. (August 22, 1999)

Some occasions received far less pomp but stayed within
BBH practices of giving all facilities and equipment to God
for His use in bringing health care to all people. With a bit of
humor Naylor writes on July 11, 1995: *Wednesday was the*
commissioning of our gobar gas plant at the nutrition centre
. . . I had to pray over the gobar gas plant—now how does one
do that? That all really brightened my day!

The same weekend of the dedication of the nursing school,
Naylor attended a more humble dedication but one of as great
significance: *I went to help dedicate a quite different building*
Sunday morning. The Tamil church in Hebbal finally got a
small plot of land. They have built a small one room building.
It was packed and they do not have chairs. There are 39 fami-
lies in the congregation. Many of them are hospital staff.
(June 14, 1996)

Baptist Hospital anniversaries offer another reason for a
celebration. Beginning with the first one in 1974 two separate
events mark the date. Some years fundraising events such as a
fête or performance by a noted entertainer follow. Letters from
January 16 and January 24, 1983 present a picture of the 10th
anniversary. *The anniversary party happened at 12. This time*

233

was just for our staff. We first had a worship service. We rec-
ognized our 10-year employees—there were 19! That is almost
10% of our payroll. I thought that was great. There was a slide
show well done. Jason had collected slides from everyone—
from the beginning.

> *Hospital Day is past history. I term it a huge suc-*
> *cess. Perhaps its most significant benefit was for the*
> *staff. They worked so hard but enjoyed it greatly.*
> *Saturday their families were there en masse. Also we*
> *had huge crowds at the exhibits on Saturday. I have*
> *heard no reports of money or attendance, but it was*
> *very worthwhile. I spent a good bit of time outside*
> *Saturday afternoon—just being visible and talking to a*
> *few people and answering questions.*

The 20th anniversary had three events that were larger than
the festivities at the 10th anniversary. The letter of January 18,
1993 holds the narratives.

> *I want to tell you about Friday, January 15. We had*
> *our Thanksgiving service at 8 AM—such a good time. I*
> *had to speak—I spent a few minutes looking back and*
> *giving thanks—the growth of facilities, services, train-*
> *ing, special events, some crises, and especially peo-*
> *ple—staff, supporters, and most of all patients! We*
> *read Philippians 3:12-16 and looked to the future—*
> *grasping the purpose for which God established the*
> *hospital. We recognized 15 twenty-year employees with*
> *a clock with the hospital seal placed on its face—they*
> *seemed pleased. There was coffee for all and lots of*
> *good fellowship. There were also photos. I think it was*
> *all very good. Our dietary contractor made special*
> *dessert at lunch, further emphasis on the positive.*

Today was the big lunch for our staff and families. It was so well organized, good food, well done—and staff did come. No program except Stan said a few words of thanks to the staff and Bill said a few words and I prayed. It was just fellowship.

January 24, 1993 tells of the fundraiser event.

Now about Saturday night. We sold over 800 tickets Santosh Benjamin was the MC. Pastor Jacob prayed. Stan welcomed. There was the choir. They did very well. In fact, it was rather remarkable. They looked lovely. The director had on a tux. I wore my navy blue with embroidery—the building dedication saree. The piano was OK—not all notes correct but a creditable performance and many complimented me including the Maharani. The next item was a classical dance for 40 minutes. The final number was a band. Quality of performance was superb. I did the thank yous and conclusion. Stage arrangements and all were good.

A huge celebration surrounded the 25th anniversary in January 1998 with a trifold emphasis on past, present, future.

The frantic preparations for the evening went on. My new red saree looked lovely on the stage and I got a lot of comments. I went to the open house. We had a few former employees who came. It was like a reunion. The man from CMC representing the Governing Board arrived about 3:30. The displays about health and the hospital were terrific. So much work all departments had done. The tea began soon after 4 in the volleyball court. Colonel Bunyan had arranged an army band to play—bagpipes and drums—10 men who are paratroopers. Terrific. We had six food tables and two tea

*tables. We served 3 items—cake, sandwich, and an
Indian savory. People just visited and talked and fel-
lowshipped. At 5 we moved to the front of the men's
hostel where we planted the 3 trees—the silver oak
saplings. The past was planted by the Wikmans, the
present by me, and the future by the Rankins. The holes
had been dug. We were helped to set the tree down in
this deep hole. We had to scoop up a little dirt and put
around the sapling and then water it. I gather this is
very symbolic. Wouldn't you know that I got confused
and excited and started to water it before I put the
dirt!! What to do!!! The main program started at 5:30.
The chimes were bad but we finished [together] on
each song. We had done fine in the practice. Everyone
read Psalm 100. Pastor George, our senior most
employee, gave the prayer of thanksgiving. Dr.
Prathap, the MC, welcomed people and the three main
guests were garlanded. We asked John Wikman to
release the memory book. We had gift wrapped six
books in silver paper. He unwrapped and gave each of
us on the stage a book. The choir sang 2 songs. The
presentation [followed]. The past was slides with narration. I mixed music in now and then. The present also
had music now and then. It was about a patient in an
accident who came to the hospital. Every area of the
hospital was represented as the narrator read. As the
present began, the big cartwheel was rolled onto the
stage with the patient in the center, each hospital division as a spoke and God as the rim holding it all
together. The presentation was so real to life. [The]
ambulance siren roared outside and then we rang a
chime four times to represent our emergency bell. At
that point four doctors came from the audience and
choir to revive the patient. What a show! So many
things happened to the man. One of the best was Grace*

praying over the patient. When he got ready to go
home, the physical therapist got him out of bed. This
guy was like a real patient—took forever to get up and
get onto the walker. As he finally is on crutches and
going home, I played "Hallelujah, Thine the Glory." I
even got tickled. Christina Eapen did such a marvelous
job with the presentation and had worked months and
then full-time since 2 weeks. It was time for the future.
The CMC person spoke first and then me. Speeches
were appropriate and kept to time. It was Jerry's turn.
In the beginning he began to talk about a missionary
appointed 25 years ago to come to the hospital. He
totally surprised me by giving me the 25-year service
pin right there in front of everyone. I got a standing
ovation. Such things are usually done in gatherings of
missionaries, but he told me later that he wanted to do
it and thought that was the time and place. For sure no
missionary has the FMB PRESIDENT to present the
pin! Jerry preached very effectively. After Jerry's
speech, employees and friends read pledges of commit-
ment. Then Jerry prayed the prayer of commitment.
Whoever could have imagined an anniversary celebra-
tion like this!

After the function the open house went on for some
time. I talked to so many people. We gathered for din-
ner at the guest house next to [me]. The Administrative
Committee, [the] visitors, Paul and Leela Dass,
Christina, and Florence—there were 28 of us. We had
the main meal catered. Barbara W. had made punch.
We used the punch bowl on the coffee table and it was
lovely. Mary had made cake for dessert. Lights twin-
kled all over trees and the front gate and the hospital
and the BBH in the flower bed. Oh, it was so pretty. It
is difficult to even describe all that it was—the whole

day. I have given thanks over and over and over. It was
[worth] all of the work.

In conjunction with the 25th anniversary the dedication of
the four apartments and the men's hostel took place.

> *We had a huge crowd of staff and students present.*
> *We sang the chorus "This Is the Day That The Lord*
> *Has Made." I told about Dr. Mays and explained his*
> *absence. I recognized the architects—Mrs.*
> *Chandavarkar and staff were there—and the contractor*
> *and his engineers. We read Scripture. Jerry Rankin led*
> *the dedication prayer. Bobbye Rankin unveiled the ded-*
> *ication stone. Barbara Wikman cut the ribbon. We then*
> *moved to the men's hostel. John Wikman prayed. Mrs.*
> *Chandavarkar cut the ribbon. The staff then streamed*
> *through both buildings. It was indeed a happy begin-*
> *ning to the day. I also recognized Bobby [Jones'] con-*
> *tribution to the project.*

The hospital did not limit occasions to groundbreaking,
dedications, graduation exercises, or anniversaries. A sunrise
service on the hospital roof began each year's Easter observance. Two accounts depict the services.

> *Today—sunrise service at 5:45. It is really one of*
> *my favorite things. It was so fresh and pleasant, so joy-*
> *ous. Jason was the preacher. We had a big crowd—*
> *some staff, Hope Church, Trinity Church. Jacob was so*
> *thrilled.* (April 15, 1980) *Today the sunrise service was*
> *lovely. From our hot houses, it was a blessed relief to*
> *feel the cool morning air. It was cloudless. It was very*
> *nice and a beautiful time. At Hope the pastor always*
> *has us pray 2 by 2. Today no one was beside me. I was*
> *praying when I looked up. One of the nursing students*

had walked all the way across the hall to sit beside me.
I prayed and waited. Finally she even had the courage
to pray in her language. About did me in. Chapel was
wonderful—they gave such attention when I made the
tomb soldiers fall down. (April 23, 2000)

Easter stands apart—holy and sacred—one day in the
spring, whereas the Christmas celebrations continue throughout December. The planning and anticipation begin as the New
Year begins. The inaugural event, Sports Day, occurs late
November. Naylor reports the 1982 event:

> *It was Sports Day at the hospital. I was an observ-*
> *er. The staff had a big time. Running races, relays,*
> *three-legged race, sack race, lemon in spoon race,*
> *slow cycling race, skipping race (girls); tug of war*
> *(first women then men), throw ball [modified volley-*
> *ball]. They are all very competitive. The other major*
> *part of it was the official inauguration of the tennis*
> *court. Gary made a speech—expressed appreciation to*
> *you—and cut the ribbon. They insisted that Gary and I*
> *hit a few balls so we did. He is a super good player. I*
> *can scarcely hit, but we were well received.*

The 1996 Sports Day is recorded in the December 3, 1996
letter.

> *Sports Day occupied Saturday afternoon. The fun-*
> *niest thing happened. We have a gardener, a small man*
> *that looks 100 and claims to be 45 who wears thick*
> *glasses and sees poorly. I always say he needs the*
> *wheelbarrow to walk around. The men were playing*
> *ring the pole. They threw rings around a pole from*
> *about 20 feet. No one could. This fellow kept wanting*
> *to, but others cut in front of him. Finally someone*

pushed him up to the line. He threw the ring right over
the pole and won a prize. Terrific!

Sports Day served as the warmup—the prelude to the big
festivity, the hospital program and dinner.

> *The Christmas decorations in the hospital are so*
> *nice—manger scenes, crepe paper streamers. Our big*
> *program was yesterday at 5. We used the back porch*
> *loading dock as the stage and sat outside. I was the*
> *chairman. Boosh Thomas brought an excellent short*
> *Christmas message on the three-fold purpose of the*
> *incarnation—to see, to serve, to save. The drama was*
> *the best yet, although, as Jarrett said, the theology*
> *might be in doubt. The Three Donkeys—story of the 3*
> *donkeys from Jerusalem who meet in heaven. The don-*
> *key that lived with Mary and Joseph and was there for*
> *birth, shepherds, wise men, flight to Egypt. The next*
> *donkey at age 12. The donkey of Easter week. The*
> *three donkeys told all of these stories; they had live*
> *scenes including donkey, sheep, baby, the morning star,*
> *three crosses, the tomb. My favorite line was from the*
> *first donkey who told about the birth: "Madam was*
> *expecting—what to do!" We doctors served food to*
> *about 700 people.* (December 16 and 17, 1984)

Accounts of two other hospital Christmas dinners and programs, 1996 and 1999, present more details about these significant occasions.

> *I believe it was one of the best we ever had . . .*
> *What a program! Dr. Prathap was MC. We had songs*
> *in 4 languages—The choir sang. We gave out longevity*
> *awards, singing competition awards, and department*
> *award. Our chief guest was Mr. Sangliana from the*

Indian Police Service. He brought a good practical message—a very nice man. After his speech came the Christmas play by the nursing students. They wowed the audience—a combination of modern scene, nativity scene, music, and choreography. We fed many hundreds in 30 minutes. The hospital is beautiful—such lovely decorations. Saturday I went through the hospital giving our Christmas gifts to the employees—we were able to give 200 Rs this time. We give same to every staff from doctor to cleaner. (December 16, 1996)

The evening went very well. We had put many extra chairs in the chapel. Our guests were Graham and Carol Houghton, here more years than I have been. He brought a strong, clear evangelistic message—I have come to tell you good news. The Callas were there. The choir did well. There were 4 language choirs, a drama, the prizes, and awards. One ward aide came forward to get her 25-year gift and certificate. She carried a wrapped box. Apparently she told Stan it was for me. She insisted that he call me forward to receive it. I was almost undone. It was a gorgeous green saree. How could she have afforded such a thing! I am so humbled. The last of program was unscheduled. The nursing students sang and did well! I was playing carols as people left; a group standing around the piano started singing and the group kept growing. We were all having such a good time when I suddenly remembered dinner and guests and responsibility. The hospital never looked more beautiful—inside and out. The lights outside were gorgeous. All three hostels were lighted. Several of my colleagues have lighted stars on their porches. Terrific! (December 12, 1999)

Naylor herself hostessed hospital-related parties. The letter for December 5 gives the account of the 1982 dinner:

> *My dinner for the other doctors turned out well last night. There were 20 of us. Rosemary outdid herself on the food. I made cheese straws and served tomato juice, chicken teriyaki, vegetable curry, curds with cucumber and tomato, cabbage with coconut, vanilla ice cream with chocolate sauce. They were so relaxed and free in my house, more than ever before. They all seemed to truly enjoy themselves. Dick was on duty but came the whole time and never was called. I was amazed that they stayed until 10:45! Sure sign of success, I suppose!*

After the nursing school opened, Naylor held parties for the nursing students. The narrative of the first one on December 11, 1996 follows:

> *Wednesday night I had nursing students and staff. How special! They were dressed in their very best clothes, hair washed—scrubbed. They brought a beautiful bouquet of roses. Primrose had a game. We sang carols. I told about BBH Christmas traditions. I read from my Christmas book the story of the birth of Jesus. We had food. I thought of their backgrounds—and my very nice things. They did so well. They were as poised as if they did this every day. I thought this is part of the social world they also must learn about. At the end one of them (who had been elected by her peers) thanked me.*

Missionaries shared together in the holiday. As long as Ted and JoAnn Swanson, Lutheran missionaries at United Theological Seminary, were in Bangalore, they included

Naylor in their holiday observance of Santa Lucia Day. The December 14, 1988 letters tells of the special time:

> *December 13th is the morning each year when the Swansons celebrate Santa Lucia Day—beginning of Swedish Christmas. I was invited to their house at 5:30 AM. I so enjoyed the time at their house. As usual we had special breakfast and then a time of worship, plus very pleasant company and fellowship.*

While Van and Sarah Williams were at BBH, they invited Naylor to their family's celebration: *Friday night was the annual tree decoration at the Williams. We also celebrated Gail's birthday. The decorating seemed to go more smoothly than usual. Wagner is more helpful. We had a lovely dinner.* (December 5, 1982)

Naylor's personal celebrations involved decorating her home, being with other missionaries, and having her private Christmas the years she remained in Bangalore. The letter of December 1, 1996 gives an idea of the joy elaborate decorations brought:

> *I am surrounded by Christmas! Last night Barbara, Marge, and Misty the student did a marvelous job! I have so many pretty things. On the front window is my wreath. In the bottom of the front window is my little paper row of cats. On the chest by the front door, little antique angels surround my little lighted Christmas tree and all sit on a linen Christmas tree towel. A ball hangs from the mirror with a red bow on top of the mirror. A red napkin covers one small table—green candles, a Christmas book. The other small table has a green and red napkin with the open Bible and a candle. The brass nativity and holly are on the TV. Stockings are on the glass doors. The nativity that hangs on a*

window is on the glass door in the living room. On piano—lovely white porcelain nativity, all my angels and 2 red candles. Dining table—my beautiful white angel centerpiece from you with its candle. On the music cabinet—a red place mat with Millie's piece on it, the crystal candle holders with red candles, another red candle, holly . . . On the way to the bathroom is now a bookcase. On it sit candles and nativity. Ornaments and red bows are on the stairs. A little Christmas tree stands in the bathroom and one in the kitchen. Now can you believe it! I was thrilled. This morning when I came down, even before I made tea, I looked at everything. Monday night I start the season by having the Wortens and Bushes for dinner, party on Sunday the 8th, nursing students on the 11th, others on the 20th, and various others as and when.

Naylor's own Christmas typically was grand. The December 17, 1982 letter gives the story of a typical celebration:

Tuesday night was my Christmas at home. The Williams came about 7. I had my Christmas napkins, candles. I had ham (the last one), cheese grits, green beans, red jello, monkey bread. How about that! I opened presents. Bob and Mary Jo had sent me air mail a book called The Nurse's Story. *Bob wrote in it that I could learn how the other half lives! A few people had brought gifts to the tea so I opened those. Van and Sarah gave me a lovely brass inlaid box that is so nice inside and will serve with all its compartments as a letter box. It was a fine evening.*

Naylor, the "consummate hostess" according to Jerry Rankin, held an open house during the Christmas season. The first, December 24, 1974, she called her Christmas Eve tea to which she invited 35 guests from the hospital, mission, and community. The December 11, 1988 letter indicates the number of friends she acquired in the intervening 14 years.

THE party is over! Actually a year ago this Sunday you arrived. Of course all day I was thinking what a wonderful time we had together at this party last year. I was so thrilled for you to meet my friends. I don't know how many people said first thing when they walked in, how they missed your being here! Many sent special greetings. The total attendance was 65. Everything looked so pretty. Every goodie was terrific. I made pictures and hope they turn out. As always it was such an assortment of people. Mr. Calla and his wife came. The Maharani came. I do realize that I have made a lot of friends. My help was great—Florence, Joann Swanson, Manorama Barnabas, Ann Baskin, and Ragini Macaden. Stan and Joe Baskin did a good job of mixing and visiting. I am so glad I did it. The guest list for 1994 grew to 178! *Tea the 18th. I am planning to have vegetables and chips and use the same dip for both— curds with onion soup mix added. We can buy seasoned cheese spread; I can make sandwiches. You sent a plain cookie recipe. I had a thing with cookie crumbs, sweetened condensed milk and dates, and the eggless chocolate cake. I may serve nuts as well. I must decorate the house. There are 178 invited.* (December 7, 1994)

An interesting piece of information concerning the many teas, dinners, and parties Rebekah hosted concerns the food. The menu had to accommodate vegetarians and non-vegetarians. All foods and recipes were eggless because many of her guests were strict vegetarians. Rebekah had recipes for dishes made without eggs. Even her cake recipe and many cookie recipes are eggless.

> *The party was a BIG success. Over 130 came. Everything looked so pretty. Many people asked about you and sent their greetings. Anita, Sarosh, Sammy and her parents came, the Calla family came, many doctors, pastors, Mrs. Chandarvarka from the architect's firm, the Maharani and her daughter—all the regulars. The best was last. After 7 Mr. Parama Shivan and Suresh and his 2 girls came. I was so thrilled. It was worth having the party for that. There were a lot of flower arrangements and bouquets as gifts and presents not yet opened. Pastor Jacob told me that when he was here a man was reading the Scripture that I had open.* (December 10, 2001)

One time a Hindu doctor asked Rebekah about the Christmas tree. She talked about evergreen and everlasting life in Jesus. Another time, a child was looking at the Nativity. The Hindu father said, "That is the baby Jesus." While the parents listened, Rebekah then told the child about Jesus' birth.

Although Naylor planned, organized, and initiated celebrations and even hostessed occasions, for two celebrations, however, she had only one function—that of honoree. The first was the Rotary Club of Bangalore, December 2, 1994. On December 1 she writes:

> *I am set for the Rotary function tomorrow. Florence got my things from the tailor and they fit. The saree is lovely. I have to think of my speech. I want to use a quotation from Jesus—I came not to be ministered unto, but to minister. I think that is how I can witness to the model of Jesus and the value system that I*

therefore have. The meticulously detailed account of the evening ensued. *I wish that you could have been there. Stan, Ragini, and Florence represented you well; I was so thankful that they could be there. My new saree is stunning. Last night after Bible study, I told the ladies that I needed help because I wanted to look perfect tonight. All 4 neighbors came at 6. They did a super job. I never wore a saree so perfectly draped, secure and neat. They had a good time doing it. Stan and Ragini were also on time. The district governor was the chief guest. There were 4 awards and mine was given last for which I was grateful. The man who introduced each of us did a superb job. For me he said that senior surgeons in most places line up the patients and they only walk in at the big moment and lay on the knife. But I am very different—considering also the psychological needs and the spiritual needs. He told all of my qualifications. I believe even you and John Earl would have thought it adequate. I am enclosing my response. I memorized it so no notes. I was given a bouquet of flowers, a brass plaque fixed on wooden base so you can stand it on a table or desk, and a certificate. Service Award to Dr. Rebekah A. Naylor, M.D., F.A.C.S. for your devoted service in the field of health care to the poor and needy at Baptist Hospital, Bangalore, India from Rotary Club of Bangalore MID-TOWN. The certificate has the same statement as the plaque. After the program we had dinner.*

The second occasion Naylor names a *function*—an understatement to be sure!

Most important I want to tell all about Saturday evening and the big function. I have seen the first round of pictures. They are wonderful. Over the stage was a large banner with the Scripture Matthew 28:19 and to God be the Glory on it, my name and 26 years in India as a medical missionary. The tea included eats served on real plates. The chief guest was a police officer, a Christian, I have known for years. The opening prayer was led by Pastor William John of Hope Church. Primrose read Scripture. Weeks ago I had given a list of Scriptures that were especially meaningful. Primrose took 8 or 10 of these and just read them one after another without any reference. It was terrific. The message was brought by Dr. Chris Gnanaken who pastors a very alive independent Baptist church here and is also a teacher at a local conservative seminary. Mr. Charles Prabakar, our hospital auditor, and one of the organizers of the function made a very nice speech. Mr. Sangliana, the policeman, made a speech. They presented me with an award, the William Carey Memorial Award conferred on Dr. Rebekah Ann Naylor "medical missionary of the millennium" May 6, 2000 by India Gospel League. It is a silver plaque tray thing with a gold-plated rose on it and filigree border. It is lovely. My speech came in between all of this. I gave a short testimony-type speech. Oh, the BBH choir sang very well. Mr. David Dass, the organizer, gave a speech. Fred Beck was asked to release the tract that they had written about me. I would judge that there were well over 500 people there. After it was over formally Paul Dass came and spoke about when I delivered their daughter Rebekah and how he used to bring her as a small child to listen to me in our chapel on Sundays. Now she is a doctor and on our staff. That was the time that I about lost it. The whole theme of the evening was a role model. The preacher had used 1 Corinthians 11:1. Others had referred to the role model theme. Paul just really summed it up. Stan

Macaden was sitting on the platform and was asked to say a few words near the end. He was gracious and did so. People were invited to come on the platform to speak to me. Many did with flowers and garlands. One garland was huge with red roses. Many hospital people at all levels of staff were there. There were pastors. A lady from KBSS brought the big garland. A huge delegation from Hope Church brought flowers. While all of this reception was going on, different groups were singing songs. Among those who spoke to me was one young man who expressed that God wanted him for something special. I wore my red saree from the 25th anniversary time and it was lovely. They had congregational hymns also and there was no one to play any instrument, so at the last minute I had to do that on our little keyboard that I had taken. Yesterday one of our young doctors, a first year OB resident, a boy from Nagaland, told me how much the service meant to him, that he was much encouraged and inspired and wanted to thank me. Well, how does one thank someone for doing such a thing as this honor? I have been writing notes but it seems so meager. After it was over, my evening was not over. The Bushes and Becks took me to the Oberoi Hotel for dinner. There was live piano music, candles, and good food. Harry did all of the driving. It was so nice. A terrific evening. I can hardly wait to show you the pictures. We will carry them around with us while I am there!!!!! (May 9, 2000)

Occasions, whether they be simple, grand, few guests, many guests, anniversaries, dedications, holidays—none could be more dear than the birthday. Indian custom on birthdays is for the celebrant to hand out sweets and candy to friends, co-workers, and family that day. The missionary community sang the birthday song and ate cake—sometimes in conjunction with a Bible study, sometimes as a reason for gathering together. Naylor remembers fondly her 50th birthday party given by her parents who were in Bangalore with Rebekah for the Christmas and New Year's holiday. Mrs. Naylor, with the help of Florence Charles, planned a small dinner party at the West End Hotel. The intimate group gathered in a private room—Santosh and Usha Benjamin, Stan and Rajini Macaden, Primrose Vasa, Norman and Kay Roberts, Ted and JoAnn Swanson, Florence, and the three Naylors—at elegantly set tables decorated with candles and fresh flowers. The multiple courses presented and served beautifully bespoke the five-star restaurant of one of Bangalore's finest hotels. With a giggle Naylor tells about the dessert. Mrs. Naylor ordered a special dessert. According to Indian custom, however, guests at this party were served their dessert first. Nonetheless the memory of this birthday remains fresh and the birthday party one of Naylor's favorite celebrations.

Critters, Contraptions, and Contrivances

"Henrietta", the first automobile Naylor drove in India

Naylor's first apartment in India

Camels, cars, and pedestrians all share an Indian street.

Bangalore street scene of a family of four on a scooter

For our light and momentary troubles are achieving for us an eternal glory that far outweighs them all. So we fix our eyes not on what is seen, but on what is unseen. For what is seen is temporary, but what is unseen is eternal (2 Cor. 4:17-18).

Critters, Contraptions, and Contrivances

Rebekah never liked bugs or animals, never wanted a dog or a cat for a pet . . . He told me to climb on the back of the motorcycle and hold on! . . . I knew how to replace the wires to the spark plugs but no one had shown me how to open the bonnet! . . . On Mahatma Gandhi are those angled spaces cars back into. When we came out of the restaurant, in the space next to our car stood a cow, backed in at the right angle chewing her cud . . . At 12 we finally took off. Lunch was not identifiable in taste or appearance so I did not eat. I killed 2 roaches by my seat. The bathroom was not describable. The Indians have a helpless, frustrated expression that is just great— "What to do!"

"Rebekah, you don't look well." Somewhat hesitant, Naylor confessed that she did not sleep well due to a "critter" running in the ceiling of her remote cabin, which was a distance from the accommodations of the others in the group. *I could not discipline my thoughts. By midnight I was miserable. I just got up, went out, crawled into my car, locked myself in and slept soundly until 6:30. I hate to admit it!* The second night, after she moved into an interior room in the main guest house, a toad hopped about her room. When summoned, Jerry Rankin captured the intruder in his ball cap. Naylor slept somewhat better. The third night, *a gigantic grasshopper with VERY long legs and wings,* leapt onto her leg as she prepared for bed; she bravely caught Mr. Grasshopper and took him outside. Van and Sarah Williams, Jerry and Bobbye Rankin, and Rebekah convulse with laughter as they recount this experience at the resort farm run by Anglo Indians, just near the entrance of the Mudamalai Game Preserve and at the foot of the Blue Hills. The main house with wide verandah and cabins and entire compound, built in British-colonial style, did provide the retreat the group needed from the sprawling urban conditions of Bangalore. Four brass "critters"—a toad, a roach, a grasshopper, and a scorpion—mementos from the Rankins of the attack of the "critters," sit on Rebekah's shelves. As her mother observed, Rebekah does not like animals. As a matter of fact they terrify her. Amidst all sorts of animals as well as various forms of transportation, snarling traffic, unfamiliar or poorly working machinery, customs alien to a Southern Baptist from America, civil unrest, weather-related disasters, Rebekah lived for three decades. Daily life offered more challenges; accomplishing the necessary required enormous amounts of time. Although India is not the only country in the world with an unruly animal population, makeshift repairs, or unique customs, India was Rebekah's world. The experiences—both the unusual and the customary in India—terrified, annoyed, exasperated, and entertained.

Rats, cobras, mice, cockroaches, wild dogs, ants, lizards, monkeys, chipmunks, crows, cows, oxen, elephants, camels—India's animal population probably surpasses its human one. Each species alternately challenged and intimidated Rebekah. The frequent encounters with them often shocked and shook her, while others left her giggling afterward. Her letters recount the anecdotes and cause the reader to be equally horrified, repulsed, or amused.

Rebekah hadn't been in Bangalore long before she had a personal encounter with the rats.

I have adopted a phrase which well summarizes the unpredictable quality of life here—"life and work in India." The latest episode includes some lovely creatures called rats! Linda [Garner] opened the big wooden cupboard to get a spoon. There was a rat. We had no way to kill it besides not being eager to do so. We locked it in the cupboard (we're so resourceful) and went after John [Wikman]. He collected a supply of weapons and came to the rescue. We soon had one dead rat, but it was quite a show . . . I observed that one had traveled alongside my bed during the night. I have now placed rat poison in strategic spots. When I say rat, I do mean rat, not mouse. Isn't that creepy! (October 15, 1974) *The rat problem has returned. We have seen three and killed two this week, the latest during my breakfast today. We finally trapped the rat in the bathroom . . . Since then there has been one execution upstairs and one downstairs. I almost managed the one this morning by myself but my subconscious hesitancy prevented victory. Linda got him. Just wait until we move to the hospital compound—then it will be rats and cobras both!* (May 1, 1975)

Such encounters continued.

A big rat (not mouse) is there—still not caught. Annamma saw it sleeping in the top of the stove eating tomato peelings! It has eaten the hose between the gas cylinder and the stove. It has chewed a hole in the lid of my garbage can. The pest control came and put poison. We have a big trap. I am terrified the rat is somewhere else. (April 8, 1987)

Rebekah's hunch proved correct.

Tonight when I reached in the closet to get my shoes, he was there! Did me in! I shut him up in the closet. When I came back from dinner Annamma and the medical student worked until they got him. He was big—about 15 inches long with his long tail. I am now trying to convince myself that he has no friends or family. (April 12, 1987) *I have a visitor in the house . . . I have a horror of it getting on me in bed.* (June 11, 1989)

Rats could appear anywhere, even in the beautiful Baldwin and the new car!

My regular piano tuner found that a rat had been very active in my piano. Some bridle tapes and bushings have to be replaced. He will do all this and put some powder to protect from a new attack. I told him to do it! (January 22, 2002) *A rat has been in the car—droppings . . . a hole in the back seat upholstery. He went in under the dashboard . . . Now I'm afraid to get in the car at night.* (April 27, 1997)

Mice seemed to be less formidable than rats.

My stove is still very sick . . . A mouse had made a nest. The maintenance man killed the mouse (December 29, 1997) *. . . I started into the downstairs bathroom and in a glance thought that I saw something in the commode. On inspection it was my mouse. He was alive! I slammed the lid down and flushed, to no avail. I put my biggest book on top of the lid and called the Turners. They came with a plunger. Art trapped the mouse in the plunger under the water until the mouse* *succumbed. Art declared the corpse small enough to flush.* (October 14, 2001)

Occasionally tales of the mice offered amusement, albeit often at Naylor's expense.

As I was seeing private patients, an American lady was in the exam room. When we took the sheet off the shelf to cover her, a mouse ran out and behind the cupboard. You can well imagine what state of mind I was in! I could scarcely concentrate on the lady for watching the cupboard. My translator insisted that we finish seeing all of the patients before we executed him. She was so tickled at me! Finally we finished and executed him by squashing him between the cupboard and the wall. (October 2, 1985) *For 2 days I had noticed that something was eating the wood in one drawer. Today a fat mouse came flying out and scared Hannah and me half to death.* (February 7, 1998) *I forgot to mention the most hilarious thing. Friday I was to give the lunch lecture. I had worked hard on it. I had my overheads to use. I realized early on that something was wrong with the group. Soon I realized what it was. A mouse in the overhead projector was running back and forth under the glass surface and was projected on the screen! Little do the others realize how I am about mice. Alex took the projector out, released the mouse, and Fred killed it.* (April 23, 1995)

Frogs did not threaten as much as they did annoy.

A frog [was] in the private examining room. The nurse helping me quietly picked him up very delicately by the hind leg and left with him. (September 14, 1990) *. . . During the day I had captured a frog under a*

basket in my dining room. Jarrett put it out for me!
(August 15, 1988)

Packs of wild dogs roam the neighborhoods, streets, and fields. When BBH had its farm, dogs presented threats not only to the people but also the farm animals. *Three dogs attacked our one sheep which was tied to a coconut tree, helpless. We have sacrificed the sheep.* (April 22, 1987)

Ants and cockroaches, like dogs, provoked problems. Roaches, according to Rebekah, were *at least four inches long and flew, usually at me!* Whatever the size, the offending intruder suffered death.

> *Two nights ago I did battle with an enormous cockroach in my bathroom.* (July 12, 1991) *Sunday morning one of my endless supply of large ants was sitting on the baby shampoo bottle. I just picked up the bottle and firmly set it down again thinking the ant would fall off. It did but the bottom fell out of the bottle (plastic). Have you ever! The ant died in the shampoo, by the way. I went down to the kitchen to make tea. The night before I had killed a roach. As is often my custom, I did not pick it up. The ants now were attacking the roach. All before tea.* (October 10, 1991)

Combat with these pests included frequent visits from the exterminators. One morning as Rebekah left for work, she reminded her *ayah* of the impending pest-control treatment. The *ayah*'s response? "Why?" Life and work in India!

Flying cockroaches, wild dogs, rats—all pale in comparison to the dreaded COBRA! Rebekah knew to look on the ground, in plants, and in trees. Soon shoes and closets as places to look were added to the list!

Dr. Achamma, our paediatrician, lives in one of our older upstairs apartments. She opened her cupboard to take some clothes out and felt something wiggling. She slammed the door and got help. It was a COBRA in the cupboard. They found, caught, killed it. Santosh told me to be sure and look in my shoes every morning!!! (June 28, 1998) *Oh, as Millie and I were sitting on the porch eating lunch, what should we see on the other side of the screen but a 5 foot cobra with the head up and hood open. I don't think Millie has recovered yet!* (September 18, 1990) Millie blanched as she repeated the same story some 15 years later! *A BIG cobra ran by the front door and path one morning this week. Sheela nearly ran into it. She was still shaking when I came home in the evening!* (May 20, 1988) *Last Saturday night the security guard came to the door. I thought he was bringing some note. Instead he had killed a baby cobra which he had carefully draped over a stick. Only it was still wiggling!* (August 6, 1987) *The man who killed snakes finally killed a big snake by my house—5 feet long. I hope it does not have friends or relations! Pillai the gardener came to my office with a big smile to tell me. Thankfully he did not bring the corpse as proof.* (May 25, 1997) *The big event just now was the capture and execution of a cobra in my back-yard by 2 security guards. It was 4+ feet long.* (April 10, 1998) *When I got home Wednesday night Annamma came running to meet me—quite excited. She was mopping when she saw just outside the screened porch a huge cobra. She claims the snake went OVER the 4-foot wall just built.* (April 4, 1997) *My phone had some temporary illness. The hospital needed to ask me about something. One of our nurses was coming. Out here in my road by the hostel she encountered an enormous cobra. Some of the fellows had it trapped under some rocks. They killed it by pouring kerosene on it and burning it. It was bigger than anything I had seen outside a zoo. That is 2 in 2 weeks.* (June 28, 1998)

Mrs. Naylor's face contorted into a grimace; with a shudder she spoke: "Those awful monkeys everywhere, jumping at me, making noises, crawling in the trees, looking in the window. And big numbers of them. I don't like them at all." Monkeys live in the BBH compound just as in other parts of Bangalore. At a celebration at which Naylor spoke, uninvited monkeys participated. *We had lunch under a shamyana in their yard. Monkeys in large numbers were running through the trees and jumping on top of the shamyana. I did not know when the tent might fall or a monkey eat my food.* (February 29, 1988)

BBH clients were often victims of bites from various animals.

A man was bitten by something on his finger. The something — carefully produced from a plastic bag — was a huge, fuzzy, striped creature with several legs. When the nurse and I were obviously a bit bothered, he brightly assured us that it was dead! (July 31, 1995)
Yesterday a man with snake bite came in. As they usually do, he had a tourniquet on his leg in the form of several very well-tied strings. He also had a stone on his head. When we asked, he said that stone was to keep the venom from coming up to the rest of his body. (May 25, 1989)

Van Williams had two major encounters in one day with both a mouse and a chipmunk running amuck.

Van was driving home with a load of people in his car when a mouse ran up his leg in the car! I would have died on the spot! They continued home with it in the car not knowing where the mouse was! That was after his day started with a chipmunk eating a hole in their screen and running around their bedroom in the morning! (August 10, 1983)

While the unwelcome animals can surprise, shock, and frighten, travel and conveyances alternately frustrate, delay, and evoke fear. Driving in India requires fortitude, daring, and ingenuity. Paved roads, narrow with two lanes, have abrupt drops at the edge of the pavement and no shoulder. Stopping beside the road is not feasible. Service stations—bunks—sit some distance apart and offer basic services. Some offer fewer than others. Road space must be shared by elephants with logs rolled in trunks, camels pulling wagons, bullocks with a cart, scooters, bicycles, rickshaws, auto-rickshaws, buses, trucks, tractors, cars, emergency vehicles, pedestrians, herds of dogs, and the omnipresent cows.

A far cry from the new, white Mustang Rebekah drove while at Vanderbilt or the new blue, Monte Carlo Chevrolet of her Dallas residency years was the first vehicle Rebekah drove in India.

Daddy, you asked about our car. The name is Ambassador—made in India—cost is about $4,000 US. The motor is Hindustan. You order them and months later you get it. Ours is a year old and has appearance of at least age 10, also the sounds of that age. It does well to stay out of the shop 3 weeks at a time—has been in twice since I came. Petrol runs about $2 US per gallon. We usually have to add oil every time we get petrol . . . Sunday . . . I drove out to make rounds *early, alone for the first time and made it OK.* (July 15, 1974)

The Hindustan Motors Limited web site gives the genesis of the Ambassador. The description states that the "Ambassador, the first car to be manufactured in India, has been ruling the Indian roads ever since its inception in 1948. Originally based on the Morris Oxford (United Kingdom, 1948), the Ambassador has been undergoing a series of changes, adapting to customer expectations." Current models vary only slightly from Rebekah's 1973 car. That India gained her independence in only 1947 gives reason that her industry lags behind that of other countries. Rebekah and Linda shared a nondescript blue Ambassador they dubbed *Henrietta*. The spark-plug wires were held on with frozen-pop sticks. Both women received detailed instructions for reattaching the wires, should the car show certain symptoms. On the first foray into town, the car died. Remembering the lesson, Rebekah set about to restore the wiring. Attempts were to no avail, for the lesson had not included how to open the bonnet. A passerby demonstrated that secret, wires were attached, and off the two women drove. That episode served as a prelude for the acts to follow.

We had a flat on our car. Linda could not get the jack to work. Fortunately Richard was still at home so he came and changed the tire. Then to the hospital after taking the tire to our regular filling station. After several trips back to get the tire, it was still not ready tonight. We put it back in our car. The spare that is now on the car has no tread. Henrietta's other most recent ailment is a reclining front seat which suddenly broke and is now supported by two bamboo poles in the back seat! (July 21, 1974) *We stopped and pho-tographed gorgeous flowers placed around the*

*Maharaja's statue for Independence Day. We got back
in the car. She would not even gasp. We pushed but
could not get it going fast enough to start. At that point
two men on a scooter came by and saw us running
along beside Henrietta—I am sure we made a hilarious
sight. They offered to help. We got in. They pushed; the
car started. Sure enough, when we got home, it would
not start again. John looked at the car; it needed a new
ignition switch and probably a new battery as well. The
battery was dead last weekend and was recharged on
Monday. No telling when we will have a car again.*
(August 11, 1974)

A year later, new cars arrived for the two missionaries.
*There are now 2 new cars at our house! Linda got hers today.
Henrietta is going to the Hellingers for the duration. We have
a driver hired by the mission who starts Tuesday. Maybe transportation problems will improve.* (May 3, 1975) Subsequent to
that Ambassador, Rebekah drove others cars—a white Fiat, a
baby-blue Fiat, and then a fine Indian luxury automobile!

Ordering a car in India isn't exactly like the American
experience of ordering a custom-built automobile. Although
the car or van or ambulance is ordered from the company, the
purchase cannot be completed until paperwork is first cleared
by government offices. One husband and wife were on station
many months awaiting the government clearance. Each
instance of ordering a vehicle presented an adventure, with
each new vehicle somewhat of an improvement over the one
being replaced. The hospital van was built in Bangalore.

*We all went . . . to see our new community health
van being constructed. Where else in the world could
you go to see where it is being put together?! I mean
piece by piece and bolt by bolt. We've been selecting
colors for the outside, inside, seats. They think it will*

be ready by the end of November. It was rather exciting to see it. (October 31, 1975)

Other cars were ordered.

You will never believe what is sitting outside. Since 5:45 last night there is this white car with bucket seats, tinted glass, floor shift, a clock. You absolutely would not believe the difference in how it drives and sounds! . . . It is also much more powerful—the pickup is so good which certainly makes it safe. Though we request-ed seat belts, there are none there. (June 8, 1990) *First, I will tell you about THE car. I had an attack of guilt— my car is good, my friends' cars are disasters, I drive so little. Finally the deed is done . . . This is a Maruthi ESTEEM LX, a 4 door sedan—small car by USA stan-dards, luxury car in India. This model has factory installed AC. Can you imagine AC in this heat and pol-lution? I may start driving!!! I did not get the one with stereo, self lock, and power windows. Real retractable factory installed seat belts. Mine will be metallic gray color—gray upholstered seats (even that will be cooler than this plastic I now have). The car is allotted. We have chassis number, engine number.* (March 28, 1996) *I have a new car as of last evening. The comfort of the seats is amazing. There is a button to open the gas tank and one to open the trunk . . . The horn even sounds nice. I am very thankful.* (April 17, 1996)

Even with new cars, situations required improvisation; problems continued. The ambulance provided transport for other than medical emergency.

I went again tonight to the Barry Moore crusade meeting. We piled 20 of us hospital people into the ambulance, Linda and I chauffeured! (February 11, 1975) *The rain continued. In the village Phil's wind-shield wipers quit so all the way back he manually moved the wiper with his arm outside. Everyone got drenched.* (November 23, 1979) *The group took Marsha to the airport. Anthony drove. When Anthony was opening the trunk, the handle just came off in his hand with the trunk locked. Marsha's purse and tickets were in the trunk. In an Ambassador you can't take the back seat out. Finally with a crowbar Anthony broke in—in time.* (July 9, 1975) *We had six cars going and five coming back. Going we had 2 flat tires, 1 broken accelerator cable, and Jason got lost. Coming back we had a flat and a broken axle.* (July 9, 1993)

There and back in one day with essentially no springs in the back seat and everything rattling and the noise and wind is wearing. I am going to appreciate my new car—if and when! (May 22, 1990) *Something was wrong. Sure enough, a flat tire. Quite miraculously a young driver in the next car agreed to help. I did a good part of the work and helped him. He jacked it up and actually changed it. The spare was very low on air. We went to 5 petrol bunks and none would give air— they turn off the air at 5:30! Finally at the 6th one, after initially refusing, the man started up his little gen-erator and put the air in. I guess three distressed ladies did him in.* (May 12, 1988)

Rebekah looked for alternatives to driving herself, especially for trips into rural areas or to Vellore.

I arrived back from Vellore before dark thankfully. We took Mark, the hospital driver, and he did well. But 3 times this afternoon he had to leave the road to avoid

265

oncoming passing vehicles (trucks & buses). It is wild.
(October 21, 1988) When I walked out of the airport a
little man was there with my name on a sign. He was
somewhat like Anthony must have been 15-20 years
ago. We piled into a somewhat ancient Ambassador. He
was a safe and good driver much to my relief.
(February 23, 1988)

When Santosh Benjamin drove to the Chikballapur hospital anniversary celebration, she reported, "Santosh is a good driver. I wish I could hire him!"

That Rebekah preferred not to drive is understandable. The traffic accidents cause anyone to hesitate. All too often patients in Casualty were victims of a traffic disaster.

I ended up with three major cases. Two of the men
had been run over by a truck. They were laborers who
were sleeping beside the road under the baskets they
were guarding. The truck backed over them and then
left the scene. Earlier in the week the orthopedists took
care of a lady whose right arm was amputated by a
vehicle as she sat by the road selling coconuts. There is
so much tragedy all around. (July 20, 1997) Rajini
went with the Kapurs and their daughter to Vellore for
the day. Rajini visited Priya at CMC for her birthday.
Coming back, about 140 km from here, they hit a bul-
lock cart. Two big trucks were coming at them with
undimmed lights from the opposite direction. The bul-
lock cart came onto the highway with no light. Mirac-
ulously only one bullock died. The cart was destroyed
and the car badly damaged—windshield gone, front
end collapsed. The family on the cart were OK except
stitches. No fractures. Mr. Kapur (driving) was bruised
in legs and his driver (in the other front seat) had cuts

*and stitches. The 3 ladies in back were unhurt.
Miraculous. It happens in a fraction of a second and
further confirms the need to avoid night driving if at all
possible.* (March 2, 1992)

*Our community health vehicle hit a cow on
Wednesday. The cow had to be put to sleep that same
afternoon. The man who is allegedly the owner came
the next morning along with some other men and created a bit of trouble, demanding money. We do not think
that he went to the police. He is to come back tomorrow morning. He must give proof that he is the owner
and a bill of sale or something.* (July 27, 1997)

Travel required either nonchalance, resignation, or sheer
endurance.

*Jason said getting home from Woodstock in North
India was unreal . . . he rode the bus down the mountains to Deradoon to fly to Delhi. An air strip was in
the middle of nowhere. The airport was a shamyana
with folding chairs to sit on. Jason struck up a conversation with a Sikh who flies and has lived all over.
Jason asked him what kind of plane was coming. The
Sikh replied, "God help us." Jason said he really started praying then!* (March 2, 1984) *The time in Delhi
seemed interminable. I was very cold. The restaurant
was not functioning. I was so sleepy. The apple and
cookies were a lifesaver. The fog was very dense. The
airline pilots strike is still going on. Very few flights
are running but mine was. Retired air force are flying
the planes. This has been true many weeks. From
Bangalore we have one flight per day to Delhi and one
to Bombay and that is all—none to Madras . . . But
just on 7th they had added a 6:15 AM flight from Delhi*

to Hyderabad to Bangalore. I had seen it there but
decided I did not want the extra take off and landing. It
never went anyway and it turned out that it is a
Russian (Uzbek) plane and crew rented for this strike
crisis. It was that very airplane that ultimately flew to
Hyderabad and Bangalore, turned around and went
back and crashed on landing in Delhi. Meanwhile we
were finally loaded by 11. He got to the end of the run-
way, turned around, and came back. Some luggage had
been loaded without a passenger. It had to be
offloaded. At 12 we finally took off. My luggage was
the very last to appear. I thought maybe they offloaded
it too! (January 10, 1993)

Beyond animals, transport, and travel stretched interminable daily tasks—each one a challenge. Each errand or task
required much effort and time to accomplish. Road conditions,
traffic, and vehicles slowed the pace. A 30-kilometer trip
(approximately 18 miles) required 45-60 minutes. Vegetables
and fruits had to be individually scrubbed and not merely
rinsed. Grocery shopping meant stops at several shops—
butcher, green grocer, a couple of food stores. Many products
were not available. Rebekah had to purchase the milk from a
reliable diary and then pasteurize the milk herself. Likewise
she purified the water. To buy a saree required three stops—
the saree merchant for the silk, a fabric shop for the petticoat,
and the tailor, who made the *choli*. Essential services such as
telephone, water, and electricity were all too frequently disrupted either by enforced shutdowns, equipment failure, or
weather-related causes.

Telephones in the '70s were the only means of communication between Rebekah and the hospital. Pagers and beepers
weren't available. The erratic service meant a messenger often
had to notify Rebekah of an emergency. To call her parents in
the U.S., she wrote them weeks in advance to tell the date and

time of the call, according to their local time. She then made with the telephone company an appointment for the call. Instant communication? NOT! Mrs. Naylor said that their calls from the U.S. often could not be completed. By the '90s the Naylors, however, could dial directly Rebekah's number. If that day her phone were in service, they talked!

My phone is just totally out of commission this weekend. It is a frustration (November 21, 1982) *Funny story: Saturday evening my phone went dead— occurs at least every 2 weeks. Rosemary told me that outside the wires get wrapped around each other in the wind. When the repairman comes, he throws a stick up in the air until they untangle. He rings up his supervisor, says he repaired it, and gets good pay. Rosemary fixed the phone in 5 minutes time. She threw the stick, the wires unwrapped, and the telephone worked!* (March 29, 1977) *I imagine you are home by now and have tried to call to no avail. My phone has been dead since Tuesday. Saturday the repairman came. He diagnosed the wire broken due to storm. He would send the wireman. The wireman came only Sunday, saw it, and left. Thus it is still dead.* (May 30, 1982)

The various domestic crises involving hot-water heater, refrigerator, and stove slowed and aggravated. Short, fat cylinders hang from the ceiling in a corner, generally in the bathroom. These geysers (hot-water heaters) are electric. If one wants hot water, flip the switch. The one in Rebekah's apartment at BBH made warm showers impossible more than once.

The geyser in my bathroom which feeds the kitchen has been gone almost a month. They tried to repair the geyser. After a week they decided they couldn't fix it. It took another week to decide to buy a new one. A week after ordering, the company said not available. Maybe some day! (November 21, 1982) *They were trying to install my new water heater after well over one month. They worked most of Friday night and Saturday night. It is making hot water though it leaks in two places. They refused to agree with me that the leaks are there.* (December 12, 1982) *My geyser is not working again and is leaking. Again tomorrow they will remove it. They just replaced it last week.* (June 21, 1999) *My famous geyser ruptured again. I did not know until I came home last night. When I went upstairs, I saw that one of the connections had been changed and realized that this had happened. I opened the cabinets. Surely enough, all of these hours later they were full of water. Everything was wet. Everything is out in the floor and wherever there is a place. They say it is fixed. This is the 6th time that it has been fixed. I cannot get the thing replaced though it is under warranty. Very disgusting.* (July 2, 1999) No hot water, no refrigerator, and no stove for several weeks at a time will not positively affect quality of life. *The . . . apparent death of my refrigerator . . . was a blow. The hospital electricians determined that the compressor was gone and the thermostat was gone. The consensus is that at age 18 years, a foreign frig which is 110V—I need to accept its demise and buy a new frig. I feel like I lost a friend. In horrendous heat I raced off to town. Three brands are possible, smaller than what I have, of poor quality— flimsy plastic . . . available MAYBE in 10 days. (April 28, 1992) I put some rolls in the oven to heat for breakfast. Soon I smelled something burning. The oven was full of flames. I turned off the stove; the flames were still inside. The house was filling with smoke. I called Alex who said to also turn off the gas cylinder. I did. The fire died. Sheela had left a pan with something in it which had caught fire. In the back of the bottom of the stove I saw a lot of fuzzy stuff. Something has built a nest. Never a dull moment!!!* (December 29, 1996) *My stove is quite sick. I can not remember what I wrote after the big oven fire Sunday a week ago. Ultimately we got a real stove repair man. There was a list of things wrong. To fix it, it had to go to his shop. It left on Monday and who knows when it will come. The man brought a fine 2 burner gas hot plate to use in the meantime. Even with no electricity 6-8 AM I can have something hot!!* (January 7, 1997) *My stove came Monday. I am so thrilled. It is totally refurbished, trouble is corrected, cleaned and painted. a new back panel, a new spring on the oven door. All of the burners light. He said it should be good for 15 years at least.* (January 12, 1997)

The missionaries generally worked together to make the milk run or used the hospital driver for the chore. That was not the case this particular Monday afternoon.

Something hilarious happened. I had to go get the milk because Anthony was tied up with mission business. I was putting the can between the seats. The lid came off. The can nicely rotated and all 4 liters spilled in the floor! By the time I realized what was happening it was too late. That milkman (who speaks no Kannada or English) was staring though the window on the other side in absolute horror . . . The sour smell still overwhelms! (November 17, 1979)

Omitted is that the foray to the dairy with safe milk was a hair-raising and lengthy trip and that the milk had yet to be pasteurized by her in her own kitchen!

Although frustrated and often *thoroughly disgusted*, today Naylor generally shrugs off the incidents. Hannah Sinclair, the BBH administrative secretary, recounted an incident that gives a bit of insight to Rebekah's adjustment to her life in India. One morning Rebekah was late to work. When she arrived, with many giggles she told Hannah the story. After breakfast Naylor went upstairs. Dressing and the brushing of her teeth complete, she turned the door knob to open the door. The knob fell off in her hand! The calls, bangs on the door, and stomps on the floor did not alert the helper downstairs. Eventually realizing Doctor Madame had not left for work, the helper went upstairs. Madame was trapped inside the room! Maintenance freed Madame, who in turn said to Hannah, "At least I was dressed! What to do!"

Critters were never eradicated. Cars and travel frustrated but improved dramatically. Equipment, appliances, hardware, and construction confounded. Mishaps and inconveniences often deterred and perplexed the strongest, the calmest of people. Despite the differences in her life in America and her life in Bangalore, Rebekah thrived, however, rather than merely survived living in India. Why? Her eagerness to follow God? Her love for the people? Her indomitable spirit? Her unique personality and character? Probably all of the above contributed. Ah, yes, life and work in India!

Trials, Tempests, and Terrors

Karnataka Parliament Building
in downtown Bangalore

Karnataka Justice Building
in downtown Bangalore

Indian market area, replete with cow

Bangalore primary shopping area—Saturday-afternoon crowd

*I know what it is to be in need, and I know what it is to have
plenty. I have learned the secret of being content in any and
every situation, whether well fed or hungry, whether living in
plenty or in want. I can do everything through him
who gives me strength*
(Phil. 4:12-13).

Trials, Tempests, and Terrors

*They have cokes in Madras (the real thing) so I had one each
day . . . We are into festivals. Friday was the puja at which
they worship the vehicles and work tools to keep away evil and
trouble. The vehicles are decorated with flowers and banana
leaves. At one electric substation workers planned to sacrifice
goats to the gods to protect them and their electricity. Animal
activists learned about it. The police intervened and prevented
the sacrifice . . . Might as well start with a weather report.
Summery—hot and dry. The ground is baked and dusty . . . It
appears that taxis are on strike in Bombay, so I am sure I have
landed in the correct country!!! . . . I guess it's a good thing I
adapt to travel so well since I live on the other side of the
world!*

Living in India presented challenges beyond animals, vehicles, and machinery. Daily existence required much energy and
travel more effort. Weather disrupted; government and civil
changes as well as international events fomented unrest and
fear. Bangalore, the garden spot of India, lies in the southwestern area of India. The pretty flowers and vegetation along with
the location make the city attractive and appealing. Being further south than Delhi and Jaipur and at 3,000-feet elevation,
the climate is less dry and hot. In the 1970s Bangalore, like
other cities in India, was not as westernized as it is today. Life

there did not resemble life in an American city. Through God's grace, Rebekah lived and worked amidst these challenges and changes. In missionary orientation and in all the years afterward, the motto was SIMPLY ADJUST.

Various church services and practices within the churches presented new experiences.

> *I have just returned from a very long day. I was to be the preacher at the 5th anniversary of a church 50 km from here. One of our young doctors, Dr. Alfred, and Krupananda went with me. The service only started by 12 . . . lasted over 2 hours. We had lunch—on the banana leaf. One thing I had not seen before. After the service, people were coming for prayer with the pastors. A few brought oil which they were to pray over. Alfred told me they would then use it for anointing or to make a sign of cross on forehead each morning. This tested my theology somewhat. I guess I will always learn and see new things.* (July 26, 1998) *The [Lord's Supper] message was by a retired missionary wife (ordained)—superb—on the 3 "lost" parables in Luke 15. The bread was a piece of chappati and then a bit of grape Kool-Aid.* (January 6, 1992)

An everpresent challenge from the onset, finding adequate supplies, food items, and household goods occupied a prominent place in Rebekah's life. She depended on items from the USA to provide or supplement locally-acquired supplies. Initially she shipped to India by sea a large wooden crate containing items not available for purchase in Bangalore: gas kitchen range, refrigerator, wringer washer, piano, two mahogany chests, sofa bed, recliner, two double box springs and mattresses, dishes, pots and pans, glassware, stainless flatware, drugs, cosmetics and toiletry items, toilet paper, medical texts, Bible-study materials and commentaries, music, favorite food items. Two other times she shipped crates from Fort Worth to India. The second crate arrived with the contents wet, mildewed, and insect-infested, with very little of the contents usable. The majority of the items had been stolen from the third crate. To wait three months for the crate to arrive, to fly to Madras to the port and customs facility, to watch the entire crate unpacked and all the contents laid out on the dock for the customs clerks to check was an ordeal, both emotional and physical. The anticipation of the much-desired items replaced with abject disappointment and despair proved to be over-whelming. After the third experience, Rebekah relied on her suitcases and packages brought in with volunteers or her parents. If the items didn't fit in the suitcases, she did without. Because she had to make her own bread, frequently letters contained a request for packets of dry yeast. Her friends often sent her boxes. Her parents with them brought items to replenish her reserves — shampoo, hairspray, hose, glue, aluminum wrap, blueberry-muffin mix, peach preserves, flavored gelatin, pen refills, party invitations, Christmas cards. *I got up and made blueberry muffins — Terrell Mays brought 5 packages and I still had one. Now no need to ration them. I may eat jello and blueberry muffins until July!* (April 2, 1989)

Shopping for food and household products entailed stops at more than one shop as well as adjustments in eating habits and lifestyle. Produce had to be scrubbed, not merely rinsed. Once a missionary friend spied at a fruit store a rare shipment of fresh strawberries. She purchased them and scrubbed each one individually before she brought them to Rebekah. What an example of selfless sharing! Potatoes, rice, flour, eggplant, tomatoes, cucumbers, coconut, mango, papaya, and chicken could be bought, but not paper products, baking mixes, cereals, canned hams, coffee. Not until 1994 were soft drinks such as 7-Up and Pepsi available to be purchased; in 1997 Coca Cola became available.

More products and more choices gradually appeared. Comments during a trip to Madras and other letters from the 1990s describe changes, one of which involved advertisements.

I was thinking today how much more advertising there is—how much more consumer goods are available—how much marketing is done . . . Spencer's [in Madras] has become Spencer's Plaza—a 3-story shopping arcade and at least some shops with nice windows. Not yet like Singapore but definite change! (October 16, 1994) Bangalore also reflected changes in stores and goods. *There is a supermarket that is bigger than Nilgiri's. There are now more imported food and cosmetic items but very expensive, some frozen foods like fish, and dressed chickens. Kellogg's now has four varieties of cereals* (November 7, 1999) *I walked all the way to Nilgiri's. They have so much more stuff than the market I have been going to out here. You may remember the good fruit stand in front on the sidewalk. Inside the store they now have vegetables.* (July 8, 2001) Generally fruits and vegetables were sold in shops or open stands separate from grocery stores. The fruit stand which Rebekah frequented sat on the sidewalk in front of Nilgiri's but had no business connection to the store. Although Nilgiri's was for years the most-visited grocery store, others appeared. *I went to Food World, the supermarket in RT Nagar close by. Next to it is a fruit and vegetable store. I bought a pound of okra and a pound of beans for the equivalent of 15 cents! I got several things in the store. Since it was before 3PM, there were very few customers and I looked at more things. Some frozen meats are there. I have cooked all of the beans and a pan full of okra, tomatoes, and onions.* (April 1, 2000)

Modernization became prevalent in other areas during the 1990s. The first two decades Rebekah lived in India, banking and securing cash involved an in-person visit to a bank, standing in a long queue during arbitrarily set hours, and enduring interminable waits for hand-produced receipts. Transfer of funds from a U.S. bank required up to three months. Rebekah explains her use of currency:

> *I had a local bank account. An advantage of being on a resident visa is that I could have a regular checking account. I put money in there as needed. I paid rupees cash for day-to-day needs like eating out, helpers, groceries, petrol; checks to pay the hospital for my housing utilities; and credit card for big things—travel, a BIG shopping purchase. I did not use dollars in India at all but kept US dollar travelers checks for out of India travel. I always made sure I could access enough money to get out of the country— one way, closest place.* (February 2008)

For comparison the March 2008 conversion rate states one US dollar equaled 40.29 Indian rupees. In 1974 one US dollar equaled 7 Rs. Petrol per liter sold in 2006 for 48 Indian rupees—approximately 200 rupees per gallon. The thick stack of Indian bills make for a fat wallet! The weekly requirement of rupees made frequent bank visits essential.

Imagine seeing an ATM for the first time and realizing the convenience of such a machine!

> *I took Resa Spann, a volunteer, and her friend Tracey Dodde to dinner. Next to the ice cream shop is a Citi Bank office with an ATM machine. This is an automatic teller machine. I knew they existed in America but had never really seen one. To my astonishment with her card, she got money, cash, right out of the machine.*

*It is available 24 hours. Money came right out of her
bank account via the credit card.* (May 1, 1996) *This
evening I went to use the ATM machine in RT Nagar.
Used to be I could only take Rs. 2000 per transaction.
But I got Rs. 5000 with no problem on one transaction.
I bet I could get more. That was such a relief and help
and it was very easy.* (June 24, 2001)

Currently numerous shops in the RT Nagar area, which is
adjacent to the hospital compound, display imported items and
locally-made products both varied and abundant. Larger shop
owners speak English and accept credit cards.

Bangalore itself made a conscious effort to be both more
modern and more attractive. *By 2004 Bangalore will be the
best city in Asia—roads, constant water and electricity, rail
city transport. They had a big "summit" on 24th. The papers
have been full of this. In the midst of it the gas stations went
on strike and chaos occurred yesterday. Probably even the city
fathers were frustrated.* (January 26, 2000) The first department store opened in 2000. With her usual humor, Rebekah
notes that the store covered several stories, had no parking,
and sported an escalator—yes, **an** escalator ascending, none
descending! Today the escalators do travel in both directions.
A newer, larger department store, Shopper's Stop, offers clothing and household furnishings as well as underground parking
garage. A road similar to a loop around a large city marked
another positive change. *A "Ring Road" has been built from
out near where Victor is across the north side, practically in
the country, over to the highway in front of the hospital. It
comes in just 3-4 blocks north of hospital in Hebbal. It is
smooth—has a yellow line in middle, has lanes for 2 wheelers,
has curbs, no lights. Incredible!* (August 3, 1998) In the early
'90s Rebekah took a computer back to India. By 2000 Internet
providers were numerous. Rebekah and the hospital had email:

I am getting a little more used to my email. (January 16, 2000) Rebekah observed that *to see now an Indian gent in traditional garb walking along a rural area while talking on a mobile telephone is common rather than a rarity.* (The term in India is *mobile,* pronounced with a long *i,* rather than the American *cell* or *cell phone.*)

Not surprising, *mobile* is not the only difference in language use. Adjusting to the Indian version of British English in opposition to American English presented challenges. Rebekah encountered such differences with her usual perceptiveness, but the occasional word or idiom perplexed. At the stationery shop she asked for *envelopes.* This time the clerk was confounded. After some explanation and hand gestures, the clerk understood the request was for *covers,* the accepted word for *envelopes.*

My friends at work never discuss any events. But India and Pakistan played each other here yesterday in the World Cup Cricket quarter finals. Big event. It was much discussed. Friday they were discussing the security arrangements, ticket scalping, the stadium. I did not want to be left out so I said—the one on Queens Road? Yes. Victor said that it is flooded. With distress I said, "What happened? It hasn't rained." Which made all laugh. They have put flood lights [on the stadium] to play at night so it is flooded! (March 10, 1996)

Other letters recount funny stories concerning word usage. *Today we interviewed for a clerk because a cashier resigned. One boy we interviewed had written that he's leaving the last job the reason was WOUNDED. I thought it meant he had an accident. But he looked OK. What it meant was WOUND UP—the project was over and there was no more job. No doubt it did leave him wounded!* (*WOUNDED* rhymes with *rounded.*) (July 24, 1998) *Sometimes their use of our colloqui-al expressions is so funny. Dr. Shyamala was talking about the challenge of the work, the needs being great, and what we do being relatively small. She said, "I am just dropping in the bucket." I thought that was hilarious, partly because it some-times seems literally true.* (May 28, 1983) Another surgeon on staff, Dr. Benjamin, recently told Rebekah that he was a "headless chicken" due to the number of patients and surgeries scheduled for that day. Rebekah had a trunk that was in essence a tin box painted black. The handwritten receipt for the delivery noted that the delivery service company's name was "The Excellent Drunk Man" and the trunk termed a "steel cabin." Street signs definitely amuse! *ZEBRA CROSSING IS A PEDESTRIAN RIGHT. (Zebras are crosswalks. I had this pic-ture of walking across backs of zebras!)* (November 30, 1988) No doubt those from India who visit America wonder about our use of English, too!

A precious incident concerns the story of Zaccheus. During one of Rebekah's and Grace Solomon's visits into a rural area, the children sang for them. Their version of the familiar story song of Zaccheus had these lyrics:

> *Zaccheus was a wee little man*
> *And a wee little man was he.*
> *He climbed up into a sycamore tree*
> *for the Lord he wanted to see.*
> *And as the Saviour passed his way*
> *He looked up in the tree;*
> *And He said,*
> *"Zaccheus, you come down,*
> *For I'm coming to tea today*
> *For I'm coming to tea today."*

Ah, tea—the familiar hostess offering to a revered, wel-come guest.

Language usage briefly challenged. Other issues and problems in India affect daily life more dramatically. Natural disasters—heat, monsoon rains, earthquakes—yearly wreak havoc in India. Living conditions in the vast slums and rural areas offer no protection from weather. Countless numbers of people are killed or injured, crops destroyed, animals killed. The wet season occurs June, July, and August, although rains often pelt the area as early as May.

Tragedy daily occurs. Friday night for 6 hours we had torrential rains. I have 2 patients in the hospital whose house in Hebbal collapsed on them. Quite a few people died in the city. Walls and other such are just caving in. Sunday night rain came harder for about 4 hours. Several nurses told me how bad so many places are and that they could hear screams in the night. Many are without shelter. This country so often is a place of excesses—years of drought and now floods. My house was really full of water. Several places in the hospital roof are leaking. The Nutrition Centre is flooded; 2 patients are there. (September 12, 1988)

Has it ever rained! All of our buildings are leaking (old and new). We need every drop of water but this coming all at one time is something else. I cannot even imagine the millions of people with no shelter, no dry place, no spare clothes, only the mud and muck. Those slightly better off face such transport problems. (October 30, 1991) *The rain just disrupted everything. The roads are in a worse state than ever. Telephones also are badly affected. The hospital has had no phone since 3 days. Wednesday night the express train from Bangalore to Delhi was derailed just 50 Km after leaving Bangalore. About 50 died.* (November 2, 1991)

The monsoon rains and resulting flooding along with the oppressive heat produce miserable conditions. *I am melting. It is sure and certain! With no current [electricity] at this hour, I cannot even know whether it is better inside or on the porch. Not a breath of air stirs in these evening hours. Official temps are 97-99. The hot season has just started.* (March 28, 1996)

Earthquakes caused much devastation. Fortunately, Bangalore was not affected often.

The earthquake killed thousands in Maharashtra. The tremors were felt here at 4 a.m. Thursday. Our patients woke up and started asking the nurses what happened. (October 1, 1993) *Stories of the earthquake in Gujarat grow more horrible by the hours. Whole towns have disappeared. As many as 100,000 may be dead. The amount of injured still isolated in places not reached is great. . . no water, little food, no shelters. Days are hot; nights are quite cool. To see this and to study Revelation gives much food for thought. A team is going from our hospital through relief efforts being organized by Christian Medical Association of India.* (January 30, 2001 #1) *Relief efforts are in total confusion though many have come to help. They are very worried now about epidemics of cholera, plague. Surgeries are being done in tents or in open without proper sterile equipment and supplies. Tetanus has become a concern besides infection itself. Many are homeless. The sewers of all are destroyed, no water in many places.* (February 1, 2001)

Rains, heat, earthquakes — not one a fluke or an aberration in the weather but part of the yearly natural weather cycle. Unfortunately, the massive number of people, the prevalent poverty, and the lack of education exacerbate the effect of each weather-related activity. A natural phenomenon, an eclipse, has far-reaching implications for the Indian people—not from a physical effect but an emotional one fueled by superstitions.

We had a solar eclipse on Saturday afternoon [February 16, 1980]. *Here it was about 90% but north of here in North Karnataka the eclipse was complete. Scientists came from all over the world to observe it. Many customs and practices are related to a solar eclipse. It was especially incredible (and sad) to me how many of these beliefs carried over to our community. Especially that an eclipse is to be a dangerous thing for pregnant women. She must not leave the house the whole day. People do not eat during the time—only before and after. Our patients wanted lunch before 11:30. They demanded that the windows be covered with black curtains. That we did not do, but the patients themselves took their bedspreads and did it. Most people refused to be in the hospital. Census fell way down. All public transportation stopped from 11:30 to 5:00 Saturday. No buses, no autos. The streets were totally deserted. Our pregnant staff took leave. Dr. Michael's wife (4 months pregnant) could not come to my dinner Sat. night because of it. Dr. Joseph told me he did no major surgery all last week because patients refused! Gail went upstairs during the eclipse to check. Nurses were in the hall with light off and doors shut to patients' room.* (February 19, 1980)

Lack of commodities such as petrol, current (electricity), and water frequently disrupted activities. The outages sometimes occurred with advance notice, often with none.

The latest local crisis is lack of petrol. Can you imagine in a city of 3 1/2 million and no gas! (July 19,

1987) *Monday, the price of petrol and diesel went up by 25% at one fell swoop. They say "temporarily" but who knows. There were long queues at the petrol stations in Delhi. Now we will be paying about Rs 14 per liter or about $3.50 per gallon of petrol. They also indicate supply will be short. Signs are everywhere asking people to conserve.* (October 17, 1990 #2) *Santosh stayed in a queue all night at a petrol bunk—still not through the line this morning.* (February 19, 1980)

Without electricity and water, hospital services are severely limited. The BBH generators cannot adequately supply current all the equipment needs. Sometimes the power was off because of breakdowns—other times for deliberate conservation.

Since 1 PM Saturday our electricity has been off. A big transformer or something blew—knocked out hospital, hostel, and my house. The Boltons, the cows, the chickens all have lights . . . Only today did I get connection temporary for my frig—from the Bolton's house . . . Four babies are in incubators. The burn patient needs heaters. The sterilizer must be run. A crisis! (November 11, 1985) *At 6 PM. last night electricity was restored—6 days and 4 hours. Our staff did such a great job trying to keep things running. The generators held out without disaster.* (November 16, 1985) *We are really having electricity problems. Yesterday afternoon it was off 4 hours. I had no dinner. The gas is finished [emptied]—cylinder not available for at least one week. I rented a hot plate from the mission plus my oven and then no current! I also had no car. This morning at 5:45 current went off again. I had a piece of bread and jam, milk, and banana. Current was off all day until nearly 4, then on . . . off again at 7, just now on. I don't know what to expect over the next several months.* (February 10, 1992) *Weather here is miserably hot. The current is off frequently.* (March 20, 1983) *From the 16th the morning electricity off-period became 8-10 instead of 6-8. The time is bad for hospital, but I am so thankful to have light early morning. When one's quiet time is in the dark, one has trouble being alert.* (January 17, 1996) *This week we had lots of additional hours cut. Candle makers should be making a profit—also the diesel fuel people supplying generator fuel.* (March 24, 1996) *The water shortage has hit in full force. I have had none at home for 3 days. There is no water in the hospital tonight. Patients and attenders are not even having water to drink tonight. It is getting hotter and hotter every day.* (April 7, 1982) *I have just finished dip and pour method of hair washing and bathing—no water for 9 days now. No cooking gas for 10 days.* (April 14, 1982)

Political and civil unrest also disrupted and caused anxiety. For example, a state or national holiday shuts cities down—no offices open, no transports operating, no shops or services available. The effects of government change go beyond disrupting daily life. The assassination of Indira Gandhi on October 31, 1984 and later her son, Rajiv Gandhi, on May 21, 1991 represent two such instances.

The heat also represents the oppressive tension that grips India tonight. The death of Rajiv Gandhi surely came as a big shock and is viewed as a great tragedy by almost everyone regardless of political position. Bangalore has apparently been quiet today. No buses have run at all and everything has been closed up tight. But the hospital vehicle had no trouble going out for staff. We were short handed in most departments but we had almost no outpatients. Medical staff came as

usual. No one yet knows what is to happen tomorrow.
Things may be closed again. The funeral in Delhi is
only on Friday. (May 22, 1991) *This is an eventful*
week both for me and for India. It seems that the right
wing Hindu party withdrew from the government yes-
terday and the Prime Minister resigned. Trouble is
expected. I do not know how things are today so far as
transport. Schools closed yesterday morning all over
India until November 3. People I talk to are very dis-
tressed. (October 24, 1990)

Rebekah kept a close watch on the economy as well as the government.

The economy issue is critical. The currency was
devalued twice in 3 days about 2 weeks ago.
Supposedly that was in an attempt to get more foreign
loans (International Monetary Fund) and they shipped
much of their gold to London. The Parliament is in
budget session. The budget came out Wednesday.
Immediately there have been large price increases.
Petrol went from 14 to 17 Rs per liter over night, cook-
ing gas from 67—80 Rs per cylinder. You think of all the
people on fixed income (or no income) and it is disaster.
Goods prices are awful. Tomatoes used to be Rs 6/kg
and now Rs 20-22/kg. Mr. Calla told us the other night
that he has little hope now for the country. At least the
government was able to secure enough votes in
Parliament to remain in place but who knows for how
long. There are further restrictions on imports. At the
city hospital administrators meeting Wednesday evening
all were saying the entire situation and budget are
going to hit us extremely hard. We are to meet again in
August on this topic. Most of us just raised charges but
now will we need to do it again? (July 22, 1991)

Even though the northern part of India saw various forms of unrest, Bangalore remained less affected and free of urban crime for quite a while.

After work I went to the bank. All of the employees were outside in an excited state. The manager said he had no money. I asked if they were striking. No, at 11:30 a.m. there had been a robbery at gun point and the man took every rupee, the first armed bank robbery in Bangalore's history. I commented it sounded like America. Well, the robber (they caught him) had just arrived from the States. He is an Indian. Sort of sad to think we are seeding the world with such violence. Anyway no money. (June 16, 1981)

Elections, beauty pageants, religious issues—such spark protests, riots, violence, even bombings.

The elections are to be this week. Violence contin-ues especially in the north. People are being killed daily. Already 9 candidates have been killed. There are more police out and about than usual. (May 19, 1991) *The Miss World pageant is over. There had been much increasing tension . . . protests all over the city with hundreds of arrests. Over 20,000 police and military were deployed.* (November 24, 1996) *You may have read in newspapers about some rioting in Bangalore. Actually 9 people were reported killed. They were fight-ing first about police brutality because a prisoner, a Muslim, was killed. The state has tried to make every-thing Kannada to the point of preventing Tamils from applying for many jobs. Yet 30% of people in the city are Tamil. The Tamilians were fighting.* (March 24, 1985)

Bombings made the news often.

I do not know if there came in your news anything about increased bombings in churches. This has been on the rise since May . . . Sunday night a Bangalore church was bombed while a festival or service was going on. No one was hurt but there was a lot of damage. Minutes before the church bomb went off a car with 3 occupants exploded not far away. Two were killed but the third was alive. The bombs were the same material. They were Muslims. I do not know what to make of that since allegedly Hindu fundamentalists are causing the problems. Even before that happened here on Sunday night, the police sent warning to all local churches to be alert and to report anything suspicious or unusual. Over the years I have become used to terrorist risks and other violence and unrest. My big concern was for the people involved and the persecution as a whole which is escalating. (July 6, 2000)

Although Rebekah observes that bombings and other terrorist activities occurred regularly, the hospital compound remained untouched. The rural setting of BBH in its early years provided security from city-related events. A devastating occurrence shattered that relative safety.

This morning I was in clinic seeing patients and doing scans. Santosh Benjamin was in the next room seeing surgery patients. I finished my present stack and went to see if I could help him. The patient, when asked where was the doctor, said, "A bomb went off and he left." I quickly went to the Casualty. The unthinkable had happened. In our own post office a parcel had exploded. The man sorting the mail was injured. He is well known to us—delivered our mail for years and just

*got promoted. He had talked to Hannah on the phone
about 10 minutes before the explosion happened. His
injuries are face and hands. He surely will be blind in
one eye and the other is doubtful. The left hand is much
gone and damaged. The right hand is badly injured but
may be salvaged. The parcel had been sent from some
place. He was sorting it to be delivered today by the
mail carrier. The post office was immediately sealed off
(needless to say, we got no mail today and who knows
when we will). We were besieged by police and government people. The TV announced that Baptist Hospital
needed blood donors. This evening the press has been
hounding us a bit—pleasant but persistent. Wouldn't
you know Stan Macaden is in a meeting in Vellore
today! So here I am. I called Mr. Calla for advice. He
said to answer all authorities but say nothing to the
press. Obviously there are big political implications.
But apart from this man's critical injury and the administrative headaches, we are so shocked by such an
event in our world and our friend so innocently struck
down. I am sure we will see results and effects in security especially in our part of town.* (February 22, 1994)

Security in India heightened. India had stringent airport
security in place much earlier than the USA did. In November
1984 Rebekah went to pick up visiting missionary Bill
Wakefield. *Wakefield did arrive last night 1 1/2 hours late. I
was so glad I had a driver because persons without a ticket
cannot go inside the airport anymore.* (November 5, 1984)
What her letter omits is that automatic weapon-armed military
members stand at the entrance doors and throughout all the
Indian airports. Body searches, luggage X-rays, and several
hand baggage searches occur during the check-in and boarding
process and remain common practice.

International news had far-reaching effects, especially the death of Princess Diana, the Gulf War, and 9/11.

Yesterday the funeral of Princess Diana was on TV all day and it captivated the attention of everyone. People were in a hurry to leave work to go and watch. (September 7, 1997) *The newspaper today announces on the first page that Americans have been advised by the U.S. Consul to leave India temporarily for one month. The Consulate says it is quiet enough but concern that there will be no fuel caused them to issue the warning now. The fuel crisis evidently will only became worse. At present I see no reason to do anything but I may send the medical student home.* (January 26, 1991) *I had no more than sent the email that evening than the horrible news came. When I put the [exercise] video in and turned on the TV, I saw the bulletins about New York. Needless to say I began to watch. Our electricity and the cable were erratic, but I had BBC off and on. I until now cannot take in and comprehend the horror and the thousands of people dead and the destruction. The passion and cruelty and hatred of people to take so many innocent lives. Then to attack the Pentagon also and hundreds more! And four planes! It has been non-stop on TV on BBC. The financial implications and the world community implications. I know from our paper that the Consulate in Madras was closed. I do not know if it was open today. We got a message from IMB in Richmond to lie low, avoid nonessential travel, avoid American places like McDonalds (that is one I do not have to worry about!!!) It made me realize again how sheltered and sequestered my life has become. Tuesday evening I had calls from Brad Beaman and Art Turner and then several Indian calls—Florence, Meera, one of our young doctors. I got up at 4:30 Wed. morning and started watching again. It has been one subject discussed at work at least some. Our rupee exchange rate was affected—not a lot but some. I pray for spiritual awakening and renewal to come out of this in America. Maybe God will give another chance to our nation.* (September 13, 2001)

Not every event brought horror. The National Games, an annual, countrywide athletic event in Bangalore in 1997, gave Rebekah yet another experience—that of safeguarding and carrying the torch!

The National Games start in Bangalore on 31st. A torch is even now progressing across Karnataka. About 6,000 athletes are to participate. We expect the city to be disrupted for 10 days. Schools are being delayed in reopening because of this. (May 26, 1997) *The National Games opened in Bangalore last night. The big torch perched on top of the jeep entered the city Friday evening. We received it at the hospital. It spent the night here. Security sat (or slept) with it all night. We had to provide food for those accompanying. Saturday morning lots of officials came. The jeep had flowers all over it. The mascot was on the front. In front of the hospital all staff gathered. It was one of our biggest turnouts ever. We had a prayer. The daughter torch was lighted from the mother torch. Our staff in relay ran with the daughter torch in front of the jeep and other vehicles all the way to beyond Mekhiri Circle where the mayor and others were waiting. What an event! The staff were so excited and pleased.* (June 1, 1997)

One hospital-related anecdote concerns the Harvard firemen, the team of medical specialists from Harvard Medical

School who over a period of several years conducted a leuko-
derma study at BBH.

*Last night I had a dinner party for the Harvard
team. The evening was a great success—Rowlands,
Williams, me, and the team—11 people! Beef
stroganoff, carrots, slaw, biscuits, lemon pie. Everyone
did eat well. Had place cards. I fixed all the tables
myself. Rosemary had enough to do with all the food!
Betty had arranged after-dinner entertainment—the
snake charmers along with their magic show. We had
that inside at the guest house. It was really a show to
end all. I had never seen the snake charmer in these 3
years. They even had a mongoose who fought with the
cobra. The magic tricks were just terrific. But the funniest part of all was seeing these sophisticated, cosmo-
politan Bostonians dumfounded and speechless at the
whole thing. I enjoyed their reaction as much as anything! They had their feet off the floor in their chairs!*
(February 18, 1977)

Those pesky cobras appear again!

*Mark took me and the Owens on a sightseeing tour
. . . a great outing. Mark has a tour plan and a guide-
book. He hands his book to his passenger and off they
go on the city tour!!! Hilarious!! We went to the bull
temple which I had not seen here. A huge stone bull sits
inside the temple. But walking to the temple [we saw]
this lady with a cobra (according to Mark) and a child
also with a cobra. The child puts the head of the snake
into his mouth. I had never seen anything like this
before.* (January 13, 1998)

Festivals and holidays alternately entertained, disrupted, and often reminded Rebekah of the people's spiritual needs.

Today is the biggest Muslim festival of the year— Ramzan, thus a hospital holiday. The men went to the mosque this morning for prayers. Then they went to the cemetery with flower petals to put at graves of relatives and then home for feasting. They have been fasting daily for 1 month, eating during darkness only. A patient on whom I operated several months ago came yesterday to tell me she was preparing my dinner and bringing it tonight. She is Muslim. Just a while ago they came bringing beriyani and so many other things! (September 5, 1978) *Monday night I went to see Meera . . . It was the night before the big Muslim holiday Id. They slaughter goats and have a big feast. I had to drive through Muslim neighborhoods and then past the slaughter house area. I never dreamed. There were thousands of people in the streets and more thousands of goats. The traffic was blocked.* (March 4, 2001) *Last Friday was a big Hindu festival at which they worship tools and vehicles. I discovered that a pooja (worship) went on Friday afternoon in our cowshed. I decided that should be addressed. I called in all of the workers and explained about our God the creator and worshipping idols. It gave me such a good opportunity along with doing an administrative task. Basically I told them that what they do outside [the BBH compound] is respected and tolerated but what they do inside will conform to our position. One fellow claimed to be a Christian and that he was just thanking God. I had a further chance to talk about Christians being different and that what he did looked no different even if his intent was different . . . I felt good about that opportunity and grateful.* (October 15, 1986) *I had been invited to lunch at the home of Dr. Seshadri, the GP [doctor]*

*who sends many patients. Just 2 weeks ago I delivered
another one of the family. They are all Brahmans. I
cannot fully describe how I feel in a home like that.
The idols and all are so overwhelming and oppressive.
While we were in one room eating, men were chanting
in another room. It was a typical south Indian vegetarian feast. I wore my best saree. This morning when I
went to work a man was standing on the sidewalk
praying to the morning sun. The day has been full of
tearing reminders of the need here.* (October 5, 1986)
*At lunch Sunday one of my long time patients, Muslims,
invited a large group to their home at the end of
Ramzan. We have had many opportunities to share
spiritually. They know many of our hospital staff. Miss
Barnabas was at lunch to my surprise and delight. Dr.
George, the surgeon who has helped, was there. Stan
and his family came late. But they separated the
women into a separate room. Before at their house that
had not happened. Of course, I knew more men! What
to do!* (June 2, 1987)

A gigantic, five-day festival occurs each fall. Divali celebrates Lord Rama's victories in battle and return to Ayodya.
The victory, according to tradition, signifies one of good over
evil. Candles, diyas, are lit; firecrackers are exploded all five
nights. The third day of the festival, "Festival of Lights," is the
grandest of the celebrations.

*The fire crackers are going off all around us light-
ing up the sky and making it sound like a war zone!
Today through Wednesday are the big Divali feast
days—lights and firecrackers.* (November 11, 1985)
*The dogs (pets) seem really upset by all this. I won-
dered what all the cows thought! Tuesday evening I
was invited to the home of the Kapurs (Macadens'*

friends) who have been so nice to me. They had an
open house. They had the entry outside all decorated
with little small lights (candles) in tiny clay pots. Lots
of goodies to eat. It is very interesting that south India
usually celebrates one day prior to north India—I am
not sure why. (November 7, 1991) *This is the time*
when they light their homes and firecrackers go off
incessantly. More lights will bring more prosperity.
(November 1, 1997)

A four-day festival in Tamil Nadu, the southernmost Indian state, includes a violent taming of wild bulls.

I think I have never seen such traffic as today. The
road was terrible. Mark said they were fighting cows.
It was bull fighting! Several men had the bull con-
tained by ropes but a man was dancing and cavorting
in front of the bull and it would try to charge him. We
saw three of these. Otherwise animals, all kinds of
vehicles, people. Just now when I arrived at the hotel
what should meet me at the door but a car driving out
the door. And another. And another. The second one
turned too sharply and he was about to scratch the car
on the door. A bunch of men just picked the car up and
moved it over!!! (January 17, 1997)

In India, holidays—both civil and religious—abound. Although government offices, schools, and businesses observe the majority of these days, a hospital cannot. Bangalore Baptist Hospital closes for five holidays each year: Republic Day (January 26), Good Friday, Independence Day (August 15), Christmas Day, and New Year's Day.

The other five holidays that BBH gives employees
are skeleton days. All services and offices function. The

employee can take the holiday within 60 days. These five days are variable but usually include Gandhi's birthday (October 2) and Karnataka Day (November 1), a Muslim festival day, and a couple of Hindu festival days. (February 2008)

Some holidays compare to those in the U.S.

Today is Independence Day—a big national holiday. At 9 we had a "flag hoisting" on top of the hospital. The flag raising ceremonies are big events all over town on the mornings of big national holidays. I got up there—wind gusting 30-40 mph, damp, quite cool. Probably 30 or so of the staff were gathered. First we had Scripture and prayer. The flag was raised and unfurled. They had included rose petals when they folded the flag. These were scattered when the flag was unfurled. They sang the national anthem. I thought it was all very nice. (August 15, 1978) New Year's Eve is observed in India. *Stan and Ragini had invited me for a quiet evening, just us. Their teenage kids were having a party on their terrace. They were grateful they were at home! I was amazed driving back to the hospital after 10 that traffic was so heavy and people everywhere. Police were also out in force! New Year's Eve is a big deal here also. The churches were all having late services last night.* (January 1, 1989)

Despite some similarities in America and India and despite Rebekah's acculturation, parts of India never became for her the commonplace. Some sights disconcerted; others filled time. Flights into India, especially in the first 20 years or so Rebekah was in India, stopped in Calcutta, Delhi, Bombay, and Madras; some required overnight stays.

Some of Calcutta began to come back as we came in—my last and only other visit was April 1975. I chose the bus as I feel more secure. But he careened along scattering everything in his path. Rickshaws manned by pullers. Crowded streets—life on the sidewalk! Huge images of the goddess Kali every couple of blocks. (November 13, 1993) *I walked the streets for an hour this evening—Incredible. So many people and much traffic. Every kind of street vendor. Every kind of shop. Saw one place selling 32 flavors of ice cream. Fresh fruit juice stalls on street, a barber—customer covered in cream sitting on a wood stool. Shoes sold by street vendors, beggars. After six years I am still amazed.* (February 22, 1980) *Now just some observations about Bombay—perhaps real enough for you to be able to imagine and share. I am in a closed air-conditioned room 6-7 floors up and yet I hear a constant din outside. People, people, people, horns of every kind; horns of a boat whistle or fog horn and a police whistle; music. This afternoon . . . I walked for about an hour. It being Sunday meant less traffic and pedestrians— maybe down to the level of Fifth Avenue in pre-Christmas rush! So many kinds of people—almost all local since it is Sunday. Some lying down, some sitting. Still the vendors. Children, well-to-do on their Sunday stroll, poor at home on the street—they look so different. The women—many are so beautiful. Saw one couple assisting a very elderly man, probably father—old age is revered. Saw one young Indian father with big diaper bag, stroller, wife and baby still trying to get something else in the car. The Gateway across the street—mobs—altars with incense, an old Indian man stuffing his possessions behind stone in the monument, the park literally covered with people sitting and talking and smoking; pigeons and crows. Then the smell—*

most incredible—food roasting, incense, sewers, urine.
The senses are overwhelmed. (February 24, 1980)
There is no doubt I have arrived in Bombay. The AC is
off. It is steamy hot. Most seats are full. People are
snoring on the floor. Children are crying. The ticket
counters are ghost-like in their darkness and absence
of activity. (October 16, 1997) *That Madras train sta-*
tion will forever be etched in my mind when I think of
India. Each day, Friday and Sunday, I saw a man (dif-
ferent) lying—one in the hall, one on the platform-
wasted, horrible looking, obviously ill and neglected.
So sad. (October 26, 1993) *The taxi ride was as*
usual—absolutely harrowing. I did not know whether
to shut my eyes or whether to be braced for collision!
The funniest part was when the pleasant driver handed
me some pamphlets and said, "You read?" I said, "Yes,
I read." They are all on traffic safety—speeding, pass-
ing. When he stopped at another light, I said, "You
read English?" No, only Hindi! I said he should know
all about these things! (February 26, 1980)

A comparable taxi ride occurred in Delhi. Rebekah and
Stan Macaden were in Delhi in pursuit of her medical license
renewal. The driver recklessly drove at a breakneck speed; this
alarmed Rebekah. She noticed his calm demeanor and suggested speaking with the driver. Stan responded softly, "Don't say
anything. It will only become worse. Close your eyes."

At times, Rebekah's appearance attracted far too much
attention.

At 8 the security guards came to my house to say
that the neighbors were tearing down our new wall
saying it was too high! Can you believe it? I went out
to see and sure enough he was making rapid progress.

Not knowing what to do I called Mr. Parama Shivan.
We went to the neighborhood police station. What an
experience! The police brought the neighbor. This is a
small station, lots of police. A teenager was in the lock-
up, a dark cell, and was peering out between the bars.
I was a novelty, needless to say. (May 3, 1987) *I took*
Richard and Frankie to Carmel at 3. I had a little skin
showing in back between my choli and wrapped saree
that all the kids wanted to touch. (July 25, 1979)
Sunday afternoon I had agreed to go to Peniel Church
with Solomon and Grace. We had the Lord's Supper.
Solomon preached. It was hot but a good fellowship.
However, I had not been so stared at in a long time.
That still bugs me a bit. (October 7, 1981)

Streets teem with people, many of whom are begging.
Some of the beggars juggle balls and perform dances and
gymnastics; some have physical maladies; some have orange
hair and skin, symptoms of malnutrition, but all are common.
Occasionally the unexpected jarred the senses. *We saw some-*
thing I had never seen. A woman, probably in her 20's, was
sitting naked in a puddle in an intersection in a neighborhood
near the Bangalore Club—smiling happily and making the
namaste sign with her hands. (July 25, 1979)

Travel to and from the U.S., mission meetings, conferences,
and vacations during Rebekah's 35 years in India always took
advance planning, a large block of time, and much endurance.
Ever observant and meticulous in recording details, Rebekah
notes differences in terminals, airlines, security and customs
practices—even people within the airports themselves.

Anthony took me to the airport. I had a fine time
watching all that went on. Every time I go out there,
they have made further improvements especially in the

*departure areas—really uptown! I did realize how
coordinated you have to be to live here (a reminder of
a known fact). I went in the rest room—to hold up
pants legs and control all of the bags and parcels
around my neck and in the hands and accomplish the
primary mission all at the same time is quite a feat. I
watched a little man empty the Red Cross donation
box, sit on the floor and count and sort, relock it, light
a candle and seal the opening—all taking more than 15
minutes. There was the man in his well starched and
clean white dhoti carefully wrapped running to catch
the Delhi flight. But instead of the usual chapals or
sandals, he had on red socks up to mid-calf and regular black oxford shoes. You can tell that it was quite a
show!* (November 18, 1978) *I take back all I ever said
about Delhi. Delhi is so far above Madras and Bombay
and well organized. No hassle of X-raying the bags in
customs. Never accosted by anyone—only one taxi
driver and he moved off quickly. Signs to buses clearly
marked. The buses just outside—covered area. An air
conditioned free bus.* (June 14, 2000) *I did write in
Madras Friday night. I got the bus in Madras from one
airport to the other. Just check in took 1 hour 10 minutes, long lines, fighting in the lines. People that ride
the Singapore Madras sector are incredible—wearing
the cotton lungi (a piece of cloth just wrapped around),
carrying everything under the sun including huge baskets of vegetables. The immigration, customs, and
security took about 45 minutes. Nowhere like it! It was
almost 10 when I got all that done . . . When I finally
fell into my seat, where was I? Business class! I was
too tired to enjoy it.* (January 11, 1987)

Well, the journey. We took off from DFW reason-
ably on time. The spectacular part of that leg was that

we flew over New York City at 33,000 feet. It was bril-
liantly clear. I have never in all my life seen so many
lights just going on forever over a huge area. Even the
pilot seemed impressed. Frankfurt was COLD—well
below freezing. There was snow everywhere but run-
ways and roads were dry . . . My feet got warm only in
Bombay! We reached Bombay 6 hours late and I
missed my flight. (January 7, 1996) *The departure was*
typical. I felt sure there would be injuries just leaving
the terminal, riding the bus, climbing the steps. It was
the worst shoving and crowding ever—and seats were
reserved! (July 13, 1996)

The trip back was quite OK. Our flight to Frankfurt
pulled away from the gate at 3:20, the exact scheduled
time. It was 9 hours and 20 minutes . . . The flight to
Bombay was 7 1/2 hours . . . It was 1 AM. Immigration
and customs were no problem. Security was very tight.
After X-raying the hand luggage and going through the
usual security check, they then searched every bag and
frisked us as we got on the bus in Bombay. (June
17, 2001)

The trips crossing continents, oceans, time zones required
multiple days and several connections. A January 1977 trip had
stops in Chicago, Montreal, Zurich, and Bombay enroute to
Bangalore. Rebekah's first trip to Bangalore as a residential
missionary in 1974 provided quite the memorable event.

My plane from Singapore arrived 12 hours late. I
missed the flight to Bangalore. At Madras I was told
taxis unsafe. Train travel with recent strike was uncer-
tain, slow, occasionally violent. I was one of only 2 or
3 Anglos at the airport, the only woman alien. I had a
2 hour wait sitting in a bus at the airport, most of that

*time alone with people milling about in the hot night
outside. The airport closed down. Some men laid down
on the sidewalk to sleep. The bus filled with airline
employees started to town. At that hour (1 AM) streets
were dark. An occasional pedestrian or bicyclist could
be seen. The entire surroundings including the dark,
deserted hotel lobby could be best described as eerie.
Finally in my room after 3 AM, luxurious by Indian
standards. I was relieved but still frightened and
uncomfortable. I had in those past hours been as close
to panic as I have ever been in traveling. By 6 AM I
had begun to try to call Bangalore—succeeded only at
9. In airport and at travel agent and back at airport I
heard the same thing—"sit down and wait please,
madam." Patience becomes a necessity. I sat. Back at
hotel—big adjustment problem—cockroaches—huge
and fat! Two days later I finally got an evening flight to
Bangalore!*

*Love Field to San Francisco 3 hours 20 minutes
Japan Air Lines to Tokyo
Tokyo-Bangkok 6 hr 15 min
Bangkok-Singapore 1 hr 55 min
Singapore-Madras 3 hr 35 min*

Although travel to and from India continues to be arduous,
the Bangalore airport now has international service. Rebekah
can fly directly into and out of Bangalore with only one plane
change in Frankfurt. Surely that inaugural trip, no small ven-
ture, gave Rebekah a foretaste of future trips—her future.
Repeating the motto SIMPLY ADJUST, she persevered.
Despite the trials, the weather, the challenges, the terror,
Rebekah continued to come and go and live in Bangalore,
unwaveringly staying the course, being herself—Miss Naylor.

Miss Naylor

In her traveling suit as she departs
Dallas Love Field, 1963

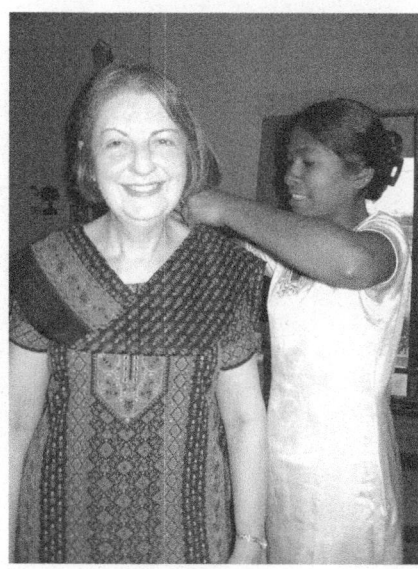

BBH employee
Madi pins a scarf
on Rebekah, who
always likes
"nice things."

Rebekah gives the "*namaste*" sign of respect to a group
of fellow believers in India.

Rebekah with her friend, Florence

Be joyful always; pray continually; give thanks in all circum-
stances, for this is God's will for you in Christ Jesus
(1 Thess. 5:16-18).

Miss Naylor

BBC is off the TV—no Superbowl . . . The concert was lovely.
The Rani was there . . . The Only Place has learned to cook
the steak just the way I like it, perfectly plain . . . The Otis man
was just here. I wonder if he knows what I think of his
"Contraption!" . . . My introverted personality makes being
among people more than difficult . . . The joke of the Mission
is my being anti-animal.

The doorbell's strident *bling, bling, bling* broke the
Sunday-afternoon nap. Rebekah—thinking the hospital needed
her—shook off sleep and ran to the door. A short, round man
dressed in a beautiful silk suit stood behind a gigantic bouquet
of roses. Who was he? Had she met him and forgotten his
name? "Doctor, Madam, I have traveled from Kashmir. I know
of you. I must see you, for I am a great admirer of yours and
desire that we become husband and wife. I have brought you
gifts." No, Dr. Naylor did not know the man. Awkwardly she
accepted the hand-embroidered shawl, roses, and nuts and
quickly dismissed him. Clearly he saw her not as a doctor but
as someone beyond that role—that of a single woman, Miss
Naylor.

Miss Naylor, a title that legally bespeaks Rebekah's marital
status, does not carry with it the stereotypical, tight-lipped,
stiff, reclusive spinster, for she is far from any of those
descriptors. Rather she is a complex woman with passions,
standards, characteristics, and concerns.

Nonetheless, Miss Naylor she is. "Why?" people ask. She's attractive, she's educated and socially polished, she's loving. She appreciates families and thrives in the nurture of her own as she always diligently works to keep the family bonds intact and strong. Friends see in Rebekah a wistfulness for a family and home of her own.

When asked about her social life in college and medical school years she is quick to answer: "Social life? Dating? No candidates and no time!" But the letters tell a different story. Dates she did have during her four years at Baylor and during medical school.

> *Sunday night was nice. I greatly enjoyed the musical. We stopped at Kips on the way back. He is quite a talker. Just after I talked to you tonight, he called. On the spur of the moment he asked me to go eat with him. I refused since I had already eaten and since my hair was wet. I can already tell he is going to be a bit pushy about this. My biggest protection is that I have a rigid working schedule. It makes me mad at myself that I wish for dates, and then I complain that one gets overly interested too fast!* (July 30, 1968)

She dated another physician for several years and eventually realized that the two were not suited for marriage. A college friend asked her to allow him to be her escort at a Baylor Homecoming weekend which she planned to attend. In India she was pursued by more than one man. Florence Charles spoke of a young professional who incessantly called Rebekah, appeared at her door, and sent her gifts. Eventually a colleague spoke to the man and asked him not to harass Rebekah. *My Kannada teacher and I had a big laugh when he told me that my old "suitor" married a month ago. That was definitely a relief.* (February 27, 1982) One gent today swoons when he sees her in restaurants and speaks of her beauty and dazzling grace. He eloquently describes her as a young woman and the stir she made in public places. Florence smiles each time the experience is repeated. Rebekah groans but is polite! *I had a hilarious letter from a patient, a young thin man I saw first last summer. His thumb hurt so he came [to the hospital]. Monday I got a letter—after just one day his thumb was so much better and "more flexible." He wanted to know me bet-ter—felt it would be "beneficial in a general way."* (August 10, 1978) A minister arrived in Bangalore with the intention of preaching in various churches and visiting the hospital. He relentlessly pursued a relationship with Rebekah. He sent her flowers and "mushy" cards and called nightly. His departure date he postponed several times so that he could be near Rebekah and work to advance his suit. When he did return to the U.S, the calls, letters, and cards continued despite Rebekah's honesty with him that the two of them had no future. Hannah Sinclair, the secretary in the administrator's office, is at all times quiet, reserved, and shy. Mention this episode in Rebekah's life, however, and Hannah's laughter erupts. Again, Rebekah had to ask for assistance in the curtail-ment of the man's dogged pursuit. One relationship held far more importance for her than did others. When this one did not continue, she experienced hurt and depression. The emo-tional upheaval in the aftermath gives a glimpse into a real person—not a automon, a robot—but a woman with feelings and dreams.

Arguments can be made that without a family Rebekah had more time to devote to her calling and her professional duties; thus she accomplished many extraordinary achievements. Arguments also can be made that because she had no family, she encountered more difficulties—loneliness, having to do the work alone, having no one to whom she could vent or confide. Both hold truth. The fact remains: she is Miss Naylor.

So who is this Miss Naylor? She is a woman with passions, one of which is sports. During mission orientation, she and Linda Garner regularly played golf and tennis, made 10-mile bicycle rides, and swam. In Bangalore, she and other missionaries held memberships in the Bangalore Club. In the early years, she frequently swam and played golf and tennis at the facility. Vacations at hotels or resorts with a pool offered great enjoyment, for she liked swimming and tanning! In her college and medical school years, she avidly followed both professional baseball and football and her school teams. This love couldn't be fed in India, however, until she had a television and BBC broadcasts aired in Bangalore.

My biggest current crisis is that Sunday and tonight I cannot get BBC. The Superbowl did not come on the TV. (February 1, 1994) *The BBC is working fine. I so enjoyed watching the opening ceremonies of the Olympics last night. I still can scarcely believe I could see it! Downhill skiing is at 3:30 today. The ice hockey game is 12:30 AM—needless to say I will not be watching!* (February 13, 1994)

Wade Garrett, while a seminary student, worked for Mrs. Naylor. He asked Rebekah to speak at his home church; she readily accepted the invitation. Wade, his fiancée, Laurie, and Rebekah made the drive. On the way home, she remarked, "The Dallas Cowboys are playing this afternoon." A bit later, she said, "The game is on the radio and is on right now." He did turn on the game, as he realized the meaning behind her comments. Wade, with a laugh, acknowledges that he never would imagined that she enjoyed football or even knew one thing about it! One of his recollections of Rebekah is her answering the door in a Baylor Bear sweatshirt!

Not unlike her passion for sports being unsuspected is that of needlework. She found stitching needlepoint a way to occupy herself on long trips, during boring or non-informative meetings, and at home. And loving beautiful pieces of art, the needlework satisfied that passion also. No doubt each stitch exactly matches the others and is perfect in size and execution. The framed pieces hang on her walls.

A third passion, music, provides relaxation and enjoyment, refreshment and entertainment. Whenever possible she attends and always has attended musicals, operas, concerts, recitals, oratorios. She had a stereo always—at Baylor, at Vanderbilt, and in India. Her car carries a sizable collection of often-used CD's.

Food ranks slightly above sports and music. Louis Carter observed that Rebekah never missed a meal during the time he volunteered at BBH. Some were interrupted; others were delayed but not missed. Letters record only one instance: *I have just finished dinner. I missed lunch which is definitely against my principles. But I missed it doing general surgery so I have no complaint.* (October 20, 1994) The recognition of the importance of food in her life only recently manifested itself. With her brow furrowed and her black eyes steadfast, she said, "I can't believe how important food was to me even as a young girl at Baylor. The descriptions of the meals go on and on. I do remember Mother in the kitchen frying chicken while I practiced my piano before school." Letters record the brownies, cakes, and cookies Mrs. Naylor brought to Rebekah during visits to Baylor and Vanderbilt and when Rebekah went home. The highlight of her day is dinner. Chocolate pie, lemon pie, steak, chicken—all her favorites. Her travel itinerary is constructed with meal times and time away from home and her work primary considerations. Even at UT Southwestern, she thinks of her teaching and surgery schedule before each day to determine when she can eat her lunch. And eat that tiny woman can do! *Incredible!* to use her term. Once she ate one half of a chicken at her favorite fried-chicken emporium in Delhi! If the meal occurs in a fine restaurant accompanied by silver, white cloths, soft live music, flowers, and attentive service, she's even happier.

Rebekah likes to surround herself with what she calls "nice things"—artwork, furnishings, and furniture; travel, restaurants, and hotels; jewelry and clothes. In India she bought fine woolen and silk hand-knotted rugs; inlaid, handcrafted chests and tables; hand-carved screens. She sought silver, brass, and ivory accent pieces for her home. Each one becomes a treasure for which she demonstrates a special affection yet never one of materialism or stemming from a desire to accumulate, but one of genuine appreciation and gratitude. As she describes each one, a rapturous expression transforms her countenance, for each is cherished.

She likes to entertain and does so with panache. *Mother, what is your sand tart recipe? Bring it, if you do not write it. I have just finished writing invitations to tea for December 24. Don't know whether anyone will come or not, but I am looking forward to doing something fancy for the first time.* (December 4, 1974)

Accounts of travel and the anticipation of those trips fill many letters. As quickly as she returned to Bangalore from the latest adventure, she began to plan the next one. Some were back to the U.S., others to places of interest such as Ceylon, London, Norway, Australia and New Zealand, the Holy Land, China, the Mediterranean. She explains that having something to which she could look forward helped her when times were trying and lonely. The planning and the anticipation occupied her thoughts and contributed positively to her well-being. One Christmas she flew to Indonesia for a holiday visit in the home of Bobbye and Jerry Rankin. Often, she took short trips to a resort in India, either alone or with another missionary. After a brief, three-day stay in a luxurious resort hotel with a landscaped pool area, air-conditioning that worked, and delicious meals served at linen-draped tables replete with silver, she wrote her parents: *You have trained me well. I am so grateful that we have the money and can enjoy these things.* These times of relaxation allowed Rebekah to sleep uninterrupted through an entire night, eat well-prepared and beautifully presented food, read a novel, write letters, sun herself at the pool, take walks, and even nap. Even back in the U.S. she has a calendar dotted with trips for at least six months in advance. Each one is eagerly anticipated and meticulously planned down to travel arrangements, mealtimes, and the mixture of alone time and speaking time.

"Nice things" includes jewelry and clothing. One year Dr. and Mrs. Naylor entrusted to a volunteer Rebekah's Christmas gift. The gift Rebekah describes as beautifully wrapped but the gold, leaf-shaped earrings are even more beautiful. The gold, a precious metal, symbolized the precious and special bond the three of them shared and the costliness the expression of the cherished gift. These earrings are the ones of choice for the dressiest of occasions and for those asking for the finest of sarees. Although relatively simple in design each piece of jewelry is unique, carefully selected, and treasured because of the sentiment enveloping it. One aspect of Rebekah's and Mrs. Naylor's relationship as daughter and mother revolves around clothes. *Mother loved to help me dress well and modeled it herself. She loved to bring me things to wear.* Mrs. Naylor sent frequent packages to Rebekah. She used volunteers and returning missionaries as couriers. Each visit she brought outfits to Rebekah. Christmas gifts today are smart woolen jackets, soft silk sweaters, chic blouses. Rebekah didn't often shop alone, whether in the U.S. or India, but relied on advice and companionship of her mother or of friends—Florence, Ragini

Macaden. Always, however, her attire was the latest in fashion, socially correct, tailored exquisitely. She does laugh, however, when she tells of her first flight to Bangalore. She wore a suit, hat, heels, and hose. She landed at the very beginning of the hot season. Her description? *I must have looked a sight!*

Clothes and her wearing of them produce more than one funny story. After her return to Fort Worth. Rebekah thought perhaps a shopping excursion might be a perfect pick-me-up. What woman doesn't want something new? Announcing she wanted to go shopping to buy something new, her mother countered with the remark that shopping wasn't necessary when so many suits were hanging in their collective closets. Admitting her mother correct, she still longed for a shopping excursion and a new garment. A furlough shopping purchase was not the usual basic black, brown, or beige of shoes and matching bag. The shoes and bag were multicolored patches of leather that were carefully sewn together but in an unmatched scheme. The red, blue, green, and yellow patches of her "crazy shoes" were not mirrored in the two shoes. Colleagues remarked on not only the bright colors but the design. Another shopping prize was a colorful dress. *I wore my new dress Friday. It was a sensation. Dr. Pulimood asked if I got that when I was home to which I said yes. He said that he was glad I could keep them up on USA styles and they had all best go buy some multicolored bright shirts!* (March 15, 1992) Not only did Rebekah want to be stylishly dressed, she wanted to please her mother. Planning a trip to Chicago, she wrote: *I realize, Mother, that you are worried about clothes. I think I can manage and look good. Shoes are OK; I have new ones. In the next few days I will go through what I have and see what needs lengthening. One difficulty conceivably could be freezing to death. It may be that you could mail my heavy coat to Chicago. Just meditate on that. Maybe a sweater and raincoat would be enough.* (August 28, 1976)

Rankin remembers that "she accompanied us to a distant village for a Christmas program. One of the village women mentioned having remembered her as coming to the program the year before. Rebekah was honored that she would be remembered until the lady said that she knew it was Rebekah because she was wearing the same saree she had worn the previous year, something even village women would notice!" Rebekah cringes when she is reminded of that and then laughs genuinely. She tells stories on herself, such as the day she realized her saree fabric was turned not only upside down but inside out! One day she walked into UT Southwestern and happened to look down at her shoes—one obviously worn, one sparkling new. She still laughs about that mishap, quipping, "At 4:30 AM, one doesn't see well!"

Laugh Rebekah does—often—at situations, at herself, in social settings, but only if she knows the people well. Carolyn White's characterization of Rebekah's sense of humor as being impish is apt. *The government and business are trying to help my cholesterol—no butter anywhere!* (October 30, 1991) The evening and morning televised news are part of her routine. The evening news she calls "news and nod time," referencing her long days and early sleepiness. Sister Flora recounted an April Fool prank she and another nurse instigated. New to BBH, new registered nurses, and properly respectful of those in the roles of surgeon and physician and intimidated by Dr. Naylor, they wanted to have a bit of fun. They deliberated several days. Knowing Rebekah's habits and routine well, they waited for her to complete rounds on the patient wards. At 8 they paged Rebekah. She ran to see the patient. Playing along with the joke, she acted as if that dummy created of bed linens and pillows on a gurney were a critical patient. Immediately she assumed the role of admitting physician. She gave orders as she rolled the gurney toward Intensive Care: "Oh, this patient is very sick. Get him to ICU. Start an IV." Other doctors were called. Orders were written, which the nurses carried out. Today Sister Flora relishes the story and the memory. She uses it as an example of Rebekah being a warm, fun-loving part of the community and her ability to welcome Flora and to draw others into this same community.

Rebekah fears and distrusts animals and elevators with a passion as great as the one she has for sports and music. *Linda got her puppy. She has been waiting months for a puppy . . . The man had said she could have her choice Sept 1. He brought them to show her Monday afternoon. Lo and behold he told her to go on and take one home. So! The puppy is 5 weeks old and is very tiny. I guess I will have to admit that she is cute . . . Needless to say the puppy is staying out of my house. It is a mission joke how anti-pets I am and everyone has wondered if I would tolerate the dog! Well, I will, since it is upstairs and Linda will care for it and discipline it well.* (August 14, 1974)

Although she could avoid the puppy, elevators were a different matter. When possible she climbs stairs. Unfortunately, in a government building during one of the interminable excursions for license renewal, she had no choice but to ride in the elevator. This ancient piece of machinery stopped. No rescuers appeared. The elevator could not be restarted. The only escape was to climb on a chair, crawl through the opening at the top of the car, and walk across a beam onto the floor above the elevator car. India's culture demands that men and women be separated. Certainly a man and a woman would never be alone in a room. A man is never to touch a woman and vice versa. As usual, she was the only woman in the car. No man could touch her. She could not touch the men in the elevator. She had to manage entirely unassisted escaping from this stopped carriage. Somehow she managed the ascent, the exit, and the crawl to safety.

Although she cringes with fear when she retells the elevator story, another causes her eyes to crinkle at the corners and sparkle bright. That little grin accompanied by giggles appear.

Did I ever tell you about the night I spent in the same hotel room with the men? It was 1981. We were to go to Hubli to unveil a plaque on a new church. A group of Indian pastors and two missionaries, a couple, were to go along; the husband was in charge of the arrangements. Saturday, my missionary friend appeared at the hospital while I was working. He had booked the wrong train; therefore, we would have to drive one way and take the train back to Bangalore. His wife could not go, not enough room in the car. The drive was 12 hours, made by five men and me. We arrived at 3:30 AM. The hotel at which we usually stayed had no place for us. One of the pastors thought he knew where the pastor lived. Unfortunately, Hubli is a railroad town. All the quarters look exactly alike. It was April and extremely hot; people were sleeping outside. At last the house was located. The wife said the pastor was at church in a meeting, but a child showed them the way to another hotel. This one had two rooms available. The driver would sleep in the car. The other missionary began to assign rooms—Rebekah, a pastor and he in one room, the others in the second room. I had never been in a room with a man. By now the time was 5:00 AM. I lay on the bed. The men were soon snoring. How was I going to manage this? I had to wrap my saree. The men awoke, one by one going into the bathroom for their morning baths. Indian baths mean lots of water is splashed on the floor. I walked into the bathroom carrying my toiletry bag and saree. No way could I wrap the saree with all that water on the floor. Finally, in desperation, I put on the choli and tied the big full-length petticoat around my waist,

picked up the saree and walked out of the bathroom.
After the church service, the same rigmarole was
repeated. That night, the missionary and I returned on
the train, using the original reservation. But, we were
in the same first class ladies' compartment using the
his wife's and my tickets! Now, why did I not think to
tell the men to stay in one room and I would take the
other? Why did I not say something? Who knows?"

And she giggled again. Her eyes darkened. Her brow furrowed as she questioned herself—another self-realization.

Why would this decisive, commanding leader of a woman
not say anything in this situation? That's part of who she is—a
person of many layers. True, she is a "no-nonsense administrator; she is strong-willed" as Jerry Rankin avers; she gives
"direct counsel" (her father's term) when she determines the
need. She has a clear vision and aims toward perfectly accomplishing that vision. She determines a goal, draws a plan of
action, and moves forward. As a surgeon and as an administrator, she performs decisively.

A certain innocence and lack of experience occasionally
surface. Perhaps her childhood contributes to that. *My world*
was mostly an adult world, especially after we moved to Fort
Worth when I was 8. (June 7, 2007). She made around-the-
world trips, went to Southern Baptist Conventions, and visited
family on the East Coast. But parties? Baby and bridal showers? Slumber parties? Choice and circumstances may contribute to the lack of experiences. *Last night we went to a baby*
shower. One girl had a new baby a week after we got here. It
was held (the shower) at the Lockards. That was my first baby
shower that I remembered. We played games. When we got in
the car I asked if you always did that at baby showers. Yes,
you do apparently. They laughed so hard and were so amazed
at my ignorance! (October 1973)

On the personal level, she shows other traits. She often refers to her compulsive and obsessive personality that causes her to want to accomplish far more domestic and work-related tasks than humanly possible in the time she allots to herself. *I have been mainly obsessed with work. Still so much clinical work.* (October 24, 1991) Leaving BBH for furlough produced anxiety. Did she see herself as indispensable or not in control if she is away? *I know it will not be run as I would nor will the quality be the same—all this upsets me. But my colleagues tell me to forget it and start again when I return.* (August 20, 1976) *Monday was quite busy. We remain very short of staff . . . I seem totally unable to control things. It is quite frustrating.* (February 8, 1994) Certainly she prefers proactive measures, with each one accomplished with prompt dispatch rather than inaction, yet she reminds herself about worry. *Doing nothing in the midst of crisis is very difficult . . . I know I should not be so worried about the bigger issues. But that is hard!* (February 22, 1998)

Since she is a perfectionist, Rebekah's patience erodes when she deems outcomes unsatisfactory. Of course, the standards she sets often are beyond the usual. Conversely, because of her standards, she does what is often the impossible. *I tried so hard not to act upset but I so want things to be right and have so much trouble when people say they will do something and don't.* (April 26, 1992) Being a perfectionist produces embarrassment unnecessarily. In India, Rebekah and the Williamses attended the wedding of the son of her dear friend Primrose. Primrose asked Rebekah to say a few words before the reception began.

The reception was a formal dinner—seated with a program and a stage on which the bride and groom and their parents sat. The tables were close together. I walked between two tables and tipped a chair up on its front two legs. When I let it down, I kept walking. The

319

saree became totally undone, unpleated in the center
front. I grabbed the fabric, stuffed it in the center, said
my words and returned to my chair. Sarah asked,
"What happened?" When I told her, she lightly replied,
"You'll get to know how it was. It's on the video. You
need to go fix it."
  "I'm not getting up."
  "You have to go greet the bride and groom."
  "I am NOT getting up."
  Sarah tried to persuade me. Finally Sarah looked
at me. As if she were speaking to a child, she com-
manded, "We are going out! Now!"
  She took me by the hand and we went out to wrap
the saree. Rebekah describes the situation as mortify-
ing but realizes that others probably did not. Some
probably were unaware of the mishap.

One trait—shyness—has stayed with her from childhood.
Today Rebekah labels herself *introverted* and even jokes about
that. *I rushed home after work (rounds and X-rays) threw on a*
saree and raced across town to eat dinner with Mr.
Manoharan and his family . . . Mercifully I could leave after
eating. They were so kind and gracious. It was just so hard for
conversation. I was my effervescent self! (August 5, 1985)
Being with people whom she does not know places a strain on
her that requires several days to smooth. *Mondays at work*
after a weekend conference are especially hard. I need time to
recover from the effort and stress. Although she is a willing
and dynamic speaker at churches for mission emphases and in
conferences relating to her educational role and research, inter-
acting in small groups as participant rather than leader and in
social occasions as guest taxes her. She prefers to remain
unobtrusive, finds conversation difficult, and speaks rarely. Yet
she yearns for friends and parties, since she recognizes the
need of community and diversion from the work and home

routine. *Dinner was wonderful. I so needed to be out of the house and with friends.* (February 4, 2007)

    Rebekah is a realist. She recognizes who she is. She speaks candidly about the facets of her personality as well as about her life's choices and decisions. Incontestably work requirements and personality circumscribe Rebekah's lifestyle. Her role as daughter exerts a strong influence too. Attending to her mother's care determines many activities. Why else would she leave India? Yet, she does this willingly, devotedly, lovingly. She berates herself should she see herself as impatient or not present at all times. What a conundrum! She knows she must have outlets, needs the work, can contribute positively to the world, yet she wants to stay beside her mother. What a constant pull! To be a caregiver, an only daughter, and a physician places an unusual strain on Rebekah. Yet she moves ever forward; she reassures her mother that she has chosen and desires to be in this role. As the years advance, Rebekah and her mother continue their strong mother-daughter relationship that is more like that of best of friends and partners. They are confidantes. They discuss every situation at length before they make a decision. They rejoice in each other's successes. They encourage. They console.

    Although Rebekah describes herself as *very healthy*, she's had her own brushes with being a patient. In her first term at Baptist Hospital, she contracted meningitis. Effecting a compromise with her physician, she agreed to stay with a missionary couple rather than being an in-patient. Restless to resume her duties, she returned to work only to incur a relapse. This was a painful reminder that she needed to follow her doctor's instruction and that recovery from some maladies cannot be rushed. Mrs. Naylor says those weeks were difficult. "My baby girl was on the other side of the world, sick, without telephone and I was here." Total recovery ensued and outside of colds and allergy attacks, Rebekah remained well. A persistent, aggravating thumb pain eventually prompted Rebekah to seek advice from a hand specialist in the U.S. and in India. The calcium deposit was scraped out in a surgical procedure, after which she sported a cast for three weeks. In time she regained the complete use of the thumb.

Whereas losing the ability to use her thumb frightened her—after all, surgeons need thumbs to use their equipment— nothing shocked, turned her world upside down, and changed her as did the diagnosis of breast cancer. Surgery is black and white; the unknown is not. Not being one who waits patiently, the intervals between the various tests and receiving the results stretched her. Thinking she knew what she would do should this situation ever arise, she had to rethink her choices. Rebekah chose a lumpectomy; the procedure required less recovery time than a mastectomy. The surgeon, Dr. Marilyn Leitch, admitted Rebekah to the hospital. This was another new experience—that of being an in-patient, not only in surgery but in recovery. Amazed at the effects of anesthesia, she reported to her Sunday School classmates that she learned much. She had always talked to patients immediately after surgery but now knows they heard nothing! The radiation treatments were scheduled early morning each day to reduce time away from home and work. Once again, she thought not of herself but of her mother's needs. Cancer free, Rebekah speaks as a survivor, a learner. *One step at a time—that's what I learned when I had cancer. A test. Wait. Results. Wait. Decisions. Wait. Treatment. Wait.* Her advice to others rings with the voice of that of patient, physician, believer.

Her standards remain uncompromised. Just as she always followed the law and the Indian justice system, she follows her personal convictions. She never fails to tell people the importance of her relationship to Jesus. Bible study, a practice her parents began in the home, continues. Those quiet times she counts critical to her life and growth. She is honest. She does not participate in any activity that might affect her witness as a Christian—a believer—nor any she interprets as incorrect for her. Rebekah does not drink alcoholic beverages and included that standard for the operation of BBH. Sometimes her outspokenness complicates the situation. A colleague tells of an Indian formal dinner to which many guests were invited. She and Rebekah were also guests. As beverages were poured, rather than quietly refuse, Rebekah made her customary comment, as she clearly spoke: "Oh, no. I do not drink alcohol." The host immediately stopped; serving the meal ceased. After an interminable wait leaving guests wondering why dinner was not served, Rebekah was poured juice which the host had sent someone to purchase! The dinner continued. A group of visiting doctors stayed in the guest quarters at the hospital compound. Their last night, they drank beer with their dinner. The same day a patient was discovered to be drinking whiskey which her husband smuggled to her. *So, we've had beer in the guest house and whiskey in the wards! What to do!!!* On subsequent visits, the beer-drinking doctors, at Rebekah's request, stayed in Bangalore hotels. Standing for her convictions, remaining true to them, and speaking boldly as needed mark Rebekah as a strong, consistent witness.

Enigmatically, Rebekah is shy yet loves parties and being a hostess. She is introverted yet places herself in speaking situations and has a career that demands she appear publicly and strongly asserts her beliefs. She is a compulsive perfectionist who obsesses over time schedules and deadlines, yet she lived in India, a country that runs on its own schedule. She does not like animals other than a soft, white, stuffed bunny from her childhood but lived in an area overpopulated with critters. Admittedly a picky eater who prefers first-class service, food, and ambience, she thrived in India. She always prefers a driver, but she has memberships to the art museums and season tickets to the symphony, both of which place her out in public and more often than not alone, driving herself. She wants "to be taken care of" but exhibits fierce independence and assumes total control. She goes so far as to give explicit instructions concerning driving route and maneuvers to the driver.

A woman of contrasts? Maybe. A woman of contradictions? *Hmmm.* A complex woman? Definitely. A real woman? Decidedly. She laughs. She cries. She has fears. She has courage. In some respects personal changes have occurred; certainly the world and her situations have changed. Her commitment has not changed. She remains Miss Naylor, a multi-layered woman of passions and strong character.

Epilogue

Receiving Distinguished Alumni Award from Southwestern
Baptist Theological Seminary, 1994

Rebekah stands outside Petro Church.

Jesus Christ is the same yesterday and today and forever
(Heb. 13:8).

Epilogue

What now? To be continued! I'm embarking on a book tour!

Rebekah's life continues as God is perfecting the work He began in her. The venue may have changed and the job description may be new, but the call from God remains—"*Follow me.*" Rebekah's life seems to be segmented: IMB, UT Southwestern, daughter, Rebekah.

For the IMB, Rebekah is chairing the Medical Missions Mobilization Summit, a July 2008 gathering in Richmond of all health personnel and volunteers to plan not only medical strategies but also evangelism strategies. Although she officially will retire from the IMB in January 2009, she will continue in some capacity to maintain her long relationship with the IMB, BBH, and the church-planting efforts in Karnataka.

The position at UT Southwestern offers challenges and satisfaction. Although she is part-time faculty, her responsibilities bespeak her unique ability to undertake multiple positions and overachieve in each one. She best tells the story not only of the affirmations but also her current work.

As I returned to the USA in 2002, entered the world of academic surgery at UT Southwestern Medical Center, and survived a very difficult year of reentry, I knew that God had directed in all of these changes. Though I miss India, God has been so good to affirm over and over that I am doing what He wants me to do for now. One way in which this has been affirmed is the collection of awards for my role in teaching. The

*introduction to this season of awards came in 2003
with honors based on my career up until that time.
Paschal High School in Fort Worth in April 2003
inducted me into the Panther Hall of Honor. Their
recognition read as follows: "First woman to graduate
from surgical residency program at UT Southwestern.
As medical missionary in India she helped develop
Bangalore Baptist Hospital, then served as administrator and surgeon." A few weeks later the Christian
Medical and Dental Association awarded me the
Missionary of the Year Award for 2003 at their meeting
in the mountains of upstate New York, recognizing my
years of work in Bangalore both in medical work and
church planting work. I was nominated for this award
by my friend and colleague Louis Carter.*

*The biggest event in the Southwestern Surgery
Department each year is the graduation dinner for the
fifth-year chief residents in June. In 2003 I did not
attend. I really was not ready for venturing into this
daunting social world of my profession nor did I fully
realize what a major event it was. But 2004 changed
that forever!!! Weeks before the June event, some of the
chief residents came to me and said that I must come to
the dinner. They knew that I was not up to the freeway
driving and getting home in the wee hours alone, so
they told me that they had hired a limousine service to
take me home afterwards!! Just a few days before the
dinner, one of them invited me to sit at his table at dinner with his wife and parents. The big night arrived. I
was enjoying a fine dinner and the early part of the
awards program. After the department awards and the
presentations of certificates by the chairman, the graduating residents took over. Among their presentations
was a special award. They called me forward and read*

a very lengthy citation. They described me as a "medical pioneer." They recognized my clinical work in India and my work there in education including accredited residency training programs, a chaplaincy training program, and the School of Nursing. They said that my lifelong dedication to others was now evident in my care for my mother. They presented a beautiful black wooden arm chair complete with the UT emblem and a plaque and said that the chair was to thank me and recognize me as their teacher, mentor and friend. I was really stunned. When the evening finally ended, I was escorted out to a waiting Town Car with a uniformed chauffeur. The chair was loaded in the trunk. When we finally reached home at midnight, the driver almost forgot the chair. Then he said, "I am used to carrying people and not furniture." A year later in 2005 at the same occasion, I received from the Department of Surgery a "Special Recognition for Outstanding Achievement in Student Teaching 2005." This was mainly based on student evaluations of my teaching during their 3rd year surgery clerkship during the 2004-5 academic year. In 2006 I was invited to attend the university-wide function in the Faculty Club on Excellence in Education Day. The Class of 2007 voted for me to receive the Core Clerkship Teaching Award 2005-6. This was recognition for teaching 3rd year students in that academic year. The Excellence in Education awards reception in 2007 occurred in October. I was invited to come. I already knew that the second-year students in 2006-7 (class of 2009) had named me as an Outstanding Teacher. That plaque was to be presented at the reception. I arrived soon after 5 p.m. in the faculty club. The administrative assistant to the dean (I did not know her) greeted me and said I was one of the honored guests. I wondered what that

meant and supposed that it was that 2nd year award.
The associate dean, Dr. Sue Cox, whom I do know,
came up to me and said that she was so excited for me.
Noting my blank look, she said, "Oh, do you not
know?" No, I did not!!! Faculty, students and adminis-
tration had awarded me the Distinguished Clinical
Science Educator Award for 2006-7 for the entire uni-
versity. This was just beyond belief. A short-tenured,
part-time faculty member!

I know that God has given me gifts. I have tried to
use these to honor Him. I work hard but yet see all this
as such incredible privileges. I am so humbled that all
this could happen to me. How good God is to bless me
and encourage me and to give these affirmations that I
am in the place He has chosen for me just now.

Amidst racking up awards, Rebekah has traveled exten-
sively on speaking engagements, found time to enjoy the Fort
Worth Symphony, and taken part in a dinner group of church
friends. Primarily she dotes on her aged mother, who turned 99
on March 14, 2008. Rebekah vowed to take care of her mother
so that Mrs. Naylor would never have to leave her own home.
She manages caregivers and organizes the household under the
constant watch of her sharp-eyed mother. Together they plan
and hostess parties. Together they plan Rebekah's wardrobe
and select her "speaking suits." Together they plan the events
and menus for the day and for parties. That relationship they
forged in Rebekah's childhood grows stronger.

Both Mrs. Naylor and Rebekah anticipate with excitement
and joy holidays, family reunions each July, visits from
Rebekah's brothers, Bob and Dick, and their wives, as well as
visits from the grandchildren and great-grandchildren, nieces,
and nephews.

So what now? In India, planning trips allowed something to which she could look forward; these plans took Rebekah through rough and challenging times. She's teaching, she's speaking, and, yes, even now she's planning a series of travel engagements—a book tour! Yet, the call remains clarion. She will listen. She will be the faithful Rebekah Ann Naylor, M.D., missionary surgeon in changing times in a changing world.

Lord, you establish peace for us; all that we have accomplished you have done for us.
(Isa. 26:12).

So what now? In India, planning trips allowed something to which she could look forward; these plans took Rebekah through rough and challenging times. She's teaching, she's speaking, and yes, even now she's planning a series of travel engagements—a book tour! Yet, the call remains clarion. She will listen. She will be the faithful Rebekah Ann Naylor, M.D., missionary surgeon in changing times in a changing world.

Lord, you establish peace for us; all that we have accomplished you have done for us.
(Isa. 26:12)

Thus the epilogue written February 2008 ends. Rebekah's story, however, does not. The call remains clear, and she obeys. Listen as Rebekah herself tells of these twelve ensuing years.

My entire working life has been focused in missions and my relationship to the IMB. Even in the years after returning from India and teaching at the medical school, I continued to work non-residentially alongside Indian pastors and evangelists in the church planting efforts. In January 2009, however, my official appointment with the IMB concluded after 35 years and 10 months. The IMB retirement celebration in Richmond occurred the summer of 2009. Friends since orientation, Barbara and Harry Bush were also retiring. Dick and Nancy came to Richmond for the retirement service, and, of course, other IMB friends and colleagues whom I had known for years attended. I struggled that week as I thought I was losing my missionary identity. That turned out not to be the case – the identity was firmly in place – but relationships and responsibilities changed. Bangalore Baptist Hospital noted the milestone for me, but they said they did not need to have a "sending off" since they did not see me as IMB but as one of the BBH family and anticipated a continued, ongoing, close relationship.

January of 2010 brought another professional milestone. I had been on the clinical faculty in the department of surgery at University of Texas Southwestern Medical School since my return from India in 2002. I loved the job and was constantly learning and having many opportunities with students and faculty. In 2009 I was privileged to receive national recognition as an outstanding teacher of surgery, the award presented by the Association for Surgical Education.

In 2009 I worked with medical missionary colleagues at the IMB to write a job description for a person to lead the medical mission effort worldwide for the IMB. I never thought this position had anything to do with me but was important for the medical missions enterprise about which I was passionate. The fall of 2009 I was approached by Baptist Global Response, our Southern Baptist international relief and development agency, about this job. BGR, as a chief partner of the IMB, administered all of the human needs ministries including healthcare. After weeks of prayer and conversations, I realized that God was leading me to do this work in the next season of life. January 13, 2010, I walked out of an operating room for the *last time after 42 years. I loved surgery. I loved teaching. But God had a new direction; therefore, I retired from the medical school.*

My relationship with the medical school, nonetheless, has continued as volunteer clinical faculty. I teach professionalism and ethics to third-year medical students during their surgical rotation. Though not making overt Christian statements in the classroom, I tell the students my professional background. Inevitably, my values come through as I teach. Also I am involved in the global health program of the school. The opportunity for senior students to spend a month in Bangalore continues; I direct this partnership.

In January 2010 I became the Global Healthcare Consultant, representing healthcare missions to Southern Baptists in the USA and to IMB personnel all over the world. The position remained with BGR until May, 2019, when I again became an IMB employee. This job has included leading medical missions conferences, speaking in churches and on college campuses, traveling overseas to consult on healthcare strategies, training and equipping healthcare professionals to serve on mission for Jesus and mobilizing those whom God is directing to go.

Doing this work has entailed a huge amount of travel which becomes wearing but is also stimulating. I have met many remarkable people. I have been privileged to see many young professionals respond to God's call and go overseas to serve. I now have relationships with younger generations of missionaries in many parts of the world.

Healthcare has become increasingly strategic in reaching our world for Jesus. More and more peoples and places are inaccessible to missionaries through the usual pathways. Healthcare is one of the only ways to reach these peoples. Healthcare professionals are unique in that they can cross every geographic barrier, every cultural barrier, every economic barrier and, best of all, they can engage in a spiritual conversation in minutes.

Those on both sides of the world who know me well know that my heart remains with BBH and the people there. Since official retirement, I have continued to travel to India, usually twice each year. My frequent visits have allowed me to form friendships with younger leaders and staff. Even as peers have retired, I remain strongly connected. Each time when I arrive in Bangalore (now a world-class airport nothing like what I knew when I lived there) and start into town, I feel that I have come home. I feel that I belong. I cannot adequately express the gratitude I feel that I have had the health and money to go, that I am wanted, and that I have dearest friends there.

The city has continued to grow incredibly to over 11 million population in 2020. The infrastructure has not been able to keep up. Traffic is absolutely mind-boggling and to go anywhere takes forever. The density of people, the noise of honking horns, the smells, the bright colors, and the scenes of tragedy assail the senses even more than ever. Bangalore is the technology capital of Asia. High rise buildings appear everywhere through the metropolis. Five-star hotels are numerous. Shopping malls dot the city. Change over these 46 years is amazing.

The hospital is even more remarkable in its changes. Today BBH has 340 beds and is staffed by well over 100 doctors in all major specialties and sub-specialties. In its clinics and in the extensive rural and urban outreach work, BBH treats almost 400,000 patients in a year. Expansion of facilities continues with an additional 100 beds under construction at the time of this writing. In 2011 BBH was the first mission hospital in India to achieve accreditation. The hospital has received multiple national awards for teaching, nursing, management, and patient care. BBH touches many hospitals across India with training and teaching.

BBH is an academic center. Post-graduate medical education (residency training and fellowships) are now accredited in eleven departments. Multiple allied health training programs offer diplomas and degrees. The School of Nursing added a new course in 2011, the Bachelors of Science in Nursing. The two nursing programs run parallel under the umbrella of the Institute of Nursing.

In the midst of all this activity, the spiritual ministry of the hospital has remained strong and a priority. The climate of increasing persecution in India has required some adjustments in methods but no pulling back from commitment to present the person of Jesus.

In January, 2019, the hospital honored me by naming the Institute of Nursing in my honor at a lovely function at the time of the hospital's anniversary. The celebration included a dinner in my honor attended by about fifty friends and retired colleagues.

When I visit BBH, my role is chiefly that of an encourager. I do engage in the spiritual ministry by leading department Bible studies as well as speaking in chapel services and retreats. Sometimes I help with administrative projects if administrators request something specific. I am careful not to give opinions unless specifically asked to do so. The many personal conversations and the social evenings over dinner with dear friends are the highlights of every visit. I always come back feeling renewed and anticipating the next visit.

In 2016 I was chosen by the American College of Surgeons, the premier surgical organization in America, to receive the annual Surgical Humanitarian Award, recognizing my surgical career, especially in India. The award was presented at a black-tie dinner in Washington, D. C., during the annual Clinical Congress. In a session of the Congress, I presented my story of years in India. This dinner and award is one of the most memorable experiences of my entire life. Dr. and Mrs. Michael Dean (my pastor), Mr. and Mrs. Donnie Smith, and Mrs. Peggy Leitch came from Fort Worth to share this incredible time. Consequent to this award, opportunities to be visiting professor of surgery at Southern Illinois University and the University of Michigan ensued.

Although I am a retired surgeon, this award affirmed my choice of profession and my place among health-care professionals as well as missionaries.

In addition to visits to Bangalore and BBH, I participate in academic, mission, health, and church activities. One is Mercy Clinic, Fort Worth. When I came back from India to my Fort Worth home church, Travis Avenue Baptist Church, I saw that the demographics around the church had changed. Most of the people are of a low socioeconomic group and Hispanic. Many do not have access to healthcare. Based on my experience overseas, I know that meeting physical needs and sharing the Gospel go hand in hand. So I began to talk to others about the possibility of our church beginning a free clinic to help the people of our community and to reach them with the Good News of Jesus.

In January 2011, a group of Travis members gathered for our first vision meeting. After much prayer, we agreed that we should move forward with a clinic. After 26 months of planning, renovation of an old house on church property, and raising some funds, the Mercy Clinic of Fort Worth saw its first patients March 28, 2013. Staffed by volunteers and free to patients, the clinic now has about 2000 patient visits per year during three clinic sessions per week. Property has been obtained, and a vision of a new facility is clear. The clinic has had great impact, transforming lives and families. My role is to serve as Chair of the Board *of Directors, but I also lend administrative help in the clinic and assist in the fund- raising efforts.*

Since spring, 2017, I have annually taught a course entitled "Human Needs Ministries and Church Planting" in the missions department at Southwestern Baptist Theological Seminary. Students in the class anticipate a ministry overseas or in churches here in the USA. This practical course enables the students to explore the biblical mandate to meet needs which they integrate with making disciples and starting churches.

Also, I have been designated permanent missionary-in-residence on the SWBTS campus. In this capacity, I maintain an on-campus office and am available to visit with students about missions and God's direction in their lives.

In these post-IMB retirement years, I have taught three-hour credit courses on India at Dallas Baptist University and Oklahoma Baptist University. Currently I am one of the lecturers for the course "Medical Missions and the Gospel" at Baylor University. Oklahoma Baptist University presented me with an honorary Doctor of Missiology in February 2018.

My college alma mater, Baylor University, recognized me as a Distinguished Alumna, January 2010. Dick and Nancy and friends celebrated this occasion with me at a formal dinner on the beautiful Waco campus. In 2014, fifty years after my graduation, I attended the induction into the Baylor Heritage Club. My fiftieth reunion of my medical school class at Vanderbilt University occurred October 2018. I had not been to any function nor seen classmates in fifty years. The two days were remarkable and wonderful. The university planned beautiful and meaningful events, but most amazing to me was that I was able to take up conversations and relationships easily after fifty years. My one close friend in the class, Godela Iverson and her husband, also attended and made the occasion comfortable for me. Several in my class told me: "You went and did exactly what you said you were going to do." I am so grateful for excellent education and institutions that molded me into a competent Christian professional.

Soon after my story was published in 2008, Mother and I began planning her 100th birthday party for March 2009. I was thrilled I could create and host this celebration for her. She enjoyed it so much. The entire family except one grandchild gathered for the Saturday afternoon party. Dressed in her finest, Mother sat enthroned in the living room. The day before, Debrah, her hairdresser for years, styled Mother's silver hair. Mother greeted everyone and mostly remembered everyone. The dining table including the cake was lovely. Both grandsons stood outside greeting and receiving every guest. For the occasion, Dick had worked for years to prepare a book entitled Merger of the Lines – Naylor-Dalton. Both family lines were traced and recorded and pictures of places and graves and events were included. On the morning of the party, Dick made a formal (lawyerly) presentation of the gift to Mother in the presence of the whole family and distributed copies to each child and grandchild. In the days and months following, she often read the book, and we recounted the events of her birthday celebration. That same year, she wrote her Christmas cards herself and mentioned the party with the exact number of persons who attended!

In January 2010 I anticipated another trip to India. For all the years saying goodbye to Mother and Daddy was always awful for me. I always cried, and cried, and cried. That time was no exception. As it turned out, the farewell was indeed goodbye, goodbye forever. By the time my plane landed in early morning about 28 hours later in Bangalore, Dick called to tell me that Mother was in the hospital, bleeding from her stomach. I left Bangalore that night to return home. Late the afternoon of Friday, January 29, I went straight to the Fort Worth hospital. Mother had been sleeping most of the day. She did wake up and know that I was there, and we talked a little. Saturday I was in the hospital with her all day, most of the time alone except for one of her faithful caregivers as Dick had gone back home. Late that evening, Mother woke up and told me that after my travel I needed to go home and sleep. She was absolutely insistent. I obeyed, leaving around 9. The phone rang just after midnight. Carol, the caregiver with Mother, told me to come immediately. That was all she said. When I reached Mother's hospital room minutes later, she was already gone – in fact, when Carol called me Mother was gone. She had arrived in heaven in the wee hours of Sunday morning January 31, 2010. I regretted that I had left her that night. But she was so ready to "go home" as she often told me.

Mother was my best friend. For almost seven decades she had cared for me, loved me, led me in walking in faith, and, most of all, prayed for me. I had cared for her for almost eight years during which our relationship became even closer. I looked forward to coming home, whether from a short outing with friends, or a day at work, or a trip to see her and give her all of the details. Now I had no one at home with whom I could share. But most of all, I lost my chief prayer supporter and encourager. I shall forever miss her.

As of this writing, both of my brothers, in their later 80's, remain well and active.

In the context of my church, and especially the ladies' Sunday School class, I have found fellowship and friendships. In recent years, I have been teaching the ladies' class of which I have been a member since coming back from India. These ladies faithfully encourage me and pray for me and what I do. They have celebrated with me big occasions like my 70th birthday. I am immeasurably grateful for the countless privileges I enjoy and for caring friends on both sides of the world.

Even when I am old and gray
do not forsake me, O God,
Till I declare your power to the next generation,
your might to all who are to come.
(Psa. 71:18)

Appendices

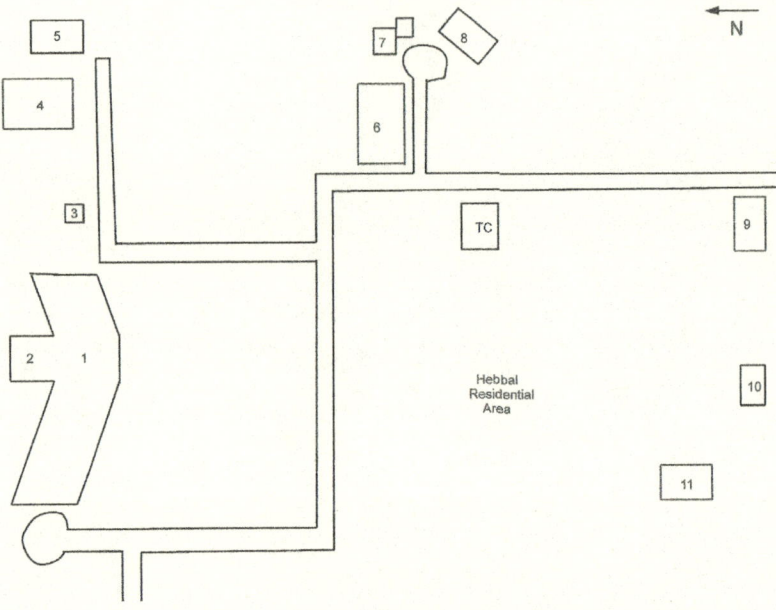

Diagram of Bangalore Baptist Hospital in 1980

1. BBH
2. Chapel Wing
3. Generator
4. Services Building
5. Nutrition Rehabilitation Center
6. Staff Hostel
7. Park Place Duplex (Naylor's home)
8. Quarry View Quarters (missionary housing)

9. Missionary Housing
10. Missionary Housing
11. Student Center
TC Tennis Court

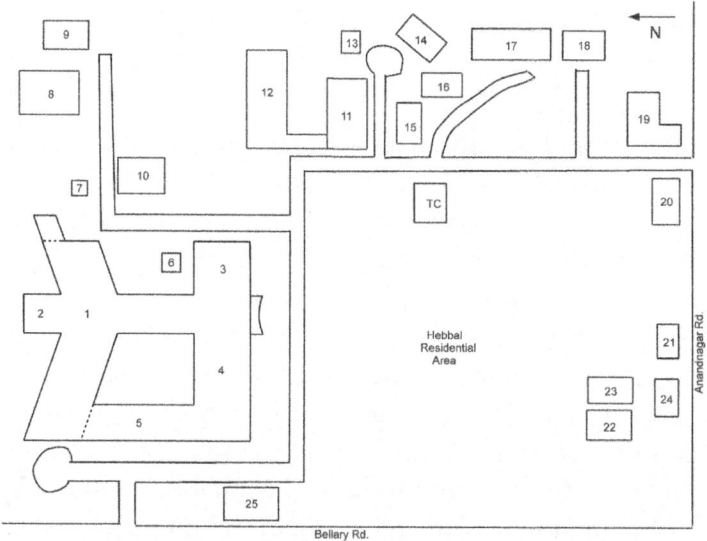

Diagram of Bangalore Baptist Hospital Today

1. BBH
2. Chapel Wing
3. Private Patient Wing
4. Outpatient Clinic
5. Outpatient Registration and Medical Records
6. Oxygen/suction
7. Generator
8. Services Building
9. Maintenance
10. Dining Room and Kitchen
11. Staff Hostel
12. Nursing School Hostel
13. Park Place duplex
14. Quarry View housing (staff housing)
15. Mays Quarters (staff housing)
16. Court View (staff housing)
17. Richmond Quarters
18. Staff housing
19. Men's hostel
20. IMB Office
21. IBS Office
22. Rebekah Ann Naylor School of Nursing
23. School of Nursing
24. Hope Baptist Church
25. CT Scan Center
TC Tennis Court

Appendix 1
Speech at Nursing School Groundbreaking

In the Bible Proverbs 16:3 instructs us like this: *Commit thy works unto the Lord and thy plans shall succeed.*

This has been our way in our hospital. God has kept His promise by enabling the work to go forward.

We are here today to begin the phase of construction of the School of Nursing. This occasion is a step toward reality of a dream expressed by the Foreign Mission Board and its first representatives in Bangalore in 1966. The property was obtained for a hospital and a nursing school. For the past five years, even as funds were raised for hospital expansion, this vision of a nursing school and regional training center was placed before donors in the USA and friends in India. Collection of money at first began slowly.

As we prayed, God affirmed in various ways that our direction was right. In 1994 we began very active efforts to raise funds for the project. Gifts began coming from many people. God brought new friends to us who began to support the hospital actively.

Our friends in USA, represented by Samaritan Medical Outreach Ministries, Inc., increased its efforts on our behalf. Early this year they contacted almost 400 people resulting in gifts and pledges totally approximately $35,000. Their efforts are continuing. I wish to read for you greetings from them:

June 15, 1995

Dear Friends:

The Directors of Samaritan Medical Outreach Ministries wish to convey congratulations to the staff and friends of Bangalore Baptist Hospital at the time of the groundbreaking ceremony for the nursing school. We pledge our prayers and continued support for the growth and expansion of the regional training centre. We know that this represents a major step in on going development of the institution as you serve people of Bangalore in South India. We are with you in spirit and share your vision and commitment to see the entire project completed.

Yours faithfully,

Dr. Terrell Mays
President

Mr. John Thomas
Vice President

Dr. Sam Law
Secretary/Treasurer

Mrs. JoAnne McCullough
Mr. John Seelig
Mr. Norman Roberts

Then in April we received the totally unexpected news that Mrs. Ruth Ray Hunt had given $250,000 toward the nursing school. Mrs. Hunt in Dallas, Texas, already has supported our capital projects in a big way. She was aware of our plans but no requests for money had been made. Indeed God worked in her, stirring her interest and concern, and thus this money came.

Many individuals, churches, and organizations in the States have contributed over $450,000 toward construction and endowment fund for scholarships. The Foreign Mission Board has given us this fine training centre building and extensive property for the school. Friends here in India and staff have contributed money and much time and effort for this project. People actually in many parts of the world have prayed. We commit ourselves today to be good stewards of God's gifts.

Appendix 2
Glossary

A and P—a required science course, anatomy and physiology

AC—air-conditioner

auto—three-wheeled vehicle in India

BBH—Bangalore Baptist Hospital

beriyani—rice with either a meat (mutton or chicken) or only vegetables or meat cooked in it and spices

bundh—cessation of all transportation

bunk—petrol station

census—number of inpatients in the hospital

chappati—round, flat bread cooked on a griddle

choli—short-sleeved, midriff length blouse for the saree

CMC—Christian Medical College, Vellore, India

Dhal—dried lentil stew

dust bins—trash containers

EMFI—Evangelical Medical Fellowship of India

fête—fund-raising event that features sale of foods, crafts, and other goods; entertainment and amusement similar to carnival rides and game booths

FMB—Foreign Mission Board (later, International Mission Board)

garlanded—flower garlands draped over the honoree

geyser—water heater

ghee—lard or butter

IBS—India Baptist Society, a legal entity

ICU—Intensive Care Unit

IMB—International Mission Board

jumble sale—garage sale

KBSS—Karnataka Baptist Sabhegala Samaikya (fellowship of churches)

KG—kilogram

KM—kilometer; 1 km equals .6 mile

Maharaja—princely ruler

Maharani—sister of the Maharaja

naan—Indian round, flat, leavened bread that resembles a flour tortilla

OPD—Out Patient Department

operation theatre—surgery

OT—Operation Theatre

PC—private-paying patient

paediatrics—pediatrics

petrol—gasoline

physiotherapy—physical therapy

post-op—post-operative, after surgery

pre-op—pre-operative, before surgery

R.N.—registered nurse

Richmond, Virginia — location of the International Mission Board headquarters

salwar kameez — woman's garment in India; loose, flowing tunic top worn over pleated, baggy topped trousers, accompanied by a long scarf

samosa — a small, triangular pastry filled with spiced meat or vegetables and fried in *ghee* or oil

saree — traditional dress for women in India — six yards of fabric wrapped around the waist and draped over one shoulder

SBC — Southern Baptist Convention

scans — X-rays or ultrasound imaging

Southwestern Baptist Theological Seminary — situated in Fort Worth, Texas; the world's largest seminary

Southwestern — shortened form of Southwestern Baptist Theological Seminary

theatre — operating room

TABC — Travis Avenue Baptist Church

throw ball — variation of the sport volleyball; ball is thrown with two hands rather than served or returned with one hand

Travis — Travis Avenue Baptist Church

UPG — unreached people group

UT Southwestern — Situated in Dallas, Texas, UT Southwestern Medical Center is the school at which Naylor teaches and the one at which she completed her general-surgery residency

Whipple — operative procedure to remove a portion of pancreas, duodenum, and stomach

Index

Made in the USA
Coppell, TX
18 March 2024